THE GHOST
HANDBOOK

THE GHOST HANDBOOK

JOHN AND ANNE SPENCER

BOXTREE

First published 1998 by Macmillan

an imprint of Macmillan Publishers Ltd
25 Eccleston Place, London SW1W 9NF
and Basingstoke

Associated companies throughout the world

ISBN 07522 1165 X

1 3 5 7 9 8 6 4 2

A CIP catalogue record for this book is available from
the British Library.

Typeset by SetSystems Ltd, Saffron Walden, Essex
Printed and bound in Great Britain by
Mackays of Chatham plc, Chatham, Kent

CONTENTS

GHOSTLY EXTRAS

GHOSTS WITH A TIMETABLE

GHOSTS . . . ON THE MENU?

ACKNOWLEDGEMENTS

Our thanks to the many people with whom we have worked during ghost research and ghostwatch vigils, including the teams from ASSAP (the Association for the Scientific Study of Anomalous Phenomena) and Bob Schott of Adventures Beyond. Thanks to Jason Braithwaite and Dr David Cross for information and background on certain reports.

Thanks also to the many people who have given their time to tell us their own stories, and to the proprietors and managers of hotels and theatres around the country, and the custodians of various castles and buildings, who have put up with our enquiries and in some cases allowed us to spend time on their premises.

We would like to confirm that none of the locations listed, including the hotels and pubs, has paid us or in any way offered inducements in order to be included.

INTRODUCTION

The concept of this book is very simple: to catalogue an interesting collection of ghosts, hauntings and associated legends around Britain in sites that are largely accessible to the public and therefore to the amateur ghostwatcher.

Virtually all the locations listed here are open to, or accessible to, the public, making the book a rich source of information for those interested in doing more than just reading accounts of ghosts. A few sites are available only by prior arrangement and a very few, included for various reasons of interest, are not open to the public. Please check before journeying.

In our experience, most of the custodians, managers and others who care for the sites mentioned are happy to discuss the haunted history of their locations if approached courteously and sensibly. When visiting these locations please respect the history of the sites and the needs and interests of other visitors there.

In addition to stories of hauntings, the book also includes 'While You're There' sections – other places of possible interest in the localities. These include ancient monuments, sites of UFO sightings and crop-circle formations, places of legend, and more. Most people with an interest in hauntings have interests in these other areas to some degree and these locations will, for many people, add extra quality to their day out ghostwatching. These other aspects of British history and culture also help to explain where many of the legends associated with hauntings start, and suggest that certain areas of the country are more prone to phenomena than others.

The book also contains a list of hotels and pubs, mostly with restaurants, that are happy to discuss the tales of hauntings associated with their premises (see Chapter 17). The amateur ghostwatcher can therefore not only visit a collection of haunted sites but also arrange to stay overnight, or take a refreshing break, in buildings that offer interesting possibilities. Your own travel arrangements may not always allow you to stay overnight in a hotel; but you might consider stopping for a coffee or lunch in one of the restaurants. In this chapter we have also, with tongue firmly in cheek, allocated 'ghost ratings' on the basis of types of phenomena, intensity, and so on.

Perhaps it is needless to say, but of course the book is not a comprehensive listing. Indeed, it would not be possible to list all the haunted sites in a country so immersed in its history as Britain, which has a wealth of ghost sightings and supernatural legends. The book covers a range of types of sites, a range of types of hauntings and lists as many of the well-known places as possible.

Lastly, while ghostwatching is fascinating in itself, it is also an introduction to the rich and fascinating story of Britain, a country with a wealth and a depth of history.

Enjoy your researches!

GHOSTS IN THEIR HOMES

There are many classifications of the phenomena we call 'ghosts'. There is a considerable difference between an interactive ghost – for example, your grandmother visits you after her death and speaks to you by name – and the non-interactive ghosts such as monks and nuns seen moodily and repeatedly walking their old haunts. The principal difference would seem to be that while the former is personal and perhaps if other people had been in the room when your grandmother appeared they would not have seen her, 'recordings ghosts' seem quite disconnected from the individual and can be seen by different people in the same place at different times.

Almost all the ghosts in this section are of the 'recordings' nature: echoes from the past sometimes visually recorded, sometimes audibly. The Treasurer's House Roman army is typical. In that case, the fact that the soldiers were seen walking at the road level as it was in Roman times rather than at the actual floor level as it was when the sighting took place, and the fact that they seemed to be going about their business in their own time oblivious of modern-day observers, suggests that a non-interactive recording got embedded.

It is believed that such ghosts represent something like a natural 'video' recording. As such they must be recorded in some way into the fabric of the area in which they are seen. No one knows how, if this is true, it happens. It cannot be a simple set of criteria or there would be many more ghosts than there are; things are happening all the time, yet few events create such lasting impressions. So the criteria must be complex and a recording made only when the conditions are right. Perhaps it is a factor of geology – the right types of local rocks, for example, combined with certain weather or climatic conditions, humidity, temperature and so on. There is also a theory that the recordings ghost is 'recorded' by a person who sights the figure when it was alive and 'passes it on' to future generations of sighters in the area.

But it seems likely that emotion also plays a part in the recording. Many ghosts of this nature are seen at times that imply brooding or unhappiness – people just before suicide or execution and so on. Few are of laughing and happy times. But we are all people of emotions: even the shade of a man walking down the street apparently nonchalantly could represent one who was in life suffering inner pain at that time. Research into recordings ghosts must try to identify the criteria that make such recordings; if all such factors can be calculated then it would presumably be possible to deliberately create recordings – which would not only vindicate the claims of ghost-witnesses, but perhaps provide for scientific advances in many areas.

If understanding the nature of recording is important, so is understanding playback. We do not know what conditions are required to get a playback, but presumably these too are complex or they would be more frequent. Perhaps it is again a factor of climate, or the mood of the observer. Perhaps there even has to be some empathy between the original mood that laid down the recording and the mood of the person who observes it.

There are reports of replayed battles – ghosts of whole armies and whole battle scenes – which would seem to refute at least some of this idea, which is otherwise compelling. Surely all the participants in this warfare cannot be sharing the same mood? Some would be excited, even overjoyed, others would be depressed, some fearful and anxious and so on. But perhaps there can be a 'collective mood' which plays a part in these things.

Another question relates to the strength of the recording. Some ghost researchers theorize that the 'power' of the recording diminishes over time. Ghosts first seen clearly are later seen 'faded'; sometimes they are represented only by sounds where previous witnesses have reported visuals. But perhaps that is misunderstanding the nature of the 'mechanisms'. It may be that the playback strength varies according to the strength of the factors involved: high humidity, low temperature or whatever. Perhaps later witnesses simply did not have such a good day for their 'sighting'. There is some evidence of this in a case related in our *Encyclopedia of Ghosts and Spirits*, that of the 'Student's Return'. In that case the witnesses saw the figure of a thoughtful student – just prior to his suicide, it seems – sometimes strongly, sometimes more faded, and at other times heard his footsteps but saw nothing, all in no apparent order. Observation of ghosts is at best random and infrequent; the data set is not enough to make judgements on – perhaps when Harry Martindale's Roman army is next seen at the Treasurer's House it will be as strong as ever.

If there is one type of building that seems almost never to be without its resident ghost it is a castle. But why castles?

During 1997 we investigated a number of sites in Scotland including Hermitage Castle, described in Chapter 1. The project had been initiated by Bob Schott of Adventures Beyond, an American with a fascination for, among other things, British ghosts. He was making a video documentary about hauntings. He had chosen Hermitage as a good site because he was convinced that such a location was full of history, full of sadness and sorrow and the emotion of the misdeeds of Lord Soulis. He was hopeful that his equipment would pick up hauntings in the castle, and that a psychic who would join the investigation – Eddie Burks – would detect traces of the spirits.

In the event less was detected than might have been hoped for, but part of our conversation seemed to take Bob by surprise. As the night wore on with little to show for our efforts, Bob shook his head and threw his arms up at the dominating walls of the Castle around us. 'This place is ancient,' he said. 'There has to be something here.' We shrugged. 'Even a 1980s house is built on ancient ground. Everywhere on earth is equally ancient; native Americans once walked where New York is today,' we suggested. Bob thought about it for a while and laughed. 'I'd not thought of it quite that way before,' he said.

We think that that position holds some truth, and there are certainly a few cases of cavaliers in modern bungalows and so on. We also know of a case that would seem to fit the normal criteria for a 'recordings' ghost: a ballroom of dancing, twirling figures, but one that 'appears' in an upper floor of a 1960s tower block. If it is a recording it can hardly have been laid down *in situ*, but it suggests that history keeps going regardless of the local changes. None the less, Bob's position was also right. The fact is that there do appear to be more ghosts reported from old castles than from modern tower blocks, and many more 'historical' ghosts in castles.

Perhaps this suggests that the theory that recordings 'run down in strength', which we challenged above, does have some validity. Or perhaps new ghosts wipe clean old recordings. But perhaps there is something about the castles themselves that we have to take into account. Perhaps the structure of these old castles is part of what makes for a successful recording. Solid stone walls, perhaps the reasonably common square or rectangular shape of the castle structures, might be factors that make for a strong echo through time.

Castles have seen a great deal of history, and were places of a great deal of concentrated emotion. Major events – which leave strong emotional imprints – have been played out in castles probably more than anywhere else in the country. As such, perhaps Bob Schott's basic idea was right – castles are a fruitful source of ghosts for the ghostwatcher and the ghost-researcher.

Ghosts are strongly associated with religion: there are large numbers of reports of nuns and monks among the spectres seen, and a great many hauntings in churches. Indeed there are few churches that do not have some local association with hauntings. Yet perhaps expectation is playing a part in such large numbers of reports. Monks and nuns are a part of history everywhere in Britain, and sightings of shapes that look like dark-robed people are perhaps sometimes erroneously assumed to be such people. If the sighting should happen to be at a place where a monastery once stood, the possibility of presuming a connection is even more likely.

Perhaps more significantly as far as churches go, there are two closer associations. First, ghosts are often assumed to be the deceased living after death. Inevitably such an impression brings religion into the equation. Second, most churches have graveyards and there is a strong superstition of ghosts inhabiting graveyards. In fact there are not a great many ghosts who spend their time in graveyards, nor should that be surprising. If we take the two clear divisions of ghost phenomena – interactive and non-interactive ghosts – neither should be overly associated with graveyards. If some ghosts are sentient – interactive – then frankly a graveyard is probably a rather boring place to spend time; the belief that such ghosts 'haunt' their former homes and the places they loved has a more logical ring to it. And recordings ghosts are not very likely in graveyards; with the exception of a few people such as, say, Charles Dickens, whose ghost has been seen in a graveyard at Rochester – where he actually did spend time and apparently hoped to be buried – most people do not spend an inordinate amount of time in such places . . . not walking about anyway!

However, let us not ignore the fact that there are a great many sightings of ghosts in churches and, whatever false or wishful thinking may be adding unnecessarily to the numbers, the true numbers have to be accounted for. Perhaps churches 'hold' recordings in the same way that castles do. They are often old, large, very solid stone structures with large voids within, all of which may play a part in 'recording' a ghost. But they are also places of emotion. The church is a place for some people to turn to at times of despair and stress, even if only once in their life, and these are the emotions that we often associate with the 'recording' of ghosts. So perhaps churches have more powerful emotions played out within their walls than many other buildings, and perhaps that is the origin of such ghosts.

The stately homes and palaces of royalty are also buildings famous for their ghosts. Whereas only a small number of 'ordinary' houses seem to have ghostly manifestations, many of the grand homes of the land can boast a ghost or two.

One difference between the two is a sense of history and an awareness of ancestry. Royalty certainly, and most of the families whose stately homes are featured in Chapter 3, have a known, long history of ancestors. Perhaps that sense of the depth of history makes people more aware of, or sensitive to, ghosts. That the families themselves are often aware of such ghosts is understandable in this light, but many sightings are reported by short-term employees on the estates, or by visitors. Perhaps their own attitude of mind is affected by the grandeur of the surroundings, and perhaps that opens up areas of the mind to greater receptiveness. Anyone who takes the time to 'stand and stare' as Davies said, can hardly fail to be moved by the atmosphere in the Tower of London, or at Hampton Court, for example.

That may also be true for the families themselves. Generally speaking they respect their own history, and regard the family estates in a proprietorial way. They own the estates they live in spiritually as well as factually. If some element of hauntings represents life after death, then it might be fair to assume that when members of the family die they continue their spiritual association with the 'family pile'.

But there may be more spurious reasons why more ghosts are reported in such places. Highest on the list is the expectation raised by the common knowledge that the building is haunted, sometimes even explained in the brochures tourists buy while visiting, and certainly known by those working there. Looking out for a specific ghost in a specific location can make every creaky door suspicious, every fleeting glimpse of shadow or movement of light seem like a figure. Built on top of genuine sightings, these spurious claims reinforce the impression that these buildings are more haunted, or at least more frequently haunted, than others.

The fact that the ghosts are often identified as famous family members, or previous kings and queens, may itself be a form of expectation. Perhaps sometimes a visitor genuinely sees or hears a ghost, but there is a temptation to attribute that often vague and fleeting glimpse to a famous person. If your one sighting of a ghost takes place at Hampton Court, how much more satisfying if you believe it to have been one of Henry VIII's Queens than one of his servants.

Perhaps the most specialist type of building dealt with in this section is the theatre. There can hardly be a theatre in the country that does not boast – and boast is indeed the word – at least one ghostly haunting within its walls. Perhaps by claiming over 500 the Theatre Royal, Drury Lane, is showing off somewhat, but if you can't show off in a theatre, where can you? And after all, they could be right ... But what, then, is it about theatres that associates them so closely with ghosts and spirits?

The buildings themselves may offer a clue, of course. Older theatres when refurbished are often restored to their former style, the ornate, plush designs providing an atmospheric surrounding for theatrical productions. Perhaps this recreation of the look of older years enables departed spirits to feel a closer affinity to the present-day structures than with other buildings. In addition, the low lighting may be reminiscent of candlelight and gas-lighting. 'Lost souls' – if that is the interpretation put on such hauntings – may find it less easy to realize that they have died because their surroundings have perhaps changed less than is the case in other types of renovated building.

We must also remind ourselves that many ghost sightings have been triggered by building work. In buildings ancient and modern, from stately homes to modern houses, building work has sometimes seemed to be the trigger for apparitions, strange lights and sounds, the release of 'recordings type' ghosts and some poltergeist activity. In addition to the occasional building work or renovation which takes place in theatres, we must remember that theatres undergo a great deal of temporary rebuilding work. New stage scenes are created for each production and then destroyed. Whole teams of carpenters, electricians and other specialist set builders frequently work inside theatres, redesigning stage sets and sometimes involving the redesign of auditoriums, for example. So perhaps with the constant rebuilding work we have a further trigger, making theatres more likely to be haunted.

And we should not ignore the nature of the work conducted in theatres. They are places of melodrama, expression and energy.

Emotions from the lightest and most humorous to the darkest and most grim are played out nightly by actors, many of whom are emotionally affected by their performances and, temporarily anyway, are stretching themselves to the most extreme of passions. If they do their work right – and they usually do – then the audience is also at least temporarily filled with emotion: awe, love, anger, and so on. Huge rooms filled with compressed powerful emotions may well be a factor in manifesting ghosts. Certainly in individual sightings emotional states seem often to play a part. Before, during and after performances, theatres are highly charged places, and perhaps this brings about either a triggering of recordings-type ghosts or even draws interactive ghostly presences back to the site of their former heights of success or depths of despair.

We should explore this possibility further, but in doing so look at the characteristics of the most highly charged individuals concerned: the actors themselves. Actors are generally a superstitious bunch and reflect their superstitions in odd ways. It is well known, of course, that Shakespeare's *Macbeth* must not be mentioned by name but is usually referred to as 'the Scottish play' to avoid bad luck on stage. But consider the way actors challenge their superstitions: green is thought to be an unlucky colour, yet the rest room in theatres is known as the green room; obviously an actor or performer needs to be physically fit in order to work yet the customary way to wish a performer good luck is to wish him to 'break a leg'. Superstitious actors have attributed omens to many theatre ghosts. The sighting of a particular ghost, for example, may herald the likelihood that the production is going to be a success.

Most importantly, actors are people who use the creative side of their brain. Whereas most people either as the product of their schooling or the demands of their work use the scientific, calculating side of their brain, actors have to suppress this in favour of the irrational, emotional side. There is now evidence to suggest that in order to experience the paranormal, whether it is to channel through automatic writing, use telepathy or PK, or to perceive ghosts, the intuitive, creative, irrational part of the brain has to be activated. Psychic Lois Bourne has commented: 'One of the greatest barriers to mediumship is the intellect, and the most serious problem I had to learn in my early psychic career was the suspension of my intellect. If, during a practice of extra-sensory perception, I allowed logic to prevail, and permitted myself to rationalize the impressions I received, and the things I said, I would be hopelessly lost within a conflict. It is necessary that I totally bypass my conscious mind.' In theatres we probably have the highest concentration of people trained to use – and using – the creative, intuitive side of their brain.

Perhaps that simply means that there are more potential ghost perceivers available. Perhaps the number of creative, emotional people makes the manifestation of ghosts easier from the ghost's point of view (assuming that the ghost is sentient), or perhaps, in the case of 'recordings ghosts', as a natural product of whatever it is that causes such manifestations. Remember also that the audience is 'absorbed' in the theatrical production underway – good audience participation means suspending disbelief and throwing yourself into the play – and perhaps if you are a member of the audience you have a higher chance of seeing the ghost than otherwise.

CHAPTER 1

~

HAUNTED CASTLES

Abergeldie Castle
(near Crathie, Aberdeenshire, Scotland)

Abergeldie Castle was built in the sixteenth century for the Gordon clan. It was rented by Prince Albert from the Gordons as a summer retreat and the Prince and Princess of Wales (later King Edward VII and Queen Alexandra) frequently holidayed there. It was a later royal, Prince Edward (later King Edward VIII, who abdicated), who in his 'memoirs' referred to a ghost story associated with the castle: 'the ghost of Kittie Rankie'. Kittie Rankie is said to have been burned as a witch on the hill overlooking the castle.

In the 1850s young Patricia Lindsay, daughter of the local doctor, was happy to play in the dungeons (where reputedly Kittie Rankie had been held) during the day, but she would not play there at night for fear of hearing the bell ringing, a portent of doom for the Gordon family.

WHILE YOU'RE THERE:

- Enjoy the memories of a Scottish version of the Swiss William Tell story. At nearby Braemar are the ruins of Kindrochit Castle where, it is said, the MacHardy clan acquired their name. The story is that the castle was owned by a cruel constable who fed local cattle to his huge wild boar. One local widow had only one cow, so her son, Sandy, killed the boar to prevent her cow being taken from her. Sandy was condemned to death but the King agreed to the widow's appeal if Sandy could shoot a pea off of his mother's head at 100 yards. Sandy succeeded, but the King asked him why he had taken two arrows from the quiver. 'If I had killed her, the second one would have been for you,' he replied. 'You're a hardy one,' exclaimed the King, and granted the name to his family.

Baldoon Castle
(near Bladnoch, Dumfries and Galloway, Scotland)

On 24 August 1669 Janet Dalrymple married David Dunbar, the heir to Baldoon. This match was arranged for her by her parents and in particular her father, the statesman Sir James Dalrymple. However, prior to this she had fallen in love with and pledged herself to Dunbar's uncle, Lord Rutherford. Rutherford was poor and considered quite unsuitable by Janet's parents. However, in the face of resistance, particularly from her mother, Janet went through with the marriage.

On the wedding night the bride and groom retired to the bedchamber but shortly afterwards wedding guests heard screams and ran to assist. On breaking down the door they found David Dunbar stabbed many times, with blood streaming from his body. Janet was lying in a corner, stained with blood, muttering incoherently and acting insane. Dunbar survived but Janet died within a month. (Another recounting of the story says that she lived for nineteen years, insane throughout.) It is said that her blood-stained ghost haunts Baldoon.

The story was the basis for Sir Walter Scott's novel *The Bride of Lammermoor* and later for the opera *Lucia di Lammermoor* by Donizetti.

SEE ALSO:
- Threave Castle.

WHILE YOU'RE THERE:
- Just across Wigtown Bay are Creetown and Gatehouse of Fleet, joined by the A75. Just off this road, clearly marked, are the neolithic sites Cairn Holy I and II, about 150 yards apart. Cairn Holy II is particularly dramatic; a neolithic tomb with a nine-foot portal stone which was blocked up after use 3,000 years ago. It was excavated in 1949 and excellent items of pottery were unearthed.

Berry Pomeroy Castle
(near Totnes, Devon)

Berry Pomeroy Castle is reputed to be one of the most haunted castles in Britain. The local village, Berry Pomeroy, was named after a Norman family responsible for building the castle. Between 1506 and 1552 the Duke of Somerset, brother of Henry VIII's Jane Seymour, built a mansion within the walls. The Seymours stayed there until severe damage during the English Civil War in the late 1600s forced them to move out. The castle was further damaged by fire in 1708.

One ghost, known as the White Lady, is thought to be the ghost of Lady Margaret Pomeroy. She and her sister Lady Eleanor Pomeroy both fell in love with one man. Lady Eleanor had her sister imprisoned in the dungeons in St Margaret's Tower, where she starved to death. The White Lady has been seen in the dungeons and along the ramparts; sightings are accompanied by feelings of fear and depression, even of malevolence. Another female ghost is the Blue Lady, and sightings of her go back to the eighteenth century. Legend has it that she was the daughter of a baron of Berry Pomeroy, raped and made pregnant by her father. She strangled the baby at birth and haunts the castle in perpetual torment. The crying of what is said to be the ghost of the murdered child is often heard. Local legend has it that she tries to lure men to their death by appearing in unsafe areas of the castle apparently desperate for help. It is held that several men have almost been killed in an effort to save her. The Blue Lady is seen wearing a long blue cape and hood.

A witness to the Blue Lady was Sir Walter Farquhar, an eminent physician of the late eighteenth century. He was at Berry Pomeroy to attend the wife of the castle steward, who was ill, when he caught sight of 'a stunning young woman, who was wringing her hands in obvious distress'. He watched her go up a stairway, then turn briefly towards him, then vanish into one of the upper rooms. He could see her clearly in the light streaming through a stained-glass window. When Sir Walter asked the steward, the following day, who she was, the steward was distressed and claimed that it meant that the sighting was a portent – his wife would soon die. The steward told Sir Walter that Lady Margaret had killed her child in the room above the staircase and whenever her ghost appeared it was an omen of the death of someone in the castle. He had experienced it when his son had died earlier. The doctor, however, was able to assure the steward that his wife was far from dying and was in fact getting better. But he was wrong; the steward's wife died at noon the same day.

Berry Pomeroy Castle has many reports of ghost sightings, shadows, photographic failures, paranormal sounds and so on. Researchers Tony Wells and Melanie Warren interviewed Mr and Mrs Barker who run the castle teashop and have stories of their own to tell. Mr Barker has given up using the men's toilet, and prefers to use the women's toilet, after seeing the shadow of a man outside one of the cubicles but discovering that there was no one there. The teashop itself is apparently frequented by a ghost that grabs the shoulders of visitors but leaves them startled to discover no one there when they turn round. Mrs Barker has herself experienced this phenomenon. Even Paramount had difficulties when trying to make a programme about the castle to be broadcast on Halloween. They were persistently plagued by failures of their lights within the castle; when checked, the lights did not seem to have faults and worked well outside the castle.

SEE ALSO:
• Modbury.

Castle of Mey
(Highland, Scotland)

Originally a Z-plan castle dating from the late sixteenth century, this is the most northerly castle in Britain. It is just six miles from John o'Groats. It is haunted by a Green Lady, the ghost of Lady Fanny Sinclair who threw herself to her death from one of the high towers. She had fallen in love with a servant, but the relationship had been terminated as it was not thought appropriate to marry 'out of one's class' and in her distress she committed suicide.

WHILE YOU'RE THERE:
• Consider a trip to the Orkneys (by plane or ferry from Thurso). The mass of ancient history here is well worth the visit. Near Stromness (where the ferry docks) is the Maes Howe burial tomb. The tomb was built in 2700 BC and is over 100 feet across and 25 feet high, containing three chambers. There are Viking runic inscriptions there which themselves deserve the visit. Nearby are also the standing stones of Stenness. On the island of South Ronaldsay is the Tomb of the Eagle, another neolithic chamber tomb magnificently set right on the cliff edge.

Castle Rising Castle
(Castle Rising, Norfolk)

Castle Rising Castle is a dominating Norman castle built on a reputedly Roman site. The castle was built in 1150 by the Earl of Sussex. Edward III had his mother, Isabella, imprisoned there – in unusually comfortable surroundings, it must be said – for the murder of her husband. She died insane in the castle. Her wild shriekings and cacklings have been reported by many visitors to the castle.

When we visited the castle we spoke to David Bailey, the custodian, and although he has not seen Isabella he has felt one of the rooms to be very 'creepy'. It is along a corridor outside this room that different visitors have also felt quite uneasy. The castle holds several events; participants of these events who have stayed in the castle grounds have told of strange noises. Queen Isabella's ghost has also been seen wandering in the ruins of the castle church.

SEE ALSO:
- Castle Acre Priory.
- Sandringham House.

WHILE YOU'RE THERE:
- A few miles to the east of Castle Rising is Raynham Hall. There have been many reports of a Brown Lady ghost in the Hall, but the subject was given a considerable boost in 1936 when a now-famous photograph was taken of the staircase and showed a human-shaped figure apparently descending. The Brown Lady has more unpleasant manifestations, however; she has been reported walking on the short road between South Raynham and West Raynham, just off the A1065, her eye-sockets empty.

Corby Castle
(near Carlisle, Cumbria)

The famous ghost of Corby Castle is the 'radiant boy'. When seen, the child is dressed in white and seems to glow brilliant white.

An account of a sighting of the 'radiant boy' is given in *The Night Side of Nature* by Mrs C. Crowe, published in 1848. The account dates from 3 September 1803. The Rector of Greystoke and his wife, having been expected to stay at the castle for several days, left without explanation after just one night. Indeed, their leaving was so sudden it almost amounted to rudeness and upset their hosts. It was much later that the Rector spoke to his host and admitted that it was the sight of the phantom that had frightened them off. He explained in a written statement, pledging his word as a clergyman: 'Soon after we went to bed we fell asleep; it might be between one and two in the morning when I awoke. I observed that the fire was totally extinguished; but although that was the case and we had no light, I saw a glimmer in the centre of the room which suddenly increased to a bright flame ... to my amazement, I beheld a beautiful boy, clothed in white, with bright locks resembling gold, standing by my bedside, in which position he remained some minutes, fixing his eyes upon me with a mild and benevolent expression. He then glided to the other side of the chimney, where it is obvious there is no possible egress, and entirely disappeared.'

It is said that those who see him achieve power and fortune but meet a violent end. One such victim is believed to have been Lord Castlereagh. His career encompassed both power and fortune: he became an MP at twenty-one, held the jobs of Chief Secretary for Ireland, Secretary for War, Foreign Secretary, and Leader of the Commons; he was responsible for British policy towards Napoleon, was largely responsible for the peace agreement that followed Waterloo and was influential in several other decisions and agreements that shaped European history. But he went insane and in 1822 committed suicide.

SEE ALSO:

• Carlisle.

WHILE YOU'RE THERE:

• To the south of Corby Castle is the well-known standing stone circle called Long Meg and her Daughters, near Little Salkeld. The formation is one of the largest of the Bronze Age circles, 560 feet across. Fifty-seven of an original seventy stones remain.

Corfe Castle
(on the A351 between Wareham and Swanage, Dorset)

The ruins of Corfe Castle dominate this area of the Dorset skyline and are a much visited National Trust property. There may have been a royal hunting lodge at Corfe in Saxon times but the castle as we know it was built by William the Conqueror as part of a ring of fortifications around his new kingdom.

Edward the Martyr, who ruled England between 975 and 978, was murdered here at his stepmother's instigation in an attempt to bring her son, Ethelred (later known as the Unready) to the throne. He ruled from 978 to 1016. While no direct connection to this history is attributed there are many paranormal phenomena associated with Corfe Castle, including unexplained light phenomena and a headless figure that drifts across the road below the castle. In 1967 a local man, John Seager, saw this figure and in 1976 three visitors also reported it, according to the local newspaper. One theory is that the figure is that of Lady Bankes, whose husband, Sir John, owned the castle in 1635. The headless woman is seen either just across the road or standing silently by the castle walls.

King John used the castle as a royal residence and prison. Indeed, twenty-two French noblemen were starved to death in its dungeons. It was Queen Elizabeth I who sold the castle from royal ownership to Sir Christopher Hatton; in 1635 he sold it to Sir John Bankes. Lady Bankes held off an attack by Cromwell's troops until Prince Maurice assisted, but it was later attacked again by Sir Walter Erle and in 1646 the castle fell to the Parliamentarians.

SEE ALSO:

- Wool.
- Clouds Hill.
- Priory Church, Christchurch.
- Town Museum, Poole.

WHILE YOU'RE THERE:

- On the cliffs above Worbarrow Bay, near East Lulworth, is an Iron Age fort called Flower's Barrow. The Romans established a garrison there. In 1678 a spectral Roman army was seen there, marching from the Barrow over Grange Hill. The sound of 'clashing of arms' was reported. The same spectral army was seen several times during the Second World War, and reported as late as 1970 by an elderly lady who saw the Roman legion at Knowle Hill, close to Corfe.

Cortachy Castle
(Cortachy, Angus, Scotland)

Cortachy Castle is the ancestral home of the Ogilvy clan and sports a phantom drummer as its ghost. For centuries there have been reports of the sound of drumming in and around the castle, usually thought to warn of the impending death of a family member. The origin of the ghostly drummer is, perhaps inevitably, the subject of much myth and folklore. Widely discussed is the belief that the drummer was a servant who fell in love with a Countess and had an affair. The Earl – a vengeful husband apparently – tied the drummer to his drum and threw him out of one of the high windows of the castle. The story continues that the servant survived long enough to curse the Earl and promised to haunt him and his family so long as they lived at the castle. There are other variations of the origin of the drummer – one being that the youth belonged to Clan Campbell who at the time were at war with the Ogilvys. The youth was imprisoned at the Ogilvys' former home at Airlie Castle and the ghost followed them to Cortachy Castle. Another story is that the drummer was from Clan Lindsay, who were also feuding with the Ogilvys; the drummer was captured by the Earl of Airlie and thrown from the battlements.

An account of the haunting comes from 1845 when a Miss Dalrymple and her maid, Ann Day, were staying at the castle. During the evening Miss Dalrymple heard the drumming sound, which she then mentioned that evening over dinner. Lord and Lady Airlie were visibly shaken and later Miss Dalrymple was told about the rumour of the drummer being a portent of family death. The following morning Ann Day heard the drumbeat moving from the courtyard and into the house, indeed approaching the rooms in which she and Miss Dalrymple were staying. The following day it was Miss Dalrymple who heard exactly the same thing and, perhaps somewhat disturbed, terminated her stay at the castle. Five or six months later Lady Airlie died, allegedly leaving a note stating that she knew the drumming indicated her own death.

Elliott O'Donnell, a ghost-researcher of the 1940s, received a first-hand account of a ghostly encounter in Cortachy Castle. He spoke to a man named Porter who as a young boy had broken into the castle in the company of another boy, Alec, to hunt for rabbits. They encountered the figure of a tall gamekeeper, which turned to move towards them. The two boys fled over the walls and ran off, listening not only to the sound of footsteps from the figure but also to the sound of a drum beating. A few days later one of the Airlie family died. O'Donnell, on hearing the story, set out to repeat this boyhood adventure. He heard drum sounds and saw a tall figure which disappeared as he watched.

SEE ALSO:

• Montrose Airfield.

WHILE YOU'RE THERE:

• Travel over to Glen Esk – not far as the crow flies but a difficult terrain to cross – and listen for the sound of pipes, which according to the locals are sometimes heard drifting across the hills. They are the pipes of a piper who was kidnapped by nine green-robed fairies, so that he could entertain them. They sailed down to his location in a boat and touched him with a wand, and he followed them into the boat. The boat sailed round the pool called Pontskinnen Pot three times, then disappeared. The piper was never seen again.

Croft Castle
(Leominster, Herefordshire)

The exterior of this grand castle dates back to the fourteenth and fifteenth centuries and is said to house at least two ghosts. In the Oak Room there have been reports of a large figure clad in leather. Many believe it to be the ghost of Owen Glendower, the Welsh freedom fighter. There are also reports of a man, apparently from the Elizabethan period, seen passing through the walls of the hall.

SEE ALSO:

- Castle Lodge.
- Kinlet Church.

WHILE YOU'RE THERE:

- Visit the Norman church of St Peter and St Paul. Stone carvings on the west door of the church set out the legend that Leominster is named after the 'Lion' King, Merewald. According to the story, Merewald dreamed of a Christian missionary bringing him news. At the same time a hermit called Ealfrid dreamt a lion was eating from his hand. The two met and exchanged stories; the King converted to Christianity and founded a church and covenant in 658 AD at Leominster. (Another belief is that the town is named after Earl Leofric, husband of Lady Godiva.)

Dover Castle
(Dover, Kent)

One of the most imposing castles in Britain is Dover Castle, beautifully preserved in good order and dominating the ancient port town from high on a coastal hillside. It is known as 'The Key of England'. The site is believed to have the longest recorded history of any major fortress in England. The Romans built a lighthouse there, the Anglo-Saxons constructed a fortified town. The present castle dates back to the 1180s and the reign of Henry II. It is believed that Henry spent £6,500 on the castle over thirty-five years, an enormous sum equivalent to one-third of the total spent on ninety other castles during the same period. It has been remodelled by both Georgian and Victorian engineers.

The castle is a major tourist attraction with many historical features, special reconstructions – for example, of when the castle acted as a key nerve centre during the Second World War – and is presently a working garrison for the Army.

Since 1991 we have been part of teams initiated by the Thanet Psychic and Paranormal Research Unit, and particularly by Kent researcher Robin Laurence, investigating the castle. The castle has many accounts of hauntings: sights and sounds of a previous era and the apparitions of several figures.

In the keep there are reports of a figure dressed in seventeenth-century cavalier-style costume. He wears a black wide-brimmed hat with plume, knee-length boots and a purple cloak. A cleaner working on the ground floor of the keep told us that she looked up from working, saw the figure by the door, and then it disappeared. Also in the keep, by the west staircase, a member of the castle staff reported seeing the shade of a lady in a flowing red dress. In the mural gallery there have been reports, also by castle staff, of a figure in blue. Members of the staff also reported seeing the lower half of a man's body walking across the doorway of the King's bedroom but found on entering the room that it was empty.

Excavations opened up what is known as the 'Underground Works', and there have been ghost sightings in this area also. One member of the staff in 1979 reported, while locking up for the night, seeing a seventeenth-century pikeman in the guardroom. The figure walked through one wall of the room, and then passed out through another. A figure in blue has also been seen in the passageways leading to this area.

In 1991 an American couple who had visited the underground works complimented the staff on the excellent reproduction of the sounds of screams and moans from bygone days which they had enjoyed while walking around the area. The staff did not disillusion them by telling them that there were no audio reproductions in that area. In case there had been an accident and a visitor was lying injured, staff members thoroughly searched the area; no one was found.

Our own investigations of the castle are recorded in the book *Ghostwatching* (by John Spencer and Tony Wells); they had their successes. Several unaccountable sounds were heard, some matching previous reports from the castle (reports which were deliberately unknown to certain team members), and a video camera recorded an inexplicable rhythmic shuddering of the door on the second floor of the keep, leading to a staircase, although the area was 'secured' by the team and monitoring devices.

SEE ALSO:

- Church of St Nicholas, Pluckley.
- Saltwood.

WHILE YOU'RE THERE:

- Over to the west, on the other side of Ashford, is Pluckley which many ghost researchers believe is the most haunted village in England. Certainly the list of hauntings related to the village is impressive and the place deserves a visit. Be respectful and diplomatic to the locals, please; not all of them welcome the tag the village has inherited.

Drumlanrig Castle
(near Thornhill, Dumfries and Galloway, Scotland)

An impressive and imposing building of pink granite standing alone in open moorland, this castle dates back to the seventeenth century. It has an unusual ghost, that of an ape that was once a family pet.

The Countess of Dalkeith, as a young girl, in the company of one of her sisters, saw this ghost on their first visit to Drumlanrig. They were retiring to bed, and as they approached their bedroom they saw what appeared to be a hairy creature coming down the corridor towards them. The candle they were carrying instantly blew out and, frightened, they ran for the bedroom.

Later in life the Countess of Dalkeith encountered the ghost again, when she saw what appeared to be a huge ape sitting on a chair. Questioned by a guest present at the time, Lady Howard, she described what she had seen; it appears, however, that Lady Howard was somewhat sceptical.

During the First World War the castle was used as a hospital and staffed by nurses. After only a short time in her post, the matron stated that she was leaving. She had, she explained, 'seen something awful in the night'. She had been staying in a room known as the 'Yellow Monkey' or 'Haunted Room'. Although it is not certain, it is believed that the monkey must have been some kind of exotic pet which perhaps lived in the castle, brought back from abroad by an ancestor of the family.

The Countess of Dalkeith's daughter, the Duchess of Gloucester, had an experience of her own at Drumlanrig Castle. Suffering from diphtheria and possibly delirious, she apparently saw a small girl at her bedside but noticed that her feet were three or four inches above the floor. The Duchess herself later speculated that perhaps the child was a ghost from the time when the floor levels used to be slightly different.

The castle also has the ghost of Lady Anne Douglas, said to walk with her head in her hands.

WHILE YOU'RE THERE:

- A short trip south on the A76 will bring you to Closeburn Castle. Look out for any swans with red- or blood-stained breasts. The appearance of such a creature is, for the Kirkpatrick family there, a portent of death.

Dunnottar Castle
(near Stonehaven, Aberdeenshire, Scotland)

Situated on the coast one and half miles south of Stonehaven, Dunnottar Castle dominates the skyline. It is virtually cut off from the mainland on the headland on which it sits. The overall impression given is said by some to be reminiscent of Edinburgh Castle which dominates the skyline of the capital city.

The site has a long history and featured in the Pict battles of around 600 AD, though the first castle was built there in the twelfth century. The present castle dates mostly from the fourteenth century, when William Keith, Great Marischal of Scotland, built an L-plan tower house which, though now roofless, still exists.

The castle was besieged by Montrose in 1645, then again in 1651 and by Cromwell's forces during the Civil War. In 1686 it was used to imprison 167 Covenanters.

In 1997 we spoke to the custodian of Dunnottar, Peter McKenzie, who first mentioned the Green Lady reported there from time to time. He did not think she was a ghost, but believed it more likely that she was an 'earth spirit'. He thought the Green Lady related to the time of the conversion of the Picts to Christianity and that she is a spirit looking for her worshippers, who have now turned to Christianity and away from her.

Several people have mentioned sighting a tall, blond-haired man clad in leather, stooping down as if to go into the guardroom. Strange but unintelligible voices have been heard in the area of the drawing room when the castle is known to be empty. The custodian also told us of his own experiences at Dunnottar.

'It was March 1995 when I saw the dog. It was like an old-fashioned deer-hunting type dog, young and scrawny-looking. It was grey, with a ginger tinge to it. I caught sight of it out of my peripheral vision, I looked up to shout at the people to keep their dog on a lead, and the thing disappeared. I hadn't realized anything was strange about it up until that moment. Three months after that a German tourist came to the ticket office and reported seeing a dog of the very same description, close to where I saw it, about ten yards away. The dog had disappeared, that's what upset him; it must have been a real surprise to them because in my experience it takes a lot to make Germans come forward like that. I told him it had been seen before, which made him feel better.

'Another time when I was approaching the castle to open up one morning I saw someone diagonally off to my right. I couldn't give you a proper description but I got the definite impression that the person came from a different society. Very old-fashioned. When I looked directly at him to see him clearly, he disappeared, exactly like the dog had done.

'On yet another occasion I was with three women tourists at the back of the castle, at the bit called the brewery. What they witnessed was a girl of about thirteen years old, wearing like a sacking-type cloth. The way they described it, it was as if the girl was going about looking for something, and talking. They were concerned in case the girl had lost her parents, but the girl didn't respond, in fact she didn't pay any attention to them whatsoever. She walked out of the doorway, the two women followed her and she – "ping" – disappeared.'

Duntroon Castle
(near Kilmartin, Argyll and Bute, Scotland)

The castle dates from the late thirteenth century. In the seventeenth century an L-plan tower house was erected, probably on the site of an earlier, demolished, tower, and it is from this time that the most well-known ghost is thought to have originated.

Duntroon Castle is said to be haunted by the ghost of a piper who was viciously murdered in the seventeenth century. Ulster Macdonnel Coll Ciotach sent a piper into the castle as a spy during the war he waged against the Campbells, who at the time owned Duntroon. The piper came under suspicion and was imprisoned in the castle, but used his pipes to signal to his master who was approaching by sea. Coll Ciotach turned back, but the piper was killed, his fingers having first been cut off. The ghostly sound of the pipes has been heard since; an echo of the piper's last stand. In 1910, during renovations, a skeleton with the fingers missing was found walled up in a section of the castle.

In addition to the sound of the pipes, there are reports of strange, poltergeist-like knockings heard on doors, of heavy objects being thrown around spontaneously, and of pictures falling off the walls for no reason. There are also reports of ghostly footsteps being heard.

Farnham Castle
(Farnham, Surrey)

Farnham in Surrey is reputed by some to be one of the most haunted towns in England, a title which it must be admitted almost every county seems to have claimed for one of its towns. Farnham Castle, at the top of Castle Street, has a long history of haunting, perhaps not surprisingly given its visual dominance of the town. For example, the Norman keep gateway has been reported haunted by an amorphous form which many witnesses have found very frightening. Occasionally witnesses have claimed the form to be that of a stern-faced woman in a light-coloured gown, perhaps dating from the twelfth century. The Great Hall of the castle is apparently the haunt of a ghostly monk, and on the stairway outside the Great Hall witnesses have reported the shade of a dancing girl. Local rumour has it that she annoyed some former castle owner, who made her dance until she was totally exhausted. She crawled out of the Great Hall and died on the stairway, where her shade is still seen dancing. On another stairway a silent figure in grey robes has been seen. In one bedroom another amorphous presence has been seen or felt. The ghost of Bishop Morley has been seen and heard in the Fox Tower, which has also been the location of many reports of a bell being heard, though the tower does not have one. Bishop Morley, who died there in 1684, lived in the tower for many years, indeed choosing to sleep in a coffin for twenty years.

Elizabeth Cox arrived at Farnham Castle as a new maid when she was fourteen. On one occasion she saw the ghost of a monk in the long gallery. He was at the far end, apparently looking out of the window overlooking the moat. Local rumour has it that the moat has seen the deaths of several victims and indeed there is a story of a procession of phantom monks, which perhaps the ghost was watching. Elizabeth described him as tall, wearing a brown habit and round cap but looking as solid as any other human. Despite that, she knew immediately she was seeing a ghost, turned away for just a fleeting moment, and when she looked back the figure had disappeared.

One local person from Farnham who spent a night in the castle woke up feeling the bedclothes being pulled off her bed and indeed had to fight to keep them over her. It was she who reported the amorphous something in the bedroom corner; crouching, almost pulsating, with a sense of evil.

SEE ALSO:
• Farnham Parish Church.

WHILE YOU'RE THERE:
• Just outside Farnham, near Waverley Abbey, is a cave said to have been the home of a white witch called Mother Ludlam. She would lend anything asked for, but when a cauldron she lent was not returned she never lent anything again. The cauldron was eventually displayed in Frensham Church, where it remains today. (But Frensham local legend has it that the cauldron was lent from the fairies on Borough Hill.)

Glamis Castle
(Glamis, Angus, Scotland)

Probably no other residence in Britain is as steeped in history, mythology and hauntings as Glamis Castle. It is the ancestral home of the Earls of Strathmore, the Bowes Lyons, and it has been said that they could well be the world's most haunted family. Forbidding though the building is, it was not intended as a fortress but as a hunting lodge in the ancient forests of Scotland. The Lyon family were given the castle by King Robert II, father-in-law of Sir John Lyon, in 1372. It is said that Sir John brought with him to Glamis an ancestral chalice which was never to be removed from their previous family home of Forteviot, and thereby brought down a curse on the family.

(Shakespeare chose Glamis Castle as the setting for *Macbeth*, though in granting Macbeth the title 'Thane of Glamis' he created an anachronism; Glamis was not a thanage in the eleventh century. King Malcolm II died at Glamis Castle in 1034, either mortally wounded in battle or murdered within the castle itself. His grandson Duncan I was killed by his cousin Macbeth, who then succeeded to the crown, although Shakespeare's story is as much drama as fact.)

One of the most famous stories about Glamis Castle is of the so-called 'monster', a distinctly politically incorrect term probably relating to a physically and possibly mentally handicapped child. The rumours have it that a first-born son, and therefore would-be inheritor of the castle and titles, was born hideously malformed and was confined in the castle where he could not be seen. Over the years this rumour has been amplified by sightings, visionary dreams and so on. Whether or not there is any reason for belief in this rumour is uncertain, but an entry in *Debrett's Peerage* of 1841 suggests a possibility. A child is recorded born and dying on 18 October 1821, the title then falling to the next-born, who was born on 28 September 1822. The speculation could be that the first-born did not die but was indeed 'the monster'. A workman repairing slates on the roof of the castle is alleged to have unwittingly found out the secret, presumably seeing the child in some concealed part of the castle, and was granted a pension and a life in Australia in return for his promise never to reveal what he had witnessed.

Glamis Castle became the scene of violence following the death of John, the 6th Lord Glamis. He was survived by his wife, Janet, Lady Glamis, whose family was hated by King James V. James seized the castle and condemned Lady Glamis to death on a trumped-up charge of witchcraft. While Lady Glamis was imprisoned, James and Queen Mary moved into Glamis Castle, ransacking the building and deliberately diminishing the value of the inheritance of Lady Glamis's son. Lady Glamis was burned at the stake and it is her ghost who is seen floating above the clock tower. Witnesses have claimed that she is surrounded by a glow, perhaps an indication of the manner of her passing. She is also identified as the Grey Lady ghost seen by many walking along the corridors in the castle. The reason that Lady Glamis's son was saved was that he was not to be executed until he had reached his coming of age, but the King died before that happened and he was released and restored to his position.

Many old castles have secret rooms, usually designed to effect escape or concealment from attackers but it is alleged that the complex structure of Glamis Castle contains at least one room whose whereabouts and access are known to only three people at any one time: the current Earl, the eldest son and the steward of the estate. Whether this room is supposedly the one which housed the 'monster' or some other secret is unknown. The quest for discovering the secret room has apparently vexed many. During the absence of the former Earl of Strathmore the Countess and a party of guests attempted to discover the secret room by the ingenious method of hanging a towel out of every window they could find and assuming that when they could see a window without a towel it would represent the secret room. The attempt failed and it is alleged that the Earl and Countess separated as a result of her attempt.

Yet another rumour is that it is the room in which Patrick, a fifteenth-century Lord of Glamis played cards with a bearded giant of a man, Lord Crawford. They continued their game into the Sabbath and were caught out by the devil, who condemned them to play for ever. Reports of a huge bearded man have been made several times; several children have woken up screaming that such a figure was leaning over their beds looking at them. (Another version of the story indicates that Lord Glamis actually played cards with the devil, having found no other opponent prepared to play on the Sabbath. During the game the Earl lost his soul to the devil as a gambling debt. A whole host of embroideries surrounded the story, including a butler looking through a keyhole and spotting what was happening, being blinded by a blast of fire from the devil who saw him looking in.)

One servant Florence Foster, left employment at Glamis in 1957 because she could no longer stand listening to the sounds of the phantom gamblers 'rattling dice, stamping and swearing'.

Another story arises from a battle between two clans: the Ogilvys and the Lindsays. A number of defeated Ogilvys asked for protection and the resident Earl of the time apparently locked them in a remote room, assuring them that there they would be safe. Whether he intended to or not, he apparently forgot about them and they all died of starvation. Their skeletons were said to have been found by a Victorian descendant. Signs of banging and knocking heard in the castle have been attributed to the imprisoned Ogilvys seeking to draw attention to their fate.

Other stories include that of a small Negro servant who appears outside the door of the present Queen Mother's sitting room, and is thought to date from the years of the slave trade from the West Indies.

Mrs MacLagan, wife of the Archbishop of York at the beginning of the twentieth century, reported being woken during the night by the sounds of workmen banging and hammering, but was told no workmen were present in the castle at the time. It is said that the present Queen Mother, as a child, was forced to move out of the Blue Room because of similar persistent hammering sounds.

SEE ALSO:

- Letham.

WHILE YOU'RE THERE:

- Travel south to the Firth of Tay at Dundee and take a look at the Tay Bridge. It is a replacement for one destroyed on 28 December 1879 during a violent storm. The disaster sent an engine and five coaches into the waters with the loss of ninety passengers. It is said that on the anniversary of the disaster a ghost train crosses the new bridge from the south towards Dundee and that it disappears into the darkness, just as it did on the original fatal ride. The event was 'immortalized' by the poet William McGonagall, whose writings are regarded as so awful that he achieved a lasting fame of sorts:

Beautiful railway bridge of the Silvery Tay
Alas, I am very sorry to say,
That ninety lives have been taken away
On the last Sabbath day of 1879.

Hermitage Castle
(near Hawick, Borders, Scottish)

Hermitage was built in the thirteenth century and is said to be haunted by William de Soulis, an early owner. It is said that he studied and practised black magic under the master wizard Michal Scot, stealing local children and murdering them in his rituals. The local rumour was that he was aided in these atrocities by his assistant and 'familiar', Robin Redcap. It is said that the dwarf-like Robin still haunts the castle, protecting his master's treasure. There are stories of blood-curdling screams heard from within the ancient walls.

Structurally the castle is forbidding. Most of the external walls are intact and some are covered in red algae, which inspire thoughts of the castle's blood-stained past. Inside can be found the pit where prisoners were dropped, never to be seen again: it is said one prisoner lasted seventeen days before dying. Varying sunlight plays on the brickwork, virtually turning the castle into its own *son et lumière* – appearing dark and brooding one minute and light and airy just minutes later as the light changes and clouds pass.

Those attempting to gain entry had to negotiate a 'murder hole': two portcullises with a space between. Here people entering could be trapped between the two gates and then, helpless, killed from above.

Inside, there is what seems to be the carving of a face in the corner of an upper window. Its identity is unknown, and it could be de Soulis – no one knows what he looked like, and no likenesses are known to exist. Jenny Much, the custodian, told us that it seems to change expression as the light changes, and sometimes doesn't even appear to be a face. We saw this for ourselves – sometimes it was remarkably clear, yet in some of our photographs it seems hardly discernible.

In the grounds, towards the chapel, is the area of the river, Hermitage Water, known as the 'drowning pool'. Enemies were killed here also. In July 1996 a visitor complained that she had been pushed from behind when walking in broad daylight in the fields next to the castle and the 'drowning pool'. No one else was there. We spoke to some of the locals in the nearby town of Newcastleton. In particular we spoke to Jane Elliot of Copshaw Kitchen. She related stories of dogs being afraid to go near areas of the castle, and the dungeon in particular. This was confirmed by Jenny when she told us that her own dog refused to go to certain parts of the castle.

On 28 September 1990 an incident occurred which Jenny described as the one she regarded as the most important. It was 7.30 p.m., and the castle was closing. During an approaching thunderstorm Jenny tried to close the castle door for the night. The key would not turn, so oil was fetched. This had no effect. Another key was brought, still with no effect. More oil was applied and the door was eventually closed with great difficulty. As the evening went on a huge storm arose; her dog was disturbed and, unusually, would not go back to the castle. As Jenny drove away both she and the dog became further agitated. At one point she thought she could hear the laughing of 'demons', and was very frightened that night.

Exactly six years later to the day, 28 September 1996, another unpleasant evening occurred. It was very dark. There was scaffolding up around the entrance door, making a dark tunnel. The batteries in Jenny's torch suddenly failed, so she had to feel her way to lock the door in the dark, and again the door could not be shut. Her dog was very restless.

She could only see the red of the dog's eyes, and was reminded of the claim that de Soulis used black dogs for sacrifice. She felt very uneasy. (If more detail were known about the history of the castle, could there be shown to be some significance to the date of 28 September?)

In 1997 we visited Hermitage and spent the night there. We have been told by the custodian that we were the first people to spend the night in the castle for over 100 years, that many teams had tried and 'quit'. Bob Schott, a video producer for the company Adventures Beyond, claimed that 137 people had turned down his requests before we agreed to assist.

The castle was basically 'inactive' the night we were there, though for a short time there was a build-up of oppressive atmosphere. We experienced a couple of strange and unexplained noises, saw a flash of light which we could not account for, and had very strange problems with the camera equipment. Just as the film crew were setting up the cameras, the cameraman exclaimed that his camera and cable had just heated up to 99 degrees and had then 'burnt out'. He seemed particularly shocked when he realized the equipment was not yet attached to any power source. All of this happened within a few moments. Then the atmosphere lightened; it seems that whatever energy had built up was suddenly dissipated. After that the strangest event of the night was discovering that the castle was slowly filling up with strange-shaped creatures with golden eyes. When we got torches on to the area we discovered that someone had left the outer door open and a herd of sheep had dropped in to visit!

The following night, psychic medium Eddie Burks spent a few hours in the castle. He, according to Bob Schott, picked up some distress around the 'pit', felt a tremendous amount of evil present, and sensed the presence of a woman in pain in the kitchen area. Bob himself returned to the castle alone to challenge the presences there; nothing significant happened, but his intuition was that something was present. We have all agreed that we would like to continue further work together there.

Research showed some interesting points. One early owner of the castle was Nicholas de Soulis, who was evil and villainous. It is said that his atrocities were so depraved they have never been revealed. The King, tired of complaints about him by the locals, exclaimed: 'Boil him . . . but bother me no longer.' It is said he was wrapped in lead and melted in a boiling cauldron!

A later owner, Sir William Douglas, starved at least one person to death in the oubliette – Sir Alexander Ramsey, one of his rivals. It appears that the legend of 'Terrible William', Lord de Soulis, is actually a combination of these two characters. Of the sprite Robin Redcap we can find no history. However, Redcap is the name of a poisonous fungi, also known as fly agaric, which may cause hallucination and is possibly used in witchcraft. This seems to tie up with the black magic rumours about the castle. And we know also that plants given the name Robin, such as Ragged Robin, are often poisonous. So Robin Redcap could come through folklore as a description of this poisonous drug.

Another famous owner of the castle was James Hepburn, the Earl of Bothwell. He was visited at Hermitage by Mary, Queen of Scots. Bothwell, after aiding in the murder of Mary's husband Lord Darnley, married her himself, which was thought to have been a politically bad move for both of them. Was this the 'woman in pain' that Eddie Burks sensed? A previous custodian claims to have seen Bothwell's ghost walking across the courtyard. The locals also say that a ghost is sometimes seen on the battlements, usually a solitary figure, possibly John Stenhouse of Hawick.

A workman recently reported seeing a figure standing in an upper window when the castle was locked and empty. That may be the most telling claim of all – there are no floors in that area of Hermitage; the figure would have been around thirty feet from the ground!

SEE ALSO:
- Newark Castle.

WHILE YOU'RE THERE:
- It is a short trip from Hermitage to Langholm, which is the historic lair of Clan Armstrong. They were cattle rustlers and outlaws noted for making their attacks during bright moonlit nights. Indeed, the phrase 'there will be moonlight tonight' meant locally that danger was afoot. Appropriate then, perhaps, that one of their descendants was Neil Armstrong, the first man to set foot on the moon. He was made a freeman of Langholm on 11 March 1972 when he visited the area.

Hever Castle
(near Edenbridge, Kent)

Building at Hever Castle began in the 1270s and was re-fortified in 1340 and 1380. In 1460 it came into the hands of Henry Boleyn, the Lord Mayor of London and grandfather of Anne Boleyn. It is said that it was at Hever that Henry VIII first saw Anne. After Anne's execution her father, Sir Thomas, lived at Hever in disgrace, dying in 1538. After his death Henry gave the castle to Anne of Cleves. A considerable amount of restoration work was done in the early 1900s by William Waldorf Astor, 1st Viscount Astor of Hever, who added several Tudor-style cottages as guest houses. The Astor family still own the property.

There are reports of a ghostly female figure seen gliding across the bridge in the grounds, not surprisingly attributed to Anne, and of a male figure thought to be a farmer who was murdered there.

Del Stephen Watts visited Hever Castle in 1989 with his mother. She took a photograph of the architecture, but when the picture was developed there was a figure clearly visible. 'I went on a trip with my mother. It was in the summer, in June, and it was quite hot. Why I say this is because everybody was wearing just T-shirts, and light clothing. But the figure that we photographed standing underneath the archway was wearing a long blue cape, very warm looking. The top half of the person is missing; it was just a light blue haze. I think it was Anne Boleyn, she was beheaded after all.' It is true that there are several reports of sightings of what is believed to be Anne Boleyn's headless ghost. 'There are about eight archways on that side and a fountain in front of the archways. My mother specifically waited until there was nobody there, she wanted no one in the pictures. At the time of course there were many tourists walking around, so we waited until there was only us two there. And all the archways were quite dark. But they were empty. And then my mother took a photograph and I saw that there was no one underneath the archways. And when we had it developed, about a month later, the figure was visible underneath one of the archways.'

SEE ALSO:
- Biggin Hill (anniversary ghosts).

WHILE YOU'RE THERE:
- Nearby Chiddingstone Castle deserves a visit. It has a very elegant ghost seen in riding habit and tricorne, riding his horse along the lanes near the castle.

Newark Castle
(near Selkirk, Borders, Scottish)

Newark was built on a mound in 1423, a rectangular tower house with end gables surrounded by a barmkin (an outer defensive wall). Today it is a ruin, but is none the less well preserved. It was the site of a slaughter in 1645 when some 500 supporters of Montrose, together with their families, who had survived the Battle of Philliphaugh, were murdered by the victorious Covenanters.

The sensitive and psychic ghost-researcher Joan Forman visited Newark Castle on two occasions and on both had paranormal experiences suggestive of hauntings. While standing in the castle courtyard at the edge of the escarpment on which it is built, she felt the pain and anguish of death there. She related it to a historian who was with her, who explained that she was wrong. Opinion was that the massacre did not take place in the courtyard but on the moor opposite and that executions took place in Edinburgh. 'I'm afraid history does not agree with you,' he said. Some time later the historian contacted her with surprising news: her impressions had been right after all. The final slaughter did indeed take place under the castle cliff and some men, women and children had been butchered in the courtyard.

On the second visit Forman went alone so that she would not be 'interrupted' by the vibrations of others and so that she could concentrate on the atmosphere. As she approached the main door she could hear voices inside, though logic suggested that there should not be anyone in the closed castle. As she approached closer the voices dissolved away. She did not feel that these ghosts were from the battle era but from an earlier or later time.

SEE ALSO:
• Hermitage Castle.

WHILE YOU'RE THERE:
• Travel east to Ednam. Around half a mile west of the village is a knoll known as the Piper's Grave. Once known as Pict's Knowe, it is a Pict burial mound. Local legend says that a piper crept into the mound to learn the tunes of the fairy folk but, failing to take a protective talisman, he never emerged again.

Peel Castle
(Peel, Isle of Man)

The Isle of Man's best-known spectral dog is the Moddey Dhoo, who frequents Peel Castle. Legend has it that a soldier sought to discover if the animal was 'dog or devil'. He returned gibbering incoherently and died three days later.

The author Sax Rohmer, of *Fu Manchu* fame, spent a night in Peel Castle and located the area where the soldier had been; he reported hearing doglike howls coming from inside the passageway. Rohmer believed that the dog dated from early pagan rituals.

WHILE YOU'RE THERE:

• If you are crossing over the Ballona Bridge, local tradition says that you must always offer a polite greeting to 'the little people'.

Rait Castle
(near Nairn, Highland, Scotland)

During clan rivalries Rait Castle, which belonged to the Comyns, was host to a particularly gruesome ambush. The Comyn clan invited the Mackintoshes to dine, intending to murder them. However, the Mackintoshes were warned of what was happening and came prepared. The chief of the Comyns believed that his own daughter had betrayed the clan, as she was in love with a Mackintosh. He cut off her hands. Wild and mad, she leapt to her death from the tower. A ghost in a blood-stained dress and with no hands has been reported wandering there in the centuries since.

WHILE YOU'RE THERE:

• A short trip of fifteen or twenty miles will bring you to the shores of Loch Ness. Look out for you know what . . .

Richmond Castle
(Richmond, North Yorkshire)

Richmond Castle is situated in Tower Street, overlooking the river Swale. There are magnificent views over the surrounding area from the 100-foot keep. The castle was built around 1071 by Alan 'the Red' of Brittany, following the award of a great deal of land in Yorkshire by William the Conqueror for his part in William's successes. Over time the castle was expanded, and the town of Richmond grew up nearby. It is believed to be connected by secret tunnels to nearby Easby Abbey.

The castle and surrounding area sports the legend of the drummer boy. It is said that at the end of the eighteenth century soldiers found the opening of a narrow passageway under the keep. Wishing to explore it, but finding that most adults were too large to fit into the tunnel, they persuaded a drummer boy from the regiment to enter the tunnel to explore it. He was instructed to beat his drum as he progressed and, guided by the drumbeats, the soldiers would follow his route above ground. The sounds led the soldiers across Market Place, towards the Frenchgate, along the river Swale and towards Easby. At Easby, about half a mile from the abbey, the sounds ceased. It is said that the drummer boy was never heard from, or seen, again. A stone – known locally as the Drummer Boy's Stone – marks the spot. Visitors to the castle are invited to take the 'Drummer Boy's Walk' for three miles around the area where the drummer boy walked. The custodian of the castle, Helen Constantine, reported to us that some visitors have claimed to hear a drumming sound in the area.

Helen also reminds us of the local legend that King Arthur and his Knights are supposed to lie sleeping under Richmond Castle, waiting for the clarion call to arms. This is a claim made for several areas of Britain, including Glastonbury and the Scottish Borders. Richmond legend tells of a potter who was exploring the tunnels and came across the sleeping knights in a huge cavern; fearful of their stirring from their slumbers, he ran out.

SEE ALSO:

• Penhill Beacon.

WHILE YOU'RE THERE:

• Close by, to the north, is Melsonby. There, Lady Well is haunted by a headless woman. Local tradition also tells of fairies that gather at Diddlesley Hill, on Gatherly Moor.

Rivington Castle
(Rivington, Lancashire)

Rivington stands at a crossroads near the M61, on the side of the Liverpool Waterworks Reservoirs.

The ruins of Rivington Castle have a long reputation for haunting. In 1967 five workmen from nearby Horwich watched for around two hours as a white figure moved within the castle grounds. At 5.30 in the morning Richard Dabbs saw a white shape on the highest part of the castle. At first it looked like a mirror reflecting sunlight, but as the sun rose he could see the white shape behind. The shape moved to and fro for some ten minutes. Dabbs told his fellow workmates, who ignored his comments, and for half an hour or so the matter was dropped. However, shortly afterwards one of his workmates went outside for something and also saw something white moving about. All four then went outside and watched the white shape moving about in and out of bushes at the foot of the castle ruins. They formed the impression that it was a figure keeping a lookout; it continually walked back and forth along the same route, travelling from the bottom of the castle to the top and then back again. At around 7.30 a.m. it disappeared behind bushes and was not seen again.

Despite the long duration of the sighting and the multiple witnesses to it, there are questions remaining. The workmen were some three miles from the castle ruins when they were observing the figure, and they were able to work out that to be visible at such a distance the figure would have needed to be around twice the height of a normal human. What they saw, however, remains a mystery.

SEE ALSO:
- Golborne.
- Samlesbury Hall.

Scarborough Castle
(Scarborough, North Yorkshire)

Scarborough Castle is a huge, magnificent-looking ruin on the clifftops. Piers Gaveston, the Earl of Cornwall, was a favourite of King Edward II. Edward ruled from 1307 to 1327 and was a weak leader, acting usually at the behest of some favourite nobleman or other. For a time the Earl of Cornwall had been one of the King's favourites; he was therefore one of those who had wielded power through the weak King and hence also fell victim to the revolt against him. He was captured at Scarborough and taken to Warwick for execution. His ghost is, predictably, headless and vicious. It lures people to their death over the battlements, particularly those foolish enough to venture into the castle at night. It is said that occasionally the ghost lunges towards people, causing them to leap out of the way, possibly attempting to make them fall over the battlements.

SEE ALSO:
- Burton Agnes Manor House.
- Whitby Abbey.

WHILE YOU'RE THERE:
- Robin Hood is famous for his exploits in Nottingham Forest and for baiting the Sheriff of Nottingham, but few know of the local tradition

of Robin at sea with a fishing fleet from Scarborough. He was fishing with them when a French man-o'-war attacked the fishing boat. Robin led a team to board the attacker, killed the captain, liberated a large quantity of gold and presented it to the poor fishermen.

Sherborne Old and New Castles
(Sherborne, Dorset)

As a reward for loyalty Sir Walter Raleigh was granted the Manor of Sherborne in 1592. He tried to make the Old Castle his home, but finding it difficult to make it habitable he built a house which is the basis of the present New Castle. The Old Castle contains a stone seat known as Sir Walter Raleigh's seat, and it is held that each Michaelmas Eve at midnight the famous explorer returns there for a rest after walking round the grounds. His ghost is reputedly without a head; no doubt a reflection of his having been beheaded in 1618 on the orders of James I. There is an amusing story of Raleigh during his life, related to the 'seat'. Shortly after having brought tobacco back from the New World, he was apparently sitting in his seat smoking a pipeful of his tobacco when he was spotted by a loyal servant, who believed him on fire and 'put him out' by throwing a pitcher of beer over him!

The Old Castle allegedly carries a curse to any lay owners. The curse was allegedly placed on the castle by Osmond, one of William the Conqueror's knights, who handed it over to the church and put a curse on anyone who should take it out of ecclesiastical hands. Lay owners who have apparently suffered misfortune include the Earl of Somerset and Sir Walter Raleigh himself.

In *Memoirs*, published in 1878, Lady Chatterton reported a ghostly experience when she stayed in the New Castle. She was four years old at the time and she and her Scottish nanny were put in a large room on the third floor, with beautiful views over the gardens and the Old Castle. During the night she was awoken by a brilliant light and saw figures of men fighting 'like the reflection produced by a magic lantern'. It appears she was watching the replay of a violent battle. Perhaps even more startling, when she tried to alert her nurse she discovered that the nurse was sitting up, not awake, but with her eyes fixed on the apparitions, apparently making signs to them, talking to them and signalling them to go away. Suddenly the apparition ended, leaving Lady Chatterton with a feeling of horror and dread. She could not sleep until the sun had dawned. She later discovered that this was known as the Haunted Room and that no one was keen to sleep in it.

At a later time the family again stayed in Sherborne New Castle, her mother and father sleeping in the room directly below the Haunted Room. Her mother was awoken by the sounds of what she described as dead bodies falling or being thrown about on the floor above. Her father took a candle and ascended the staircase to see what was happening, opened the door but found it empty.

SEE ALSO:

- Purse Caundle Manor (anniversary ghost).
- Cadbury Castle.

WHILE YOU'RE THERE:

- A short cross-country trip will take you to Winterbourne White-church. Take a look at the church in the village and at the field just west of the village crossroads, known as the Round Meadow. According to the local story, the Round Meadow was the chosen site for the church but the site was cursed. Each time bricks were left in the field ready for building they would be mysteriously moved into another field. This was interpreted as divine intervention and the church was built near the quarry where it stands today. Round Meadow is supposedly still cursed today; whenever the field is mowed, it brings rain and storms.

Stirling Castle
(Stirling, Stirling, Scotland)

Described by the poet Alexander Smith as the brooch that 'clasps Highlands and Lowlands together', Stirling houses arguably the mightiest fortress in Scotland. It was built in the fifteenth century as a replacement for a wooden fort that used to stand on the site and remains today as impressive as the day it was built. Mary, Queen of Scots was crowned in the chapel there in 1543 and lived a great deal of her life at Stirling Castle.

Of the ghosts of Stirling Castle perhaps the most famous is the Green Lady. She is said by many to have been Mary, Queen of Scots' maidservant, who at one time saved the Queen's life. According to legend, the servant had a premonition that Mary was in danger, went to the Queen's bedroom and found it on fire. She pulled her mistress to safety. Appearances of the Green Lady have been held to be premonitions of fires and disasters at the castle. One cook quartered in the castle reported that while making soup he could see someone watching him and turned around to see the form of a woman dressed in green; he fainted.

There is also a Pink Lady, the apparition of a young girl dressed in pink who is alleged to walk between the castle and the nearby church. It is thought she dates from the time when womenfolk and children watched the men jousting in the area known as Lady's Rock.

WHILE YOU'RE THERE:

- Keep an eye on the skies. You are in the area of one of the largest UFO waves in the subject's fifty year history. Identified with the town of Bonnybridge, near Falkirk, a few miles to the south down the M80, the sightings (one count numbered them at around 8,000 reports!) arise all over the area. Bright luminous balls of light, and triangular-shaped objects, have been prominent.

Threave Castle
(near Castle Douglas, Dumfries and Galloway, Scotland)

Threave Castle started life in 1370, built by Archibald 'the Grim', 3rd Earl of Douglas, Lord of Galloway. It was a major part of the Douglas defences against King James II, who was determined to break the power of the Douglas clan. In 1455 James II's forces besieged and eventually took the castle. The Great Tower of the castle remains fairly intact; around it are the ruins of what is thought to be the first 'artillery' wall in Britain. It seems the castle was built to withstand siege, being self-sufficient. The inside well can still be seen, full of water.

The castle is situated on an island in the river Dee and can only be reached by a small 'ferry' rowing-boat which takes four people at a time. We were there in 1997 along with a video production crew from California, Adventures Beyond, run by Bob Schott. We were told that a caretaker at the castle sometimes heard voices there when she was quite definitely on her own. Peter, our ferryman, took us to the castle and we were left there to spend some time while it was quiet, hoping we would be able to hear the ghostly voices. During the quiet of the night we were able to hear not the sound of a ghost but music, which was coming from quite a distance but was modern enough to suggest an 'ordinary' origin. We realized that sounds in that location can be deceiving and can travel unexpectedly long distances. This does not, of course prove that the voices reported are not ghostly but that further investigation should be done in future.

While we were on the upper floor of Threave we had all been examining a chimney-like opening in one wall. All of us had taken turns standing in the small, fireplace-like opening below it. One member of the team, Al, suddenly had a very uneasy feeling, backed out of the opening quickly and for some time refused to go back.

While looking in the visitors' book, open on the table downstairs, we noticed something that might be of interest, though it could equally be unimportant. It seemed that ghosts were on people's minds while they were in the castle, at least at certain times. The entries for 2 and 3 June 1997 seemed to have a higher numbers of entries referring to 'ghosts' and 'ghostly' than entries for other days. Had there been something of an atmosphere on those days? It could, of course, have just been a gloomy, dark day; or a bunch of schoolfriends playing around; or one entry leading others to copy.

SEE ALSO:
• Baldoon Castle.

Tower of London
(London)

Held by many to be the most haunted building in London, if not the world, the Tower is also probably the building with the longest royal history. Its core is the Keep, or White Tower, built by William the Conqueror.

The earliest report of a haunting is that of St Thomas à Becket during the building of Traitor's Gate. The story states that St Thomas's ghost's disapproval of the work caused 'him' to bring it to rubble twice by striking it with his cross. Henry III apparently finished the work in the end, naming the work St Thomas's Tower after St Thomas, and the haunting was not reported again. Richard III is popularly, though possibly incorrectly, blamed for the murder of his two nephews, the twelve-year-old King Edward V and his nine-year old brother Richard, the Duke of York. What are thought to be their skeletons were found in the Tower in 1674 and buried in Westminster Abbey. Their spirits have been seen several times in the Bloody Tower where they were imprisoned, dressed in their white nightgowns, standing hand in hand.

Another haunting associated with St Thomas's Tower was reported by a deputy governor of the Tower who, when returning to his quarters together with his wife, was asked by a Yeoman if they had visitors. They replied that they had not, but the Yeoman said that he had seen a face looking down from one of their windows. This did not faze the couple, apparently the wife only commenting: 'Oh, is it there again?' The face had apparently been reported many times before.

In 1817, in the Martin Tower, Edmund Swifte, the Keeper of the Crown Jewels, was having supper with his family. Mrs Swifte saw a luminous cylinder in the air, 'like a glass tube' oscillating from white to light blue. The object revolved, passing close to Mrs Swifte's chair and causing her some distress. The family watched the apparition for some three minutes before it faded away.

The Martin Tower is also the site of several reports of the apparition of a large bear, which many believe harks back to the days when the Tower housed the royal menagerie.

Northumberland's Walk is named after the Earl of Northumberland, who was a prisoner in the Tower and for whom the Walk was his exercise area. His ghost has been seen on the Walk by many people; for a time some sentries preferred to remain in pairs in the area rather than be alone.

The executed Queen of Henry VIII, Anne Boleyn, is reputed to haunt the Queen's House within the Tower of London; this was a building in which she was imprisoned for four days prior to her execution. The Queen has been seen by many witnesses, including several sentries who have charged the apparition with bayonets only to pass right through the form.

Lady Jane Grey and Guildford Dudley were both executed on Tower Hill; ghosts of both have been reported. Guildford Dudley's ghost has been seen in the Beauchamp Tower apparently sobbing gently as if contemplating his own death, and Lady Jane Grey's ghost was reported in the mid 1900s. A guardsman called Johns saw the figure of a woman on the battlements and identified it as Lady Jane Grey; he called another sentry who also witnessed the figure.

Sir Walter Ralegh is frequently reported in a spectral form at the Tower. He was imprisoned there and walked the battlements for exercise prior to his execution.

Poltergeist activity has been reported in the Tower, for example in the kitchens drawers have been seen opening and shutting spontaneously. This, it seems, occurs around the New Year.

The list of ghostly reports is as varied as it is long, with ghostly choirs, precognition, time slips and other varied and often menacing hauntings. Reports have been received from visitors, from the Yeomen and from other employees working in the Tower. All in all it probably deserves its reputation as one of the most haunted locations in the world.

SEE ALSO:

- London's various locations; mainly palaces and theatres.

WHILE YOU'RE THERE:

- Lombard Street is in the centre of the City of London's Banking and Finance area. But in 1647 a violent and hideous ghost was seen there which slammed windows and could vanish away into the ground while creating noises like claps of thunder.

CHAPTER 2

~

HAUNTED CHURCHES AND PRIORIES

Bisham Abbey
(Bisham, Berkshire)

The reputation of Bisham Abbey as the most haunted building in Berkshire possibly relates to its original use in the thirteenth century as a house of the Knights Templars. One of Queen Elizabeth I's confidantes, Lady Elizabeth Hoby, lived there. Lady Hoby apparently had six children. The youngest, William, did not come up to her expectations and she beat him to death. However, there are no records of William's birth and the tale may be legendary. One version of the story says that he was beaten because of a failure to be tidy in his workbook; in 1840, during renovations of the abbey, workmen found old school books that related to the Hoby family and in one of them the writing was smudged and blotted. However, it may be that the discovery of the book has embellished the legend.

After her death in her eighties Lady Elizabeth's ghost was seen at the abbey looking sorrowful and regretful. In the most dramatic of accounts she is said to walk through the corridors washing her hands rather in the manner of Lady Macbeth. One account of her apparition was given in 1910 by Admiral Vansittart. While playing chess with his brother under a painting of Lady Hoby, he saw her 'leave the frame' and walk around the house. Charles Harper has reported that the ghost is always seen as a 'negative', i.e. a white dress but with black face and hands.

SEE ALSO:
• Windsor Castle.

- To the west of Reading is Tidmarsh. It is said that on clear nights in June, with a full moon, the ghost of a boy drowned in a stream rises again – around 100 yards from the rectory.

Borley Church
(Borley, Essex)

Whether the now-destroyed rectory at Borley was actually the most haunted building in England, as claimed by many, it can almost certainly take the title of the most *written about* haunted building in England. But this focus of attention on the rectory has served only to detract from the equally impressive but less examined hauntings associated with Borley Church.

The church itself is built on the site of a wooden church. It was replaced by a flint and rubble building in the twelfth century and the present church incorporates some of this into its present wall. In the fifteenth century the chancel, north wall and west tower were added; the red brick south porch was added in the century after that.

In 1974 Denny Densham, film director and cameraman, set up tape recorders in Borley Church as the basis of a BBC documentary. During the winter months around midnight the tape picked up a series of knocks and raps from the empty church. On another occasion two tape recorders both picked up sounds of a heavy door being opened and slammed shut accompanied by a squeaking bolt. But the porch door and chancel door had not been opened, as the observers were able to watch, and the bolt on the chancel door was not squeaky. The following week sophisticated microphones were set up and an additional cassette machine positioned in the church; half the vigil team stayed in the church and half remained outside in the churchyard. Members of the team felt a presence and a feeling of being watched, and felt the temperature drop. They heard, and the tape picked up, a clattering as if something was thrown in the aisles. They heard knockings and rappings, again the sound of the door opening and closing and being bolted and the sound of a human sigh.

In July the team again 'staked out' Borley during the night, and again felt a change of atmosphere. Again they heard the sound of the door shutting and the sounds of footsteps, despite the fact that the floor where the sounds were coming from was heavily carpeted. The team saw a glowing light near the chancel door and heard a terrifying grunt.

In 1974 several photographs were taken by psychical researcher Ronald Russell, of which he comments: 'Sandwiched between perfectly normal frames we got 'ectoplasmic' stuff in the churchyard, shadows where no shadows should be, and a thin light near the north door. As a photographer I'm at a loss to explain this as camera or film malfunction'. Together with another team, Russell also recorded noises, footsteps and crashes similar to those recorded by Densham.

Nor was Russell's photography unique. In *Picture Post* in 1954 a photograph taken in Borley churchyard by Thurston Hopkins has a 'black mist' on it that the photographer did not see when taking the photograph and which he cannot explain.

There are many accounts of electrical interference, equipment mal-function, abnormalities on photographs and so on, all of which are common to various areas of psychical research and which seem particularly prevalent at Borley.

The church is also one of many where there are a number of reports of organ music heard from inside the locked and empty church.

The famous ghostly nun of Borley has been seen in the churchyard. For example, a Mr Cole of Great Cornard saw the nun in 1951 standing under a tree looking sad and dejected. He described her as looking normal, with a black hood, white collar and black skirt. He approached her and she disappeared. Others have seen a figure in black walk towards the priest door of Borley Church and disappear.

The Reverend Harry Bull, the Rector of Borley from 1892 until 1927 and famously associated with the hauntings at Borley Rectory, was one of the first to hear the strange tapping noises in Borley Church. A subsequent rector, the Reverend Alfred Clifford Henning, from 1936 to 1955, also reported phenomena. In 1946 he reported the story of a Miss Byford who was teaching Sunday School at the church; the children arrived early and sat down to wait for her and heard footsteps coming along the path. They heard the sound of a key in the lock. Thirteen-year-old Kathleen Finch went to the door and called out to her teacher but got no reply. Miss Byford arrived shortly afterwards and found the door locked; there was no explanation found for the previous sounds. Also in 1946, on 21 April, John Durrant and his fiancée visited the church and heard footsteps and the sound of the latch being lifted. The door did not open, so Mr Durrant opened it from the inside and found no one standing there.

Of particular interest perhaps is the observation by historian and folklorist Graham McEwan, in his book *Haunted Churches of England*, that there are links between the hauntings at Langenhoe Church and those at Borley. Both villages belonged to the same family at one time, the Waldegraves, and there were times when the two churches were served by the same rector. There are also phenomena in common. McEwan lists: 'The phantom of a sad faced nun; sibilant murmurings, in which the words are indistinguishable; music resembling plainsong; unaccountable, sometimes offensive, smells; the mysterious locking and unlocking of doors; the involvement of bricks; mysterious footsteps; and the unexplained ringing of the church bells.'

Stone-throwing in poltergeist cases is probably one of the commonest manifestations, and Borley Church has at least one such account. In the early 1980s an elderly couple and their daughter visited Borley and heard the sound of music coming from the church. They decided to go in and listen but found the church empty and the organ locked up. While inside the church they took the opportunity to admire the Waldegrave monument and were suddenly assailed by dozens of small pebbles falling from above. Although falling all around them and close to them, not one actually hit them.

Wesley Downes in *Essex Ghost and Hauntings No 1* in the spring of 1994 relates the story of a 'timeslip photograph' at Borley. A group of investigators felt their attention was being drawn towards the chancel door and one photographed it. To quote Downes's account: 'When the film was developed, they were amazed to find that the photo revealed not the chancel door as it exists nowadays, but a wider, higher and more Gothic style doorway, with the interior of the church well lit and an obscure figure of what appeared to be a veiled bride.' Downes points out that 'four people can testify the sequence of events'.

SEE ALSO:
- Four Sisters Crossroads, A12, Stratford St Mary.
- Abbey Ruins, Bury St Edmunds.

WHILE YOU'RE THERE:
- Drive carefully and watch out for strange objects parked in fields by the road. Ros Reynolds and her boyfriend were driving very near here in 1982 when they saw a UFO, first in the sky and then hovering in a nearby field. Ros believes that she was abducted by aliens and taken aboard the craft.

Abbey Ruins
(Bury St Edmunds, Suffolk)

There have been several sightings of ghostly monks in the abbey ruins at Bury St Edmunds in Suffolk. Several people have seen the apparition of monks in brown clothes gliding around, particularly by the abbey gateway, but in fact the best-known spectre is that of a nun, Maude Carew. There are houses built into the west front of the old ruined church and it is there in 1446 that it is believed Maude poisoned the Duke of Gloucester while he was imprisoned. She is seen in the present buildings as a Grey Lady passing through both rooms and witnesses, to their consternation.

SEE ALSO:

• Borley Church.

WHILE YOU'RE THERE:

• There is also a haunting at the nearby museum at Moyses Hall. The museum houses the relics of William Corder, the murderer of Maria Martin in the red barn at Polstead. Among other items is a book bound with his skin. His execution at Bury was attended by 7,000 people and afterwards his head was removed from his body, but it was thought to be an omen of bad luck to those who held it and it was therefore buried.

Castle Acre Priory
(Castle Acre, Norfolk)

The Priory at Castle Acre is thought to date from soon after the Norman victory at the Battle of Hastings in 1066. It is a wonderfully peaceful site, set in the atmospheric, historic village of Castle Acre.

Liz Gray and Alex Kemp, who work at the Priory, told us that phantom monks were seen by two ladies together. The ghostly figures were seen to walk under the gateway and along the walkway that leads to the Priory. Another ghost has been seen sitting by the fireplace in the solar of the prior's lodgings. It is thought that this figure is not a monk but comes from the time when the building was used as a farm building.

SEE ALSO:

• Castle Rising Castle.
• Sandringham.

WHILE YOU'RE THERE:
• North of Castle Acre is Syderstone; on the common there have been reports of a phantom highwayman.

The Chapel of St Peter ad Murum
(near Bradwell-on-Sea, Essex)

St Peter ad Murum is one of the oldest chapels in Britain. Built in 654 by St Cedd from the ruins of an old Roman fort that had stood on the site, the chapel is actually positioned on what is thought to have been the gate-house of the fort. It was re-consecrated in 1920, having been a beacon tower, smugglers' hideaway and cattle shed in its long history. In recent years there have been many reports of strange lights shining from within the chapel but without apparent explanation, and also of shadowy figures moving around inside making no sound.

SEE ALSO:
• Mersea Island.

WHILE YOU'RE THERE:
• A ghostly Roman on horseback has been seen at Bradwell-on-Sea; a similar phenomenon to that reported on nearby Mersea Island.

Chicksands Priory
(near Shefford, Bedfordshire)

Built in 1150, the priory became an officer's mess for the RAF/USAF base at Chicksands just after the Second World War. There are several hauntings reported in the priory. In 1954 a serving airman, asleep in his room, awoke early in the morning and switched on his light to find 'at the side of my bed a woman with a ruddy face and untidy hair, wearing a dark dress with a white lace collar. She appeared to be holding a notepad. She moved to the foot of my bed and vanished.'

In 1957 what appeared to be the head and shoulders of a nun was seen in contemplative thought.

The identity of the ghosts is unknown but the association with the nun is obviously thought to date back to the time when the building housed a large number of nuns. This came to an end in 1538 when John Orrey, the Prior of Chicksands, and Margaret Burton, the Prioress, acknowledged the suppression of the monasteries and priories and gave up the building. The local legend is that the nun seen was made pregnant by a lover, possibly one of the canons also stationed at the priory, and was walled up alive after having witnessed the execution of her lover. This may arise from the comments of Dr Richard Layton, writing to Oliver Cromwell in 1534, who confirmed that two of the nuns at the priory were pregnant. There is a plaque commemorating the fate of a nun, Berta Rosata: 'By virtues guarded and by manners graced, Here alas is fair Rosata placed'. However, the authenticity of the plaque has been called into question and it is believed to date from the eighteenth century rather than from the time when the priory was active.

In the 1960s the shade of a woman dressed in black was seen in the picture gallery next to the King James's Room and was seen to disappear through a wall. Another member of the staff saw 'a fascinating woman dressed in white glide past me. I heard the rustle of her dress and saw the long white train as she moved past. It was about ten o'clock in the evening, some time in January'.

SEE ALSO:
- Bedford.

WHILE YOU'RE THERE:
- Take a short trip to Cardington and admire the sheer size of the two airship hangars still dominating the skyline. It was from these hangars on 4 October 1930 that the airship the R-101 set off on its ill-fated voyage to India. The airship crashed near Beauvais in France with great loss of life. Over a year earlier the celebrated psychic medium Eileen Garrett had had a premonition of the disaster: while exercising her dog in Hyde Park she had looked up and seen the airship above her then saw it burst into flames and dive behind some buildings. But it was a vision – the only airships that could have been in the skies at that time were in their hangars at Cardington and there are no reports of an actual crash. Furthermore there were psychic messages to Emilie, wife of a deceased pilot, W.G.R. Hinchliffe, warning of the impending disaster of the airship. These were coming through mediums Garrett and Mrs Beatrice Earl. After the disaster, messages were received from the captain, Flight Lieutenant Irwin, commenting on the problems they had encountered. It is said that the hangar is an 'unlucky spot' even today.

Church of St Mary and St Gregory
(Frithelstock, Devon)

Sometimes it is not haunting but the possible interpretation of a paranormal event which is of most fascination, and occasionally an account brings with it the possibility of some insight into the paranormal, albeit with a tendency to ask more questions than are answered.

Just such a case arises with an account of a paranormal incident at the priory ruins that adjoin the Church of St Mary and St Gregory at Frithelstock. The church was founded in the early 1200s by Sir Robert de Bello Compo and Bishop Walter de Stapledon, who created it for a group of Augustinian monks. Theo Brown, in *Transactions of a Devonshire Association* (Volume CVIII, 1976), tells us that Mrs Barbara Carbonnell, in 1932, was on a committee charged with the excavation of Frithelstock Priory and she went there to meet a colleague. She took with her her daughter and her daughter's son, Christopher, then aged seven. When the car stopped, Christopher ran into the ruins first and they found him standing inside the wicket gate, crying that he was glad he had come because 'I love this place'. Mrs Carbonnell pointed out that neither he nor his mother had been there before. Christopher was adamant. 'I have been here before. I have long, long ago when I was a very old man.' To dismiss such a claim as pure fantasy in a child of seven would possibly be somewhat reckless, but had the event ended there, there would be little of substance to go on. However, Christopher ran to the west end of the ruin and cried out, 'Oh, what have they done to my tower, my lovely tower – with the stairs that went windy up, where I pulled the bell?' Climbing on a grass-covered heap, he looked up into the sky, indicating that that was where the roof used to be. This time it was his mother who reminded him that he had never been there before and he looked back obviously puzzled and bewildered. Mrs Carbonnell asked when he had been there and he said, 'Long, long ago I rang the bell. Oh, my lovely tower'. What is significant is that there was no evidence that there had ever been a tower in that position and indeed Mrs Carbonnell thought it unlikely one would be positioned at that particular place. Later excavations, however, revealed that there had indeed been such a tower there. Graham McEwan, in *Haunted Churches of England*, points out that Mrs Carbonnell did not speculate how the child acquired knowledge but he suggests, 'Did the spirit of one of the long dead monks linger at the spot, using the boy's mind and mouth to voice its sadness at the changes time had wrought to his beloved priory?'

- A trip south down the A386 will bring you to Okehampton Castle. It is said to be visited by a spectral black dog but with luck you won't see it – those who do are said to die within the year. Not much better is the nightly procession of Lady Howard's coach, which is said to pass the castle – the coach, driven by a headless driver, is made from the bones of her four husbands.

The Church of St Nicholas
(Pluckley, Kent)

Although just about every county in England has its claim to be the most haunted village in the country, Pluckley is one very haunted village that certainly qualifies as a fair contender for the title. The Church of St Nicholas is particularly well known for its hauntings.

There is a classical Lady in White report from the churchyard, which also appears to have a ghostly white dog. Perhaps most famous is the Red Lady, thought to be Lady Dering, who is buried in the Dering Chapel. Her ghost, holding a red rose at her breast as she was apparently buried, has been seen in the churchyard. The Dering Chapel is also the scene of strange sounds and ghostly lights.

SEE ALSO:
- Saltwood.

WHILE YOU'RE THERE:
- Reported in the village are the 'Screaming Man', a spectral coach and horses, and a host of ghosts inhabiting private properties. In the nearby Park Wood, a soldier – known as the Colonel – committed suicide and his shade is said still to walk there.

Deerhurst Priory
(near Tewkesbury, Gloucestershire)

Most ghost sightings tend to be of short duration, but this is the tale of a ghost seen for a good quarter of an hour – an incredibly long time to the witness considering the frightening nature of the experience – at Deerhurst Priory in November 1968. The witness was Mrs Olive Bryant. Her husband was in the church pursuing his interest in church architecture and Mrs Bryant was sitting in her car waiting for him. At one point she looked up and saw what appeared to be an elderly woman some forty feet away. The woman was dressed in clothes that seemed to date her to the period of the First World War: cloche hat, long green coat with a broad collar, black shoes, open-back gloves and lisle stockings. Of more concern to Mrs Bryant is that the woman seemed to be mentally disturbed. She was looking straight at her, unmoving, and clearly aggressive. Several minutes of such intense staring passed, and Mrs Bryant relieved her anxieties by looking away. The Bryants' dog, sitting in the back of the car, was growling throughout the experience, apparently frightened and restless. Mrs Bryant looked up, hoping that the woman had by now left, but she was in exactly the same position and still staring exactly as before. Mrs Bryant looked away momentarily and, when she looked back, found that the woman in green was virtually leaning on the radiator of the car, staring through the window just as intensely. Although Mrs Bryant still believed she was dealing with a disturbed person, she recognized that no one could have cleared the forty-foot distance in that space of time.

Some minutes later a car stopped nearby and a woman, possibly the organist as she was carrying a bundle of music, got out and walked towards the church. As the car had approached the hostile aggressive woman in green had herself walked away from Mrs Bryant's car and was walking towards the church. The organist was just a few yards behind her.

Just moments later Mr Bryant emerged over the stile looking agitated and determined to leave quickly. 'You could cut the atmosphere in the church with a knife,' he said. When Mrs Bryant asked her husband about the woman in green, he was adamant that he had passed the organist but that she was walking alone. He was equally certain that there was nowhere that the woman could have left the path that he himself had just walked down.

Taking all the factors into account, Mrs Bryant was forced to consider the possibility that the woman she had seen had been an apparition.

SEE ALSO:
• Sudeley Castle.

WHILE YOU'RE THERE:
• Take a trip through Cheltenham and take care whom you meet there, particularly if it is a lady in black holding a handkerchief to her face. This spectre has been seen many times by various people, particularly in Pittville Circus Road. Reported often in the late 1800s, she was

seen as recently as 1970 by Mrs Doreen Jackson while on a driving lesson – causing her to brake suddenly, much to the surprise of her instructor.

Ellesborough Parish Church
(near Wendover, Buckinghamshire)

The church organist of Ellesborough Parish Church, just after the Second World War, saw the ghost of a figure he described as 'a tallish man dressed in medieval garb'. The organist, who had been playing the church organ, had heard the front door of the church open and saw the figure 'glide in' and vanish near one of the memorial tablets.

At least two other people have reported similar experiences since, suggesting that the ghost is of the 'recording' type, non-interactive and always seen doing the same thing by whoever is present at the time.

SEE ALSO:
- Haddenham.

WHILE YOU'RE THERE:
- Nearby is the Prime Minister's country residence, Chequers; in the adjacent fields in 1991 a pattern of unique crop-circles were found. They were of the 'Maltese cross' shape but with one of the arms ending not in a circle but in an arrow pointing towards the east.

Kinlet Church
(Kinlet, Shropshire)

Sir George Blount was a landowner in the Wyre Forest in the sixteenth century. The family manor house was at Kinlet. The Blounts had a church, now Kinlet Church, built beside the house. The church is still in good form today. The church houses a monument to Sir George, his wife and their two children, John and Dorothy. The circumstances leading to a haunting began when Dorothy, the apple of Sir George's eye, eloped with a servant very much against her father's wishes. Sir George swore a revenge through time on Dorothy and her family and is said to have haunted them after his death in 1581. One of his more dramatic spectral entrances was apparently riding a coach and four out of the local lake, creating an enormous noise with the pounding of hooves, the snorting of the horses and the rumbling of the coach's wheels. It is said that the family saw this apparition while they were having dinner, and it came into the hall through the doors and across the dining-room table.

In 1720, 140 years after Sir George's death, in a bid to remove his apparition – which was therefore presumably still haunting the locality – the building was destroyed and a new manor built further away from the church. (This building is now a boarding school; there are no known manifestations there.) An exorcism is said to have been held in the church to lay Sir George finally to rest, and there is a rather curious theory that his spirit was trapped in a glass bottle which was either left in the church or cast into the sea.

SEE ALSO:
- Castle Lodge.

WHILE YOU'RE THERE:
- Visit nearby Ludlow; the church, the castle as well as Castle Lodge have their hauntings. The churchyard and the rectory are haunted by a grey-haired lady apparently wearing a dressing-gown; the castle is haunted by Marion de la Bruyère, who killed her lover and then committed suicide after being betrayed by him.

Newstead Abbey
(near Ravenshead, Nottinghamshire)

Newstead Abbey is the ancestral home of the Byron family, of which the most famous member is the poet Lord Byron. For around 400 years the abbey was the priory of the black Augustine monks, but fell to King Henry VIII's dissolution. It was at this time that the abbey was given to the Byrons and it remained in the family for the next 300 years.

The most well-known ghost is that of the Black Friar, a spiteful and malicious monk who seems to be seeking revenge for the dissolution of the monastery. He is described as cold and dark. According to legend, whenever a family member died the monk would make an appearance gloating at the death, or would, just to rub salt in the wound, appear on happy and cheerful occasions looking sorrowful and downcast. Lord Byron believed the ghost appeared looking cheerful during his marriage ceremony to Annabella Milbanke, a marriage which Lord Byron described as the unhappiest event of his life.

Byron is possibly referring to the family ghost in his poem *Don Juan* when he writes:

By the marriage-bed of their Lords,
'tis said,
he flits on the bridal eve and 'tis held as faith,
to their bed of death he comes – but not to grieve.

David Cross, with psychic medium Jenny Bright, has done a lot of work researching the ghosts of Newstead Abbey. David and Jenny ran their 'Ghost Tours' from there for some years. They told us of a young electrician who had been rewiring the abbey a few years ago; he saw the monk and died in his early twenties of a strange illness.

The abbey also has a White Lady, said to be Sophia Hyatt, a deaf-mute who idolized Byron and lodged at Weir Mills Farm on the estate. She was run down by a coach and four in Nottingham but got her wish 'never to leave Newstead' – she's still there in spirit! The White Lady Restaurant at the abbey takes its name from her.

Byron's beloved dog, Boatswain (Bosun), is frequently seen today in the grounds and on the abbey roof. He was recently seen by a gardener working there. There are also a number of other hauntings not specifically related to known people. Heavy footsteps were heard in the Great Hall by a maid in the 1840s; a column of white vapour was seen in one bedroom which the servants became reluctant to enter (Lady Wildman took it as her bedroom so they had to go in or be fired!); there is a ghostly smell of perfume in one particular spot. In the so-called Ghost Room many guides and visitors report feeling a 'heavy cloak put round them, dragging them down to floor', and they often report feeling light-headed there.

David and Jenny have themselves heard ladies' voices, laughing and giggling on the stairway leading up to Lord Byron's bedroom – not too surprising, perhaps!

WHILE YOU'RE THERE:

- Consider a 'ghostly tour' with David and Jenny. Ghost Tours of Nottingham arrange a number of ghost-related events, paranormal weekends, and so on. The tours, while entertaining, are also informative and useful to those genuinely interested in ghosts and the paranormal. Jenny is a well-known psychic medium with an impressive history of work in the field, and is often seen on television documentaries on the paranormal.

Parish Church of St Mary
(Beaminster, Dorset)

The ghost report which relates to the Parish Church of St Mary is an old one but is apparently a well authenticated story. It first appeared in the *Gentleman's Magazine* in 1774 and is currently recalled in the present-day official literature of the church.

During the spring of 1728 the body of a local boy, John Daniel, had been found in a field near his home. His mother testified that he suffered from fits and he was buried without inquest. At the time the Parish Church of St Mary was being used as a schoolroom. On 27 June 1728 a number of boys were playing in the churchyard; some were inside the church and they heard something that sounded like the striking of a brass pan. The boys searched the building but could find no one. As they were ending their search they heard a second noise from the stairs leading up to the gallery, sounds of a religious service followed by singing. When these sounds had stopped one of the boys, looking for a school book, entered the schoolroom and was shocked to see within the room a coffin lying on a bench. He called the others, and five boys together returned to the room where they all saw the apparition of the dead John Daniel sitting some distance away from the coffin. He was holding a pen in his hand and had what looked like a book next to him. Four of the five boys had known him in life. In fact one of the boys was Daniel's half-brother and immediately recognized him and the coat he was wearing. This boy picked up a stone and threw it at the apparition; immediately the ghost, the pen, the book and the coffin disappeared.

A local magistrate, Colonel Brodrepp, investigated the claims of the boys and found that their stories agreed even to the minutest detail. He also discovered that their description of the coffin was exactly like the one that Daniel had been buried in. Interestingly, one of the boys had not known Daniel in life yet his account was also exactly corroborative. This boy, however, added one piece of information. He said that there was a white cloth around one of the hands of the apparition. It later transpired that the woman who had laid Daniel out for burial had indeed removed such a white cloth from the boy's hand – he had apparently suffered a small injury days before his death.

Inspired by the ghost report, the body of Daniel was exhumed and it was discovered that in fact he had been murdered by strangulation. There is, however, no record of anyone having been brought to justice for the crime.

SEE ALSO:
- Sherborne Old and New Castles, Sherborne.
- St Peter's Church, Dorchester.

WHILE YOU'RE THERE:
- A few miles to the east is the Cerne Abbas Giant. Carved into the hillside above Cerne Abbas, the figure is 180 feet long and 40 feet wide. Most notable is his huge erect phallus, which has led to fertility beliefs: that barren women can conceive after sleeping on the carving; and that women seeking to keep their lovers faithful should walk around the figure three times. The figure is believed to have been carved in 1539 and is certainly mentioned in writing in 1751 in Hutchins's *Guide to Dorset*.

Priory Church
(Christchurch, Dorset)

The Priory Church at Christchurch is largely known for its auditory ghosts. In 1972 while the church was being renovated many people heard odd tapping sounds. It might have been assumed that it was the stonemasons at work, but in fact the noises were often heard on Saturdays and Sundays when the workmen were not present. The fact that the church was undergoing restoration, however, is consistent with many ghost reports, where it appears that building work can either trigger or stop a series of hauntings. Around the time these sounds were being heard, one door on the south of the priory was known to open inexplicably from time to time, and there were strong smells of incense not originating from any obvious source. Canon Leslie Yorke had not heard the sounds but accepted that 'there have been many unaccountable noises in the priory and I certainly trust the integrity of those who tell me they have heard the tapping sounds'.

The Priory Church is not, however, without an apparition. One woman saw the ghost of a monk pass by her and walk into the Draper Chapel. Other people have reported seeing a monk in the chapel and noted that 'he' disappears inexplicably. It is thought that it could be the ghost of John Draper, the last Prior of Christchurch, who died in 1552. The chapel is named after him and indeed the church has reason to be grateful for his intervention. His association with Thomas Cromwell apparently persuaded Henry VIII to allow the church to remain standing when the monastic buildings were destroyed.

SEE ALSO:
- Town Museum, Poole, Dorset.

WHILE YOU'RE THERE:
- On a spit of land stretching from Milford on Sea to half-way to the Isle of Wight is Hurst Castle. Once a prison that held Charles I, it is now reputedly haunted by a ghostly monk.

Roche Chapel
(near Roche, Cornwall)

Roche Chapel is a ruin set high on the rocks and a well known local tourist attraction. Several local people have reported the sounds of something unseen moving around within the chapel confines. A few have reported seeing a 'fleeting shadow'.

Local legend attributes the sighting to the ghost of a miner who sought sanctuary at the chapel while under attack from 'demons'.

WHILE YOU'RE THERE:
- A trip to the east will bring you to the village of St Cleer. In a field adjacent to the village is the largest neolithic monument in Cornwall, which many believe also to be its most impressive. It is Trethevy Quoit, a fifteen-foot-high double-chambered tomb also known as the Giant's House and King Arthur's Quoit. The capstone is over twelve feet long, supported by six uprights, a seventh having fallen.

St Albans Abbey
(St Albans, Hertfordshire)

The abbey's monastic background is ever present in its hauntings, and there have been many accounts of processions of monks walking through walls and locked doors. One account from around fifty years ago was from the verger, who opened the building early one morning and watched the procession of Benedictine monks walking towards him and through the stonework.

One local woman from St Albans saw 'approaching me four very tall monks, who swayed slowly from side to side, as they moved along the pathway from the Great Gateway to the west front of the abbey'. As she watched them she could see that they were carrying between them what looked like a coffin and she found it a good time to turn and run. The same woman also heard sounds from within the abbey.

But it is the sounds and music which are perhaps most exceptional. One woman recounted: 'For many years, I lived near the abbey, and one evening I was walking home along by the railings on the south side path, and enjoying the last fingers of the summer sunlight, when from within the abbey I heard the sounds of the most beautiful music and choral accompaniment that I have ever experienced.' She wanted to hear more and tried to enter the abbey but found the door locked. As soon as she touched the door handle the music ceased; the abbey locked and empty became silent.

There have been many other witnesses to beautiful choral music echoing from the abbey when it is closed and empty. In the 1930s such an account was reported to the local Rotary Club by Frances, the widow of Canon George Glossop, of St Albans Abbey. Canon Glossop had heard the music when he was working on a sermon late at night and became convinced that it was the music of monks from the past. Three months later Canon Glossop was listening to a performance of the music of Dr Robert Fayrfax, who died in 1521. This was being played in the abbey and Canon Glossop recognized it as the music he had heard before. Robert Fayrfax is buried in the abbey.

In the 1930s a witness saw candlelight from the abbey's Lady Chapel and also heard music, but realized that the abbey should have been shut and closed at two o'clock in the morning, as indeed it was. During the Second World War the Fayrfax Mass was also heard being played on the organ by a 'fire-watcher'. He saw the keys played as if by an invisible hand, could see the music and a lighted candle on the organ and watched figures of monks taking part in a service.

There are at least a dozen other good accounts of strange music from the abbey at times when it is known to have been closed.

SEE ALSO:

- Verulamium.
- St Albans.
- Salisbury Hall.

WHILE YOU'RE THERE:

- Take a walk – or perhaps a cycle would be more appropriate – down Fishpool Street. In 1919 a cyclist dismounted to allow the passage of a chaise drawn by two white ponies being driven by a man in a white panama hat. When the chaise had passed the cyclist looked round to watch its progress and discovered it was instantly gone.

St Michael's Church
(Deptford Green, London)

In 1996 we received a letter from a Miss Pat Lee, relating to a time when she had lived in Church Street, Deptford, and had taken a photograph in the old churchyard of St Nicholas of Deptford Green. Miss Lee comments: 'The experience has always remained with me. I will always remember that cold December day as I set out from Fletcher Path, Church Street, Deptford, SE8 to visit the Church of St Nicholas at Deptford Green. I quite clearly remember the skulls at the gate and as I entered they looked as if to say you have arrived at last.

'It was an experience walking around the churchyard and at the same time the atmosphere was of a deep spiritual sadness. God only knows why.

'The tower caught my eye, and I started to remember the day when I was with other people on a history tour. We went up the stairs to the tower one by one, candle in hand. When I reached the top the view was beautiful. You could see St Paul's Church.

'When all of a sudden a "light" appeared in a tree. It was a "spectral light". In the light I clearly saw what I believe to be a medieval-looking man sitting in the tree looking at me. Dressed in black, tall hat, buckled belt and bearded and with boots on. As if to say: 'Do you know who I am?'

'Camera in hand I took the photo, stared at him hard, and then he was gone.'

WHILE YOU'RE THERE:

- Hare and Billet Road in Blackheath, nearby, is said to be haunted by the ghost of a Victorian lady who hanged herself on the branch of an elm tree there when spurned by her lover.

St Osyth's Priory
(St Osyth's, near Clacton-on-Sea, Essex)

St Osyth's Priory was founded in 1121 by Richard de Bellmeis, the Bishop of London. It houses the bones of St Osyth, an abbess killed in 653 AD. Her life was associated with strangeness. It was said that she fell into water and remained there for three days, but was restored to life by St Modwen. Her death is similarly shrouded in legend. Osyth of Essex was the daughter of King Frithewald of Mercia and Queen

Wilburga. She was betrothed to Sighere, King of Essex, but took an oath of chastity. Sighere agreed to this and presented her with the nunnery of which she became abbess. But the area was prone to attack by Danish pagans, one such invasion taking place in 653 AD. A sea captain became enraged because she would not revoke her vows for him, nor worship his gods, and he took his revenge by killing her. It is said that he decapitated her, that she picked up her head in her hands and staggered several hundred yards to the Church of St Peter and St Paul. Finding the door closed, she hammered on it and fell to the ground. On that site a fountain of clear water is said to have gushed forth, the water able to heal the sick. Other accounts suggest that it was more likely that her throat was slit, making this famous last walk more possible.

Hauntings at St Osyth's Priory are varied. St Osyth herself is said to have been seen around the priory buildings and there is also an account of a ghostly monk in white seen walking the estate with a lighted candle at night. In the late 1970s a Mrs Joyce Bennett lived near the priory and related an account of her own. She came to St Osyth's as a nurse (the priory housed a convalescent home from 1948 to the 1980s) and was alerted by a cleaning lady outside the nursing office to come to her. The cleaning lady told her that 'the carpet had been trying to throw her up against the wall'. Mrs Bennett could not understand what the woman meant, particularly as the carpet was fixed, but shortly afterwards watched as the carpet suddenly moved and the cleaner was thrown against the wall. The cleaner left then and never returned. She later found out that this had happened on two previous occasions also.

On another occasion Mrs Bennett went into the laundry room and found another person there at the machine. Knowing she was the only nurse present, she was surprised to find someone there and asked her what permission she had to be there. Suddenly there was no one there and where she had stood there was an 'icy patch'. A lady who visited to do the weekly wash told her that such things happen all the time and that in the same room a monk was sometimes seen walking through a wall by a washing-machine.

On yet another occasion Mrs Bennett spoke to some new patients who were sitting by a window looking out. She asked them what they were doing and they told her, 'We are watching the monks walking side by side through the archway'. They asked what the monks were doing but when Mrs Bennett looked out she could see no one. There were no monks in St Osyth's at the time. She later discovered that near where the monks were seen was formerly the monks' graveyard and where they often gathered before going into the church for evening service.

SEE ALSO:

- Mersea Island.
- Langenhoe Church (site).
- Berechurch, Colchester.

WHILE YOU'RE THERE:

- South of Colchester is the village of Virley. A boatload of excise officers was found on Sunken Island, near Mersea, all with their throats cut in the early 1800s. They are now buried, all beneath their upturned boat, in Virley churchyard. They had fallen victim to the many smugglers who operated in the area and who exploited local ghost stories to frighten away prying eyes – even going as far as using a 'ghost cart' to carry away their booty, painted luminous and with muffled wheels.

St Peter's Church
(Dorchester, Dorset)

On Christmas Day 1814 two church wardens were sitting down resting after hard work decorating the church. They suddenly realized that sitting between them was the Reverend Nathaniel Templeman. This might not have been too extraordinary had it not been for the fact that Templeman had died the previous year. 'Templeman' looked at each of the church wardens, shook his head (as he always did in life, when he was showing his disappointment), then got up and floated along the aisle, sank downwards and disappeared from view.

Since that time there have been several reports of Templeman's reappearance in the church but quite what he was disappointed with is uncertain.

SEE ALSO:

- Parish Church of St Mary, Beaminster.
- Athelhampton House.

WHILE YOU'RE THERE:

- Near the coast is Abbotsbury and overlooking the village, 250 feet up the hill, is St Catherine's Chapel. In the south doorway are wishing holes: traditionally you put your knees in the lower hole and your hands above, then make a wish.

Whitby Abbey
(Whitby, North Yorkshire)

Whitby Abbey was built in 657 AD, destroyed by Viking invasion and rebuilt by the Normans in 1067. It is said, however, that the founder of the original abbey, St Hilda, remains as a ghost and is often seen through one of the present abbey's windows.

She is also associated with the reported apparition of a hearse-like coach driven by a headless driver, pulled by four headless horses which race along the cliffside and plunge into the sea. The 'headless' aspect of the haunting would appear to arise from St Hilda's efforts to destroy all the snakes in the district by steering them to the cliff edge and decapitating them with a whip, though the connection seems to be a somewhat tenuous one.

There is also a story that the abbey is haunted by the ghost of Constance de Beverley. She was a nun who fell in love with a knight and, as punishment, was bricked up alive in the Whitby Abbey dungeon. Her ghost is allegedly a pathetic one: seen on the stairway, she begs and cowers for release from her imprisonment. The abbey is presently administered by English Heritage. It was once one of the most devout outposts of religious life in England, a double monastery for monks and nuns founded by St Hilda, who pioneered the conversion of Anglo-Saxons to Christianity. Hilda was born into the nobility, a great-niece of King Edwin of Northumbria and sister-in-law of King Ethelhere of the East Angles. The Venerable Bede, the first ecclesiastical historian, comments that she taught her flock 'to observe strictly the virtues of justice, devotion and chastity . . . but above all things to continue in peace and charity'.

After the Norman conquest it was the Knight Reinfrid, inspired by Bede, who took up a religious life and commenced the building of the present abbey, although today only ruins remain. The abbey had been a victim of Henry VIII's dissolution of the monasteries.

The abbey ruins, standing on the hillside and as described in the Admiralty's *North Sea Pilot* as 'a conspicuous feature' for mariners, is an atmospheric and dominating part of the skyline. As such it formed the setting to several of the most moody scenes in Bram Stoker's novel *Dracula*.

SEE ALSO:
• Scarborough Castle.

WHILE YOU'RE THERE:

- A short trip inland will bring you to Goathland; just to the south is Wade's Causeway. This is the best preserved Roman road in Britain; and the longest, running for over one and a quarter miles.

Most of the ghosts reported seem to be haunting the buildings they knew in life, whether or not we conclude that there is actually any presence there, or just a 'recording' of their previous activities. In other chapters we note cases of ghosts in the open air, at Cawthorpe, for example, what might be the ghost of a nun looking for her now-demolished former home. But we might spare a thought for the Grosvenor Centre ghost who must be feeling very lost indeed . . .

Grosvenor Centre
(Northampton, Northamptonshire)

In 1970s the Grosvenor Centre was built on the site of the Grey Friars monastery. It is said that the building disturbed the resting places of those buried there and that at least one of those so disturbed has become somewhat restless. There have been reports by the cleaning staff working after the shops are closed of a monk-like figure – hooded and gowned – floating along the empty corridors.

SEE ALSO:

- Dallington Church.
- Ringstead.

WHILE YOU'RE THERE:

- Visit the Norman church of St Peter. In the early eleventh century the parish priest, Brunning, asked his servant to visit Rome on a pilgrimage. But the servant turned back after having a dream. Brunning suggested a divine purpose and told the servant to expect more. The servant dreamt again, and was 'told' to search the church. He did so and discovered an ancient tomb. It was the tomb of St Ragener, nephew of St Edmund. Brunning, the servant, and a crippled girl knelt at the altar and at midnight the church filled with white radiance, while a dove sprinkled holy water from the font on them. The girl was cured.

CHAPTER 3

~

HAUNTED HOMES AND PALACES

Athelhampton Manor
(near Dorchester, Dorset)

Athelhampton House is regarded as one of the best medieval houses and landscape gardens in England. It contains many priest's holes built by Owen, regarded as one of the most famous makers of priest's holes in history. There are stories of grey ladies and black monks but these do not feature greatly in the list of hauntings of Athelhampton. The grey lady is alleged to have passed through the walls of the East Wing from the landing to the State and Yellow Bedrooms. The housemaid once asked her to leave, which she apparently obediently did. There is also a story of a ghostly cooper working at barrels in the wine cellar. Furthermore, there is the story of two duellists from the Civil War occasionally fighting at evening time in the house.

The house is mostly associated with its animal ghosts. In 1957 the MP for Bristol West, Robert Cooke, then owner of the house, was concerned about his cat, which was ill. While working in the study he heard the cat on the stairway, though he could not find it. The following morning when he told the gardener that he was pleased the cat was up and well, the gardener told him that in fact the cat had died the week before and was now buried in the garden. The ghost most associated with Athelhampton, and indeed the one which they describe in their own literature, is an ape which belonged to the Martyn family in the sixteenth century and is indeed part of their coat of arms. Supposedly since the end of the Martyn line in 1595 the ape has run the house searching for a new owner, and is frequently heard scratching behind panelling in the Great Chamber where he is alleged to be walled up in a secret staircase.

All in all a very mixed bag of hauntings.

SEE ALSO:

- St Peter's Church.

Beaulieu
(Beaulieu, Hampshire)

The home of Lord Montagu, Beaulieu is probably now most famous for its motor museum, housing such cars as Donald Campbell's *Bluebird* and a sample of conventional road traffic through the decades. It has theme park-like rides, music festivals and so on.

The site of Beaulieu was originally populated in 1204 by Cistercian monks who built a variety of ornate buildings, including the Abbey Church, the Domus Con Versorum and the Great Gatehouse. The last two form an essential part of the present house and public area. Other buildings included the Outer Gatehouse, the Refectory and the Infirmary. The monks wore either white or brown, as many visitors would see in later centuries. The property came into the Montagu family in 1673 and has been beautifully maintained ever since.

A Mrs Bertha Day, who worked at Beaulieu, heard singing one night just like the service in a church. 'It was lovely singing, I'll always remember it – it gave you a wonderful feeling of peace.' Interestingly, Lord Montagu observes that there used to be other types of ghosts such as 'grey ladies' but 'they disappeared when electric light was installed'.

A Mrs Varley who was shooting a film documentary at the Palace House also heard singing. 'It was the sound of many voices in repetitive singing, which faded and strengthened like the sound from a primitive wireless.' When she repeated the tune she had heard to a friend of hers he told her it was a well-known Gregorian chant.

The most commonly seen ghost is that of a monk dressed in brown. One witness to the monk in brown was Colonel Robert Gore-Browne, who lived on the estate and maintained the vineyards. He saw 'a figure in brown, with a skirt that reached the ground. I thought it was a woman, actually ... But when I got to the brow of the little hill there wasn't anybody there. I looked on either side of the path and I'm pretty sure she wasn't there either. It may have been a ghost, it may not. I'm suspending my judgement.'

SEE ALSO:
- East Cowes.

WHILE YOU'RE THERE:
- Directly across Southampton Water is Netley. Of the old Royal Victoria Military Hospital only the chapel now remains, the rest having been demolished in 1966. The Grey Lady may still be walking about there, but perhaps hopefully not; she used to appear to patients of the hospital who were about to die.

Brede Place
(Brede, East Sussex)

Brede Place was built around 1350. Although slightly altered during the Elizabethan period, it is essentially intact today as it was originally built. Indeed, even in the 1920s it was still lit by candles, and had crude toilet and sanitation facilities. On the west side of the house is a chapel used by the family. The primary haunting at Brede would seem to be a priest, and indeed what are believed to be the bones of a priest were unearthed during excavation in the haunted chapel.

Several people have found the ghosts at Brede to be unpleasant and oppressive. Many have curtailed their stay there unable to continue to sleep in the bedrooms. Jenny Churchill, for example, mother of Sir Winston and sister of the then owner, Mrs Clara Moreton Frewen, stayed in the main guest bedroom but could not stand the hauntings and abandoned the room during the night, spending the rest of it in her hostess's room. On the following day she left and, it is said, never returned. Clara Moreton Frewen's daughter, Clare, later Clare Sheridan, frequently visited her parents at Brede, often in the company of her children Richard and Margaret. Clara was told by the vice-president of the Theosophical Society, A. P. Sinnett, that the house was haunted by a kindly old man who had lived there hundreds of years ago who 'endeavours to be helpful to you'. Clare Sheridan, working with a medium, began to accept and communicate with the ghosts at Brede Place as indicated in her book, *My Crowded Sanctuary*. In particular she became friendly with the ghost of 'Martha', allegedly a Tudor maid who had been hanged for stealing. It seems that Clare Sheridan was alone in befriending Martha, for many other people approaching 'Martha's Gate' – which crosses one of the private roads at Brede Place – find the atmosphere hateful and oppressive. Clare also came to terms with the ghost of 'Father John', presumably the priest whose bones were unearthed at Brede Chapel.

Margaret, Clare's daughter, hated the oppressive and frightening atmosphere of Brede, as she revealed in the book *Morning Glory* (written using the pseudonym Mary Motley). She described how she would lie awake in her bed at night listening to the sounds of the adults in the dining-room downstairs and praying for their conversation not to end – but eventually of course it did, and when the silence indicated that everyone in the house was now asleep her anxieties would increase. Other members of the family shared her feelings. Oswald Frewen, who had fought in the Battle of Jutland and was a distinguished Naval officer, refused to enter certain rooms at night. Margaret's uncle Hugh was so terrified during a visit to the cellar that he would never discuss what he had seen there. Her grandfather would not go into parts of the garden at night alone. Margaret also found a presence on the porch which other people commented on. When her grandfather collapsed and died at that location it reinforced her fear that something malevolent was there.

SEE ALSO:
- Hastings Castle.

WHILE YOU'RE THERE:
- Herstmonceux Castle, about nine miles to the west, was built in 1441 in a lake that has created a moat around it. It once housed the Royal Observatory. It has a variety of ghosts, such as a man sleepwalking, a woman on a white donkey, a phantom drummer, a Grey Lady and a White Lady.

Buckingham Palace
(The Mall, London)

Built for the Duke of Buckingham during the reign of Queen Anne, the palace was obtained by George III for the Royal Family. However, it was not much beloved by the Royal Family until the reign of Queen Victoria, who as a young queen enjoyed her life there with Albert. Sadly, after the Prince Consort's early death Queen Victoria found the palace less attractive, probably because of the memories it held, and in later life she lived there less frequently. It is believed that few of her descendants have regarded the palace with great warmth. The palace stands near the site of the Leper Hospital of St James the Less, which was run by monks and later also by nuns. One ghost at Buckingham Palace appears to date from that time. A monk is frequently seen walking around the Grand Terrace looking over the palace gardens. The figure is described as bound in chains and looking sad. It is thought that the monk died in the priory's punishment cell for committing misdemeanours now long since forgotten. The monk is regarded as an 'anniversary ghost', seen only on Christmas Day.

A more recent ghost is also noted at Buckingham Palace. Major John Gwynne, Private Secretary to Edward VII, committed suicide in his first floor office, shooting himself in the head. He had been the victim of social ostracism resulting from scandal. There are occasions when the ghostly sound of a gunshot is heard from Gwynne's office room.

SEE ALSO:

- London's various locations; mainly palaces and theatres.

WHILE YOU'RE THERE:

- Take the air in nearby Green Park and ask the park wardens to point out the so-called 'tree of death'. It is believed that it was a favoured tree for suicides and that an evil 'cackling' represents the spirits of those who died there. There are also reports of a shadowy figure standing under it, which fades away if approached.

Castle Lodge
(Ludlow, Shropshire)

Castle Lodge has origins which extend back to the fourteenth century though the present building is the result of various alterations. Some time before 1572, Thomas Sackford, an important figure in the Court of Queen Elizabeth I, leased the house from its then owners, the Ludlow Corporation, and in 1580 substantially rebuilt the house in much the form that it exists today. Castle Lodge has had many owners over the years and has, in its history, served as a school and a hotel. Threatened with being turned into a modern office block, it was bought in 1992 by the present owners, Bill and Gwen Pearson, who are actively restoring it to its former glory and retaining its sense of history. It is open to the public, who will find that the building has a wonderful 'period' atmosphere.

Bill and Gwen have reported certain elements of poltergeistery; mischievous and not harmful. One builder working in the lodge thought that Bill was 'messing him about' by playing with a handle on a door on which he was working. The handle kept moving down despite his attempts to stop it. He was convinced that Bill was doing it from the other side until Bill showed him that the handles on each side of the door are in no way connected – they are not even in the same position on each side. The handle the builder was watching could only be moved from his own side! Gwen was washing her hair one day and found her comb missing; they searched the whole house looking for it but were surprised not to be able to find it. When it did turn up it was inside the plastic wrapper of a loaf of bread.

Early in 1997 Gwen reported yet another piece of mischief. The television in their bedroom is always set on 'standby' – the small red light providing Gwen with a sense of orientation if she has to get up during the night. One night she found it was not only out, but that the plug was pulled from the socket. Another night Gwen heard children running about in the room above her bedroom, but knew that there was no one else but her and Bill present. She went upstairs but found only that the room was icy cold, much more so than usual or than any other part of the house. On returning to her bedroom she could hear the sounds again, but she could never see anything in the room; she re-checked several times that night. This continued from 1 a.m. to 5 a.m.

But by far the most famous ghost, and one that Gwen has herself seen, is a young girl who they are certain is Catherine of Aragon. 'Kate', as she is locally spoken of, is generally seen moving fast through the upper corridor towards a room where she stands by a window looking out before disappearing. She is described as around fifteen years of age, short, with long blonde hair, wearing a cape and red gloves with tassels. She is buoyant, jolly and bouncy, moving in quick, sweeping motions. She appears quite solid but on one occasion an iron frame bedstead was in the upper hallway, blocking her path, and she was seen to run straight through it. In 1996 one visitor to the Lodge left at a pace, his wife apologizing for the manner of his leaving. He was sick on the lawns in the Castle grounds. His wife told Bill and Gwen only that he had seen a ghost which had upset him. Around a year later, in early 1997, he apparently summoned up the courage to return to the Lodge to explain himself. He described seeing 'Kate' exactly as many others have done, which Bill confirmed to him. Whether it brought him any comfort to know others had seen what he had seen is unknown.

Bill is in no doubt that it is Catherine, even though there is no official record of her staying in the house. However, when the building was a hotel it displayed a plaque which referred to the building as a 'former home of Catherine of Aragon'. Locals have told Bill and Gwen that the story of her ghost goes back far beyond their days of ownership; she has been reported in the building for decades. She is known to have stayed at Ludlow Castle, across the town square, and there was a connecting tunnel between the house and the castle. Perhaps it was a 'playhouse' for her as a child, or even just a friend's house. Whatever the truth, if it is Catherine's ghost then it seems to have been a house in which she enjoyed happy times.

SEE ALSO:

- Wenlock Edge.
- Croft Castle, Leominster.

Charlton House
(Greenwich, Greater London)

Charlton House is a former mansion house, now a local Community Centre. It is famed for a variety of ghosts, and the wardens have allowed research teams of ghost-researchers, including ourselves, to spend many days and nights on the premises. They also host guided 'ghosts tours'. Accounts of our experiences there, which include the sighting of a 'ghostly monk-like shape' during an experimental seance, are related in *Ghostwatching* (by John Spencer and Tony Wells).

The most famous reported ghost in Charlton House is that of Sir William Langhorne, who lived in the house until his death in 1714 at the age of eighty-five. It is said that he always regretted not having an heir and that his ghost is said to pursue, and molest, female victims to this day.

The ghost of a young female servant has been reported, carrying a baby in her arms. During rebuilding after Second World War bomb damage, workmen discovered the mummified body of a baby in a chimney.

SEE ALSO:

- The Queen's House, Greenwich.

WHILE YOU'RE THERE:

- Take the Ghost Tour. You probably won't see a ghost but you stand an above average chance of spotting a ghost research team sitting all over the staircase having not much more luck than you!

Chingle Hall
(Goosnargh, Preston, Lancashire)

John Wall, one of England's last Catholic martyrs, is thought to haunt Chingle Hall where he was born, causing knockings and footstep noises which are sometimes responsive. Chingle Hall, a moated manor house, is claimed by some to be the most haunted house in England. Built in 1260, it now has the shape of a cross, and it has hiding places built into it. The cross shape and priest holes were built during refurbishments in the 1600s. It is thought to be the first domestic building in the country built of brick. The Priest's Room, on one occasion, was found filled with smoke though no reason for this could be found. The Hall is said to also sport the ghost of a monk.

Visitors can take guided tours at the weekends. The Hall has also catered for several teams of ghost-researchers, many of whom have reported paranormal phenomena during their visits, including strange blue lights seen and photographed, sounds of laughter, table tilting, and doors unlatching themselves.

SEE ALSO:
- Samlesbury Hall, Blackburn.

WHILE YOU'RE THERE:
- A short trip through Preston to Higher Penwortham will place you in the area of the 'Fairy Funeral' said to be seen on the road to Penwortham Wood. This might not be a good idea, however, as seeing the procession is thought to be a portent of death. Two men are alleged to have seen the miniature cortège coming from the churchyard at midnight; one saw that the face in coffin was his own. He died within the month, falling from a haystack, and his funeral passed along the same route as the Fairy Funeral procession.

Clouds Hill
(near Bovington Camp, Dorset)

When T.E. Lawrence ('Lawrence of Arabia') rejoined the RAF in 1925 he bought a brick and tile cottage on the slopes of Clouds Hill as his retreat from Bovington Camp nearby. To the present day the rooms are as Lawrence left them, simple and austere, reflecting the almost monastic way of life which Lawrence sought. It was at Clouds Hill that Lawrence would take the opportunity in solitude to read, play Beethoven and Mozart, and where he revised his biography, *The Seven Pillars of*

Wisdom. Lawrence regarded his cottage as heaven on earth, and told Lady Astor, 'Nothing would take me away from Clouds Hill'. When discharged from the Air Force in 1935 at the age of forty-six, it is probable that he saw for himself a long, largely solitary, peaceful retirement at Clouds Hill. However, five days later he was dead, killed in a crash on his Brough Superior motorcycle when returning home to the cottage.

Perhaps because of the complexity of the man, perhaps because there is a tendency to analyse deeply everything relating to the death of our heroes, the crash has been the subject of controversy ever since. Some have said it was just an accident, others have speculated on recklessness caused by a preoccupied complex mind, others have suggested it was suicide. Some have darkly suggested Lawrence was the victim of political assassination.

Lawrence was an incredibly complex and tortured individual. He might have sought, indeed he would have been showered with, fame following his exploits as Lawrence of Arabia. By the time he was thirty he was a legend. However, he refused to accept any rewards or declarations for his services and indeed spent the remainder of his life trying to escape from the legend. When the First World War broke out Lawrence had been employed on mapping work and was posted to the Intelligence Department in Egypt. He became passionately committed to encouraging the Arabs to create a nation for themselves and to liberate their land from the Turks. The Arab revolt began on 5 June 1916, and Lawrence later that year was sent as chief advisor to Prince Feisal, the principal Arab leader. He virtually invented terrorism, preferring short aggressive interferences with communications, railways and so on to full-scale war. Lawrence made endless journeys encouraging the Arabs, dressing as they did, eating their food, riding camels, and no one was more delighted when the Arabs succeeded in destroying the 4th Turkish Army and entering Damascus on 1 October 1918. Lawrence returned to England, but already he was afraid of his own success. He became convinced that Britain would betray the Arab nation he had fought for. When he attended the Peace Conference of 1919 as a representative of Arab interests his fears were justified. In 1921 Winston Churchill, then Colonial Secretary, sent him back to the Middle East and eighteen months later he was able to feel that 'England is out of the Arab affair with clean hands'.

It says something for the passion in Lawrence's mind that his nearly completed manuscript of *The Seven Pillars of Wisdom* was stolen and within three months he rewrote it from memory.

From almost immediately after his death there were stories of his ghostly form seen entering the cottage dressed in the full Arab dress for which he was most famous. In the decades since, many visitors have reported a man in Arab dress walking into the cottage, several of those witnesses not even realizing the significance and naturally puzzled why a figure in such a dress should be there. Those who have followed the silent brooding figure into the cottage have found no one there. There are some locals who believe that the apparition of Lawrence appears when England is in dire trouble.

A second form of ghost appears to relate to the death itself. Several people have reported hearing the roar of a motorbike rushing towards them but when they believe it should be very close to them, the sound suddenly stops.

If we accept that Lawrence's ghost exists, and that in some way it represents Lawrence returning to or remaining at a particular site, then it is perfectly logical that it would be Clouds Hill. Apart from Arabia, Clouds Hill probably represents where Lawrence's mind worked through his beliefs, his dreams, his plans and he will be forever associated with it. It seems in any case to reflect his statement to Lady Astor. It is interesting that the ghost is in Arab dress rather than British military uniform, but perhaps that is how Lawrence would have seen himself. As for the echoes of the fatal crash; whatever caused the crash, it cut off Lawrence early from a long retirement at Clouds Hill. Perhaps it is this regret which has created the haunting.

Ghost researcher Peter Underwood received correspondence from a Mrs Brown who reported seeing what she believed was the ghost of Lawrence, not at Clouds Hill but a few miles away at nearby Wareham. On 17 May 1967, together with her husband, Mrs Brown visited Clouds Hill and then went on to Wareham. It was early evening and they were sitting in the cab of their touring motor caravan when Mrs Brown looked up and saw a figure she was certain was Lawrence standing on the bridge in front of them. 'He was standing in the first niche of the bridge, his arms resting on the parapet, and he looked round slowly to meet my eyes and, as long as I returned his gaze, he never turned away.' Mrs Brown, clearly moved by the experience, commented to her husband, who looked up but saw nothing. Mrs Brown reports that the figure was dressed in RAF uniform, which surprised her, though she was later shown a photograph of Lawrence in India wearing the uniform she had seen. Mrs Brown recalled: 'His face was very, very red; his eyes seemed to be screwed up against the light, although in fact the sun was behind him.' She has never seen him since, despite visits to Clouds Hill and Wareham every year, but she remains 'overwhelmingly convinced' of her sighting.

Did Mrs Brown's visit to Clouds Hill earlier in the day inspire her to think of Lawrence, or did her being there allow her an affinity which gave her a perception of Lawrence? And why were his eyes screwed up looking *away* from the sun; did she in fact see Lawrence as he was not at sunset but at dawn, standing on the bridge watching the sun rise in front of him?

SEE ALSO:

- Wool.
- Corfe Castle.

Hampton Court
(Kingston upon Thames, London)

Gifted to Henry VIII by Thomas Wolsey, Hampton Court Palace in London is largely associated with that king and his succession of wives.

Anne Boleyn, the second wife of Henry VIII and frequently reported as a ghost at Blickling Hall in Norfolk, has been reported in Hampton Court. She has been described as sad-looking, drifting through the corridors wearing a blue dress.

Catherine Howard, the King's fifth wife, is more commonly associated with Hampton Court. She fell out of favour with her husband after indulging in an extra-marital affair with Thomas Culpepper and was confined to her suite of rooms in Hampton Court. Only nineteen years old, she must have realized the probability of her execution, particularly given that that fate had already fallen on her cousin, Anne Boleyn. Desperate to win back favour with Henry but prevented from doing so by political factions opposed to her family, she planned to speak with him when he attended a service in the Chapel Royal, which was separated from her own rooms by a long gallery. She fled down the gallery, making it to the chapel door, but was arrested by guards and returned screaming to her rooms. Henry apparently ignored her crying and banging. Her ghost has been reported several times making this frantic and desperate run down the long gallery; many people have heard her screams.

The ghost of Henry's third wife, Jane Seymour, has also been reported at Hampton Court. She is seen dressed in white, moving soundlessly and holding a candle. There have been so many sightings that some workers have left Hampton Court for this reason alone.

Jane Seymour died young, after only a year as Queen, soon after giving birth to the son, Edward, so desired by her husband. After her death Sybil Penn was appointed nurse to the young Prince Edward. In later years Sybil Penn was granted a pension and residence in Hampton Court. She died there of smallpox and was buried in the Church of St Mary's at Hampton. After the church was demolished in the 1820s her ghost was seen at Hampton Court. One report, for example, was from a guest staying in one of the grace and favour apartments who awoke to see a woman bending over her bed. The guest asked what the woman wanted, to which she replied that she needed a home. On being told that the room she was in was not available, the ghost disappeared. Other witnesses have seen her in and around other parts of Hampton Court, and reportedly heard the drone of a spinning-wheel which Sybil Penn had used when she was making baby clothes for the young Prince Edward. In the nineteenth century one family occupying Sybil Penn's rooms at Hampton Court reported hearing the spinning-wheel. The wheel itself was found in a sealed room nearby. Another witness to Sybil Penn was Princess Frederica of Hanover. Penn's identity has been established by comparing witness accounts to the effigy on her tomb.

Another sighting of ghosts in Hampton Court was by a police officer on duty in 1907. During a night shift he saw a party of people in evening dress walking towards him, but as they got to within around thirty feet of where he was standing they dissolved into thin air. The description given by the policeman suggests a fairly contemporary party, but their identity has never been clarified.

The actor Leslie Finch, after giving a performance at Hampton Court and in the company of Lady Grant, saw a woman in a grey Tudor costume walking towards them and assumed that she was an actress. It was apparent, however, that Lady Grant saw nothing and he realized he had seen a ghost.

Hampton Court boasts a whole host of other ghosts: two cavaliers seen in the mid nineteenth century, the ghosts of a monk, a dog, clerics, Wolsey himself and Thomas Culpepper.

If the recordings theory of ghosts is correct, then Henry VIII and those around him had a knack of creating psychic imprints for the future to behold.

WHILE YOU'RE THERE:

- Ham House, just outside Richmond Park, is a Jacobean mansion haunted by the spectre of the Duchess of Lauderdale. She was seen by a six-year-old who woke up in the night to see the hideous old woman scratching at the walls by her bed, searching perhaps for incriminating evidence that had been hidden there.

Kensington Palace
(Hyde Park, London)

During his last illness George II was confined to his rooms at Kensington Palace, at a time when his concern was for news of his ships coming from the Continent to Britain during European wars of the time. He apparently spent a great deal of time looking out of his window at the weathervane to see if the winds that were holding his ships in foreign ports had changed, and groaning in a heavy German accent: 'Why don't they come?' For George they never did come; he died before the winds changed. There have been many reports of the ghost of the King looking out of the window towards the weathervane and even of hearing the ghostly question: 'Why don't they come?'

SEE ALSO:

- London's various locations; mainly palaces and theatres.

WHILE YOU'RE THERE:

- Holland House, which used to be situated nearby, was almost completely destroyed in 1940 during wartime bombing. It had been a spectacular Jacobean mansion and was already famed for its ghosts and hauntings. The headless Earl of Holland had been seen wandering through the Gilt Room. But part of the east wing survived the bombing and was restored as a Youth Hostel; students staying there in 1965 reported seeing the Earl's ghost still walking.

Levens Hall
(Levens, Cumbria)

The Hall dates from the fourteenth century, though most of the existing structure was built in Tudor times.

Levens Hall has its own spectral black dog which runs around people apparently threatening to trip them up. Although it may appear to people in company with each other, only one person ever sees the dog at any given time. Generally speaking it will disappear into a bedroom, and even when the house is searched throughout no dog is ever found.

Levens Hall also has the Pink Lady. She appears to be a serving-girl wearing a dress with a pink print and a servant's cap.

Another ghostly figure is the Grey Lady. She is alleged to be the ghost of a gypsy woman who came to Levens seeking charity but died of starvation and cursed the family. The curse was that the family would have no sons. This curse ended in 1895 when Alan Bagot was born to the family, but sightings of the Grey Lady have continued. In 1954 a seven-year old girl described her in detail and in a way which matched earlier descriptions.

The Hall is currently under investigation by Jason Braithwaite for ASSAP, the Association for the Scientific Study of Anomalous Phenomena.

SEE ALSO:
• Sizergh Castle, near Kendal.

Littlecote House
(near Ramsbury, Wiltshire)

Littlecote House was built around 1500 on the site of an earlier house. It belonged to William Darrell, whose family had lived on the site since 1415. Its most notorious history arose on a night in 1575. A local midwife known as Mother Barnes who lived at Great Shefford, a few miles away, was asked by two men who came to her door to go with them. She was, however, to be blindfolded so that she could not identify the house, in reward for which she would be paid well. Despite the obvious danger, she accepted. Inside the house she saw a 'tall, slender gentleman having upon hym a longe goune of blacke velvett'. He instructed Mother Barnes to assist a lady in a bedchamber through delivery, threatening her 'Yf shee be safely delivered yow shall not fayle of great rewards, but if shee myscarry in her traveyle yow shall dye'.

Mother Barnes attended the woman, who to her astonishment and perhaps fear she discovered was also masked. A baby boy was safely delivered, though the woman, Mother Barnes realized, lay dying. Then came perhaps the most awful part of the story. On the instructions of the man in black velvet the baby was thrown on the fire. The woman was taken back to her home.

Mother Barnes was able to identify the house, particularly from the number of steps she had counted going up to its front door, and she later gave a statement to a magistrate 'including the quoted section above' which identified Darrell as the man in black velvet and Littlecote House as the house she had been taken to. Even prior to that Darrell had been known as 'wild', a reference to his bawdy lifestyle. Darrell was not, however, brought to trial and lived on until dying when thrown from his horse in 1589. (There is a story – legend of course – that he was thrown from the horse after a vision of the child's ghost appeared.)

The identity of the woman who died in childbirth is unclear, but she is widely thought to have been Darrell's sister and the child the product of incest.

It is said that horses still react badly at the point where Darrell died and again the local legend is that his own ghost appears to frighten modern-day horses.

The murdered child's mother is held to haunt Littlecote; there have at least been reports of a sad-faced woman holding a baby seen in the room where the murder is believed to have been committed. In fact this has been called into question, but psychic Tom Corbett could find no sense of such a ghost in what is known as 'the haunted bedroom', though in fact it is only a tradition which indicates which bedroom is *the* bedroom.

Following the death of Darrell, the house came into the possession of Sir John Popham, the Lord Chief Justice under Elizabeth I. The Popham family retained the house until 1922, when it was purchased for the Wills family by Sir Ernest Wills, the tobacco magnate. It was open to the public in 1960 and in 1985 was purchased by Peter de Savary.

During the ownership by the Wills family, Sir Edward, brother of Sir Ernest, stayed at Littlecote with his wife. One night his Pekinese dog was acting in a very agitated way and pointing towards the door. Sir Edward walked into the passageway and saw the figure of a woman walking away from him which then disappeared. Sir Edward could not find the person and returned to bed. The household was informed about what could have been an intrusion the following day, and a housemaid said that she often saw 'a lady wandering around wearing a sort of pink dressing-gown'. Apparently the ghost was quite happy, agitated no one and was not frightening.

Another most famous haunting of Littlecote is 'the woman in the garden'. One of the Littlecote tourist guides saw the woman and went to call her into the house. But almost immediately she disappeared and could not be found. Tom Corbett, when he visited the house, saw a figure in the garden and identified her from a portrait hanging in the Regency Room; she was apparently Mrs Leybourne-Popham. Corbett got the impression that not only did she remain in the garden but she was somehow unable to enter the house, though there was no known history of the house which would have explained that. Her portrait does show her in the garden rather than in the house itself.

In 1985, after Peter de Savary had moved into Littlecote, there was a sale of the effects of the previous owner. De Savary met, in the gardens, a lady dressed in a tweed skirt who accused him of being wicked and threatened that he and his family would suffer for his actions. As he reported in *Hello!* magazine in October 1993, he was confused and asked what he had done to upset the lady. 'You have taken my baby's things,' she replied. When he offered to return them to her she indicated that she could not have them and explained where the clothes belonged. The appropriate clothes were located and replaced as instructed. The lady smiled and said to him, 'You and your family will be blessed in this house forever,' and then she vanished. De Savary had presumably met a ghost in the garden, although it seems unlikely from his description that this was Mrs Leybourne-Popham; his description was of someone in contemporary dress, like 'you would find in Hungerford doing her shopping'.

Among sundry rumours of other ghosts is the belief that the house is visited by Gerald Lee Bevin, who rented Littlecote in the 1920s. While he was at Littlecote he was above repute: religious and a teetotaller. At the age of fifty he apparently, however, turned to crime and swindling. On 8 February 1922, together with a woman friend, he absconded by plane to Paris (the first time a criminal had absconded by plane in fact); he was eventually caught at Innsbruck, brought back to England and jailed. He eventually died in Havana at the age of sixty-six and many people believe that it is the calm and peaceful side of his soul that returns to the home where he found his greatest tranquillity.

SEE ALSO:
- Mildenhall.

WHILE YOU'RE THERE:
- To the west of Ramsbury is Avebury, site of the largest prehistoric monument in Europe, covering twenty-eight acres. The henge originally consisted of three stone circles; the outer made up of 100 40-ton sarsen stones (of which twenty-seven still exist). Many of the 'lost' stones were broken up and used to construct the village itself in the seventeenth and eighteenth century. You are also in the heart of crop-circle country – some of the first and most elaborate 'pictograms' were found in the fields around the area.

Longleat
(near Warminster, Wiltshire)

The Thynne family, who have occupied Longleat House for generations, have, like so many other well-established families, a legend of omens associated with animals. In their case the story has it that the family is doomed to die out should the swans of Longleat ever fly away and never return. Visitors to Longleat will be familiar with the large numbers of swans that nest around and on the lakes, as they have done for hundreds of years.

In 1916 the 5th Marchioness of Longleat was looking out of one of the windows of the house and saw five swans flying low and heading for the house. As she watched they came close to her window; one of them broke away and flew off into the distance, while the other four settled on the lake. Such a flight pattern and break-up of formation cannot be that unusual, but something seems to have convinced the Marchioness that it indicated that her eldest son, Viscount Weymouth, was dead. He was at that time fighting with his unit in France. For the whole day his younger brother, later Lord Bath, and his three sisters tried to reason with their mother's fears. However, the following day she received a telegram reporting that her son had been killed in action, as she feared.

The 5th Marchioness seems to have been deeply psychic herself. Another event shows her psychic abilities. One morning she came into the Great Hall to join the family and as she entered the room through an arch from the hallway she appeared to brush aside what seemed to be curtains. She asked the people in the room: 'Why are there men on the roof? And why are these dust-sheets hanging here?' Those in the room could see that there were no dust-sheets and no one was aware of any men on the roof.

Shortly afterwards fire broke out at Longleat, damaging the roof. For some time workmen were working on the roof and in order to prevent dust spreading into the house, canvas dust-sheets were hanging in the archways including the one into the Great Hall.

Although not traditionally known as a house associated with skulls and mortal remains, Longleat has an interesting account of what happened after a gardener dug up a skull in the grounds. It is highly possible that it was from old monastic burial grounds, disturbance of which seems to have caused ghost phenomena in many old buildings around the country; Longleat is built on the foundations of a priory which was removed during the Dissolution of the monasteries. Lord Bath had the skull buried in consecrated ground; however, prior to that it is known that five people handled the skull, all of whom associated unpleasantness with doing so. Lord Bath himself – in a mischievous moment – put the skull on his head and rode around on his bicycle with it. Before the day was out he had fallen from the bike and hurt himself badly. The four other people had all within that day received some kind of injury.

Probably the most persistent report of a haunting relates to the corridor known as the Green Lady's Walk, so named because of the portrait of Lady Louisa Carteret, dressed in green, which hangs in the dining-room at Longleat. Her ghost is alleged to walk the corridor in grief. The legend of the origin of Lady Louisa's ghost goes back to Queen Anne's day, when Lady Louisa married the 2nd Viscount Weymouth. Their marriage was, allegedly, miserable and unrewarding, the 2nd Viscount being a vicious and unpleasant individual. Lady Louisa fell in love with another, and they were found together in Longleat House by her husband. The two men fought a duel, resulting in the death of the lover. Legend has it that he was buried beneath the cellar flagstones by the Viscount. There are, inevitably, some facts which support the legend or on which the legend was built. The 2nd Viscount moved away from Longleat, moving to a nearby village of Horningsham and allowing Longleat to fall into disrepair. Also four generations later, when central heating was being installed at Longleat, a body was found under the flagstones in the cellars, dressed in clothing which seemed to indicate the Queen Anne period. Several people, including Longleat's librarian Miss Dorothy Coates, felt unable to walk along the corridor, and many people often took extended roundabout routes through Longleat to avoid it. Miss Coates once described walking along the corridor as 'sometimes you daren't look behind you, you just dare not'. Lady Louisa died in childbirth on Christmas Day 1736 and allegedly roams the corridors looking for her long dead lover.

Another haunting relates to the Red Library. Miss Coates believes that there is a presence in the library but 'it's companionable, friendly. I have worked in here a lot and all the time I have been conscious that there was somebody standing, just out of view, watching me. I think of him as the 'nice kind gentleman'. I know it's a man, and I know it's friendly. Every time I look around, of course, he isn't there.'

There is also a family confirmation of Miss Coates' feelings. As a child, Lady Caroline had asked her nanny, 'Who's that old gentleman who's just gone through the door'. The nanny investigated immediately. She could see no one, however, though the child was quite certain someone had passed that way. It is believed that the ghost is Sir John Thynne, the Elizabethan who was responsible for the original building of Longleat. A German reporter from United Press International, Guy Montas, spent the night in the Red Library and believed he saw the image of Sir John Thynne for several minutes.

In fact the list of alleged ghosts in Longleat is long and includes a malevolent presence thought to be a servant, an unidentified presence that knocks on a door, ghosts of Cardinal Wolsey, a cavalier and others.

The site was originally a priory dedicated to St Radegunde, Virgin Queen of France. Longleat was founded in 1270 by Sir John Vernon. The priory was dissolved in 1529 and the land was purchased by Sir John Thynne in 1540. During Sir John Thynne's building of the mansion there was a huge fire. It is alleged that at this time a ghost barred the way of servants going up the staircase. One of the servants attacked it and it 'melted away'. A vision appeared later that night with a face like a horse and long bony claw-like fingers. This terrified the servants, who ran out of the house with the ghost mocking them. When they re-entered the house they found the ghost smashing furniture and creating such terrible mayhem that the decision was made to burn the house down and start building again.

One alleged ghost, that of Bishop Ken, is commemorated by the Bishop Ken Library. He stayed at the house as a religious refugee for twenty years and is alleged to have been seen by several staff and security officers. However, Tom Corbett, a psychic who allegedly successfully located several of the house's hauntings, indicated that he did not believe Bishop Ken was haunting the house; and the then Marquess of Bath agreed that he could not see why Bishop Ken should be haunting it.

SEE ALSO:
- Frome.
- Warminster.

Lyme Park
(near Disley, Cheshire)

Lyme Park is situated in thirteen acres of parkland and is administered by the National Trust. In 1725 a Venetian architect, Giacomo Leoni, remodelled the mansion, introducing some of the beauty of Italy into the surroundings. For example, a courtyard of the old Tudor house was remodelled into a mock cortile of a grand palazzo. The Italian impressions were enhanced by using marble and by the creation of a classical portico.

Lyme Park was the home of the Legh family for 600 years, since 1346 when it was granted to the family by the then King to Sir Piers Legh, rescuer of the Black Prince's standard at Caen. His son, also Sir Piers, fought for the King in France and was at Agincourt with Henry V. He died in 1422 following the battle of Meux. It was the son's wish that he should be buried at Lyme Park; his ghostly funeral procession is occasionally seen.

It is a belief of 'recordings' ghosts that their 'batteries' eventually 'wind down' and so it would seem to be the case with this procession. Originally seen in its full glory, it is now believed that only one solitary mourner remains, the rest of the procession having 'disappeared'. The mourner is a woman dressed in white, unusually, but with her head bowed in sadness. She has been named Blanche locally, and the local legend is that she was an unknown mistress of Sir Piers who because of proprieties of the time, was unable to attend the actual procession and therefore attends now.

SEE ALSO:
- Whaley Bridge.

WHILE YOU'RE THERE:
- See Capesthorne Manor, near Macclesfield. Dating from 1722, the house and chapel have survived to the present time in extremely good

condition though there was considerable rebuilding after a fire in 1861. One of its owners was the MP Lieutenant-Colonel Sir Walter Bromley-Davenport. Several of his guests, themselves public figures, witnessed apparitions there, including Sir Charles Taylor, MP for Eastbourne, who saw a Grey Lady apparition floating past him near a stairway in the west wing. Sir Walter himself has seen several such spectre-like figures around the stairway and in other locations. The Grey Lady has been seen walking the corridors, head bowed, and descending into the vault below the chapel. In 1958 Sir Walter's son saw the apparition of an arm reaching towards his bedroom window frame, but when he walked towards it the arm vanished. There was no person in the room at the time, and no possibility of the apparition being from outside, as the ground level was thirty feet below the window. In 1967 a butler working at the house, Mr Elio Cenzaleghe, confirmed that the family ghost was a grey lady seen many times.

Penfound Manor
(near Poundstock, Cornwall)

Penfound Manor dates back to a Great Hall belonging to Edward the Confessor and his wife, Queen Edith. The ghost of the manor, a woman called Kate Penfound, dates from the English Civil War. It is a story so detailed that many believe it is more than legend, but if it is factually true, records do not exist to support it as they are likely to have been destroyed during the English Civil War. The Penfounds were ardent Royalists, and the Royalists often destroyed church records to prevent the Roundheads getting valuable local information.

Kate was the daughter of the smuggler Arthur Penfound, who developed the manor between 1635 and 1645. She fell in love with John Trebarfoot, a neighbour from nearby Trebarfoot Manor. Unfortunately the Trebarfoots supported the Cromwellians and therefore had become hated adversaries of the Penfounds. The lovers, in the classic style, decided to run away together. Kate's father, however, caught them and shot them both dead in his anger.

Locals accept the haunting of Kate matter of factly. She is described materializing in her room, walking down the staircase, through the Great Hall and then disappearing. She is said always to materialize on 26 April, this being the anniversary of the day she and her lover were killed. Owners of the house have discovered that workmen and others avoid the house on 26 April because the ghost 'walks that night'. Some tourists going round the house seem to have identified Kate psychically.

There is another record of a haunting locally at Poundstock village church. In December 1356 William Penfoun, clerk of the church, was brutally murdered when a group of armed men broke in and cut him down with swords and staves. It is not known why Penfoun was attacked but it is thought possible that it could have been revenge for infidelity with one of the men's wives. The two ringleaders of the attack, John Bevill and Simon de St Gennys, were pardoned, and since that date William Penfoun has been seen in ghostly form in the church, presumably angry at the lack of revenge.

The Manor used to be open to public but is presently not so.

WHILE YOU'RE THERE:

• Journey south on the A39, take the B3263 towards Boscastle, and just a little way beyond there you will find two incredibly detailed labyrinth rock carvings which possibly date from the Bronze Age. Each is around a foot across and a couple of feet off the ground. Such labyrinthine and spiral carvings have been found all around the world; many believe they represent the journey into the afterlife.

The Queen's House
(Greenwich, Greater London)

The Queen's House was built for the Queen Consort of Charles I, Queen Henrietta Maria. It is now part of the National Maritime museum. In 1966 a clergyman on holiday from Canada, the Reverend R.W. Hardy, took a photograph of the circular Tulip Staircase within the Queen's House. This has become one of the most analysed photographs in ghost research. Although we are told that there was no one on the staircase when the photograph was taken, the print shows the image of one, or possibly two, figures apparently climbing up the stairs. Clearest of all is a hand on the banister rail wearing what may be a wedding ring (third finger, left hand).

Assuming that the photograph is genuinely ghostly, the identity of the person remains unknown. Inevitably there has been speculation that the figure is that of Queen Henrietta Maria herself. For any furtherance of that theory, the route most analysts are taking is to find a portrait of the Queen with the ring in question on the right finger, but as yet that has not been forthcoming.

CASTLE ACRE PRIORY
A ghostly male figure has been seen in an upstairs room

THE TREASURER'S HOUSE
Built on the site of the Roman Road, the *Via Decumana*

Credit: Paranormal Picture Library

CELLAR OF THE TREASURER'S HOUSE
In this cellar a parade of Roman soldiers was seen and heard, regarded as
one of the most impressive ghost sightings ever reported

Credit: Paranormal Picture Library

CASTLE RISING CASTLE
Visitors have heard the wild screaming of the mother of Edward III
who was imprisoned here for the murder of her husband

THREVE CASTLE
During a visit here the authors noticed that entries in the visitors' book
for certain days referred to ghostly feelings on the part of the writers.
Were the castle ghosts more active on those days?

Credit: Paranormal Picture Library

EPWORTH RECTORY
Former home of the Wesley family, Epworth Rectory is the site
of one of the world's most famous poltergeists

HERMITAGE CASTLE
The authors and a small team of researchers were the first people
in over a hundred years to spend the night in the castle

Credit: Paranormal Picture Library

THE LANES, BRIGHTON
The ghost of a nun has been seen passing through the bricked up doorway in the wall

Credit: Paranormal Picture Library

THE PAVILLION, BRIGHTON
This extraordinary former home of the Prince Regent is thought to be
haunted by one of his servants who has not yet 'left service'

Credit: Paranormal Picture Library

MARKYATE CELL
Home of the most famous highwaywoman of all, Lady Katherine Ferrers

Credit: Paranormal Picture Library

POTTER HEIGHAM BRIDGE
A ghostly carriage has been reported crashing into this bridge;
an 'anniversary ghost' said to appear on the 31st May

Credit: Paranormal Picture Library

ACLE BRIDGE
Ghosts and fresh blood have been reported appearing on the bridge, the scene
of gruesome murders, with an 'anniversary ghost' said to appear on the 7th April

Credit: Paranormal Picture Library

An attempt to duplicate the picture deliberately was made by Brian Tremain, the National Maritime Museum's photographer. His 'reproduction' makes it clear that a photograph taken with a long exposure would include several ghostly images of anyone that passed up the staircase. We only have Hardy's recollection that no one passed by, but could he have been mistaken? The possibility that this happened is extended by the image of the ring on the hand; both 'figures' seem to have a ring on the identical finger.

SEE ALSO:

• Charlton House.

The Royal Pavilion
(Brighton, East Sussex)

One of the most charismatic individuals of the Hanoverian line of the monarchy was King George IV. He had served as regent during the last years of his father, King George III's, life when the King was confined, mad and blind as a result of suffering from porphyria, to his rooms in Windsor Castle. Throughout his life George IV, as Prince, then Regent and finally King, was generally despised by the public for his extravagance, the scandals of his private life, his selfishness and his lack of involvement in serious politics. As a young man he had been good-looking and charming but his indulgences led him to obesity, gout, idleness and extreme egocentricity. When he tried to be the monarch it appeared just like another of his indulgences: 'like a King in a play, or in a wooden cut in the History of England' as described by Lord Palmerston. Others have more graciously pointed out that his eccentricities raised the image of the monarchy from a dowdy, dull, workmanlike image to one of spectacle. There are those who have described George IV as less of a British king and more of a Roman emperor. What has perhaps been less emphasized by history is that George IV was probably the most intelligent of the Georges, a conversationalist and raconteur who could banter with the greatest wits of England, a lover of the arts with impeccable taste and a sense of exceptional style. No surprise then that this charismatic king should have produced so extraordinary a building as the Royal Pavilion in Brighton. Having created a London home for himself at Carlton House near St James's Palace, he required a residence by the sea and purchased a farmhouse in Brighton, to which he applied his exceptional gift. Over time he transformed it into the mock-Arabian assortment of buildings topped by onion domes and minarets that now so dominates the town.

The Prince himself has been reported haunting underground passages beneath the Royal Pavilion, though not in recent times. A better known haunting in the Pavilion arose at a banquet in the early part of the twentieth century. A caterer was ensuring that the set-out and arrangements for the banquet were correct when he noticed a dark shape, sufficiently identifiable as female, appearing from the kitchen area and gliding round the tables as if assisting him in checking out their suitability. The shape then disappeared through a doorway. Concerned by the intrusion, the caterer tried to approach the figure during its time walking around the tables but could not get close to it, never more than twenty or thirty feet. Once the figure had passed through the door he ran into the corridor, but found no one outside. An attendant at a door at the other end of the corridor was questioned but had seen no one for at least an hour. Later the caterer was informed that the description he gave was of Martha Gunn, also known as the Brighton Bather, thought to hark back to Regency times. The description of her clothing was believed to be a Regency costume. Others have speculated that the ghost may have been a housekeeper of the Pavilion, charged with ensuring that the Regent's dinner parties were immaculately presented – certainly the Regent's character seems likely to be demanding of such attention to detail and may well have impressed strong emotions in one of his former staff; emotions that perhaps lingered on after her death.

SEE ALSO:

• The Lanes.

WHILE YOU'RE THERE:

• A trip towards the east along the A27 will bring you to Wilmington. Carved in the hillside of Windover Hill is the Long Man, the largest representation of a human figure in western Europe. The carving is 230 feet tall. It is first mentioned in writing in 1779 but the present state of preservation is to the Duke of Devonshire, who in 1873 had the figure restored and outlined in yellow bricks.

Rydal Mount
(Rydal, Cumbria)

William Wordsworth's love and poetry of the Lake District has come down to us from 150 years ago. He moved to Rydal Mount in 1813 with his sister Dorothy and made it his home for the rest of his life, dying there in 1850 at the age of eighty. In 1909 a Miss Ward was staying at the house when she woke up during the night and 'saw perfectly clearly the figure of an old man sitting in the armchair beside the window'. She identified him immediately as Wordsworth. He was apparently sitting with both hands on the arms of the chair, leaning back, looking down and with a rapt expression. Moonlight coming in through a window 'lit the top of his head'. Miss Ward found the experience 'solemn and beautiful' and not frightening. Eventually the figure faded away. Later Miss Ward learned she had been sleeping in Dorothy Wordsworth's room.

SEE ALSO:
- Tebay.
- Cark Hall / Holker Hall, near Cartmel.
- Gaythorne Hall, Tebay.
- Reston House, near Ings.

WHILE YOU'RE THERE:
- Go east towards Seascale, stopping at the town of Gosforth. In the churchyard is an ancient cross carved with snakes, dragons and wolves, all interwoven with Christian imagery. It is thought to be of Viking origin, from the tenth century, and depicts the triumph of Christianity over paganism.

Salisbury Hall
(St Albans, Hertfordshire)

Probably the most famous illicit love affair in history is the sixteen-year liaison between King Charles II and the actress Nell Gwynne. Charles was crowned on 23 April 1661, married the Portuguese Princess Catherine of Braganza on 20 May 1662, and started his affair with Nell Gwynne in 1668. Although clearly fond of his wife and aware that his marriage to her had brought with it a necessary dowry, it seems that his relationship with Nell Gwynne was the true love of his life; it was sustained until his death on 6 February 1685.

It is almost certain that Salisbury Hall featured strongly in their relationship. In 1668, when their affair started, the Hall was purchased by what would seem to be nominees. James Hoare paid £7,100 for the Hall, almost certainly buying it on behalf of the King, who set it up as a home for Nell Gwynne where they could meet in secret. Just one year after Hoare purchased it, possibly in order to prevent the ownership of the Hall being discovered, title was transferred to Jeremy Snow; he and his wife Rebecca probably acted as housekeepers and confidants for the couple. Certainly Snow renovated the Hall to a standard befitting a king and was later rewarded with a baronetcy.

In 1905 Sir Winston Churchill's widowed mother Jenny and her new husband George Cornwallis-West lived in the house. Cornwallis-West wrote in 1930 in his book *Edwardian Hey-days* that his first exposure to ghosts was at Salisbury Hall. He described how one evening he entered the dining-room and saw standing in the corner 'the figure of a youngish and beautiful woman with a blue fichu round her shoulders'. The woman apparently looked at him and then turned and disappeared through the door into the passage. Cornwallis-West followed her but found no one there. He thought she was a former nursemaid who had been known as 'Old Girlie', and became certain that he was seeing her crisis apparition; that this was the time of her death. He contacted his mother and discovered that she was in good health. It was much later, when speaking to his sister Daisy, that she reminded him that people had often said Old Girlie looked exactly like Nell Gwynne. Cornwallis-West realized that he may well have seen the apparition of the King's former mistress in her old home.

A second ghost at Salisbury Hall is believed to be that of a cavalier, sometimes seen with a sword sticking through him; apparently he had a grisly death at the Hall in some former time. The cavalier was said to have been wounded in battle at South Mimms and sheltered at the Hall to recover from his wounds. However, knowing that he was about to be captured he impaled himself on his sword.

In 1956 the house was taken over by Mr and Mrs Walter Goldsmith, who took on the task of renovating it. Mrs Goldsmith had an experience which was to make her rethink her scepticism of ghosts. Early one morning, at approximately 2 a.m., she heard footsteps in the passage outside her bedroom. The passage had once led to a Tudor wing of the house that was destroyed in 1818. She thought it was her husband, but discovered afterwards that it was not and noted that the footsteps had gone one way but did not return. Later she spoke to someone who had lived there during the mid 1930s and who confirmed that her family had also heard strange footsteps in that corridor. Further confirmation came in a letter the Goldsmiths received in 1959 from a Mrs Rosamund Stutzel, who had lived in the Hall as a child. She described the ghost often felt by the children in the bedroom over the entrance hall and also that the children were awoken by 'something' standing by the bed. It is believed that the ghost in its former life occupied the Tudor wing but used to stand at the end of the corridor, and now walks the path it used to walk although the wing no longer exists. Alternatively, if the ghost does not represent the survival of spirit but a recording then there are a number of people who have heard the sounds embedded in the building from centuries ago.

SEE ALSO:

- St Albans.
- St Albans Abbey.
- Verulamium.

WHILE YOU'RE THERE:

- A trip to the south of nearby Hemel Hempstead will bring you to King's Langley. Keep an eye out for a procession of ghostly monks that has been reported in the Priory Orchard.

Samlesbury Hall
(Blackburn, Lancashire)

Like any centuries-old manor, Samlesbury Hall has its share of ghosts. The most commonly reported is that of the White Lady, seen by several staff members and visitors to the Hall over the years. One witness, for example, described seeing the figure of the White Lady, young, dressed in a long flowing white dress, running through the corridors. Interestingly, although the witness was with her husband he could see nothing. Generally the ghost is said to walk or run through the gallery and corridors moaning or crying softly. She has also been seen in the Great Hall, occasionally embracing a ghostly male figure.

The local legend claims that the White Lady is Sir John Southworth's daughter Dorothy. Sir John was the Sheriff of Lancashire in 1562 and a staunch Catholic. Dorothy is alleged to have fallen in love with a Protestant knight and they sought to elope together. One of South-worth's sons lay in ambush to prevent this family disgrace. Dorothy's lover and two companions met her but Dorothy's brother leapt from concealment, slaughtering all three of the men. It is alleged that the bodies were buried under the chapel at Samlesbury Hall and Dorothy confined to a convent. Three human skeletons discovered during excavation offer some substance to the story, though it is possible that it has been derived from or embellished by the discovery of the skeletons in the first place.

SEE ALSO:

• Chingle Hall, Goosnargh.

WHILE YOU'RE THERE:

• Take a trip into nearby Preston and watch out for the spectral, headless hound reported in the streets there. Like so many such legends, this one foretells of a tragic event.

Sawston Hall
(Sawston, Cambridgeshire)

Sawston Hall played a crucial part in the power struggle between Mary Tudor ('Bloody Mary') and Lady Jane Grey. Chief conspirator was the Duke of Northumberland, who had married his son, Guildford Dudley, to Lady Jane Grey. On the death of Edward VI he prevented knowledge of the death from becoming widespread, and in order to ensure that his daughter-in-law would take the throne he sought to imprison Mary in the Tower. Unaware that Edward was already dead, Mary was travelling to London to his bedside. Northumberland set up an ambush but sympathizers were able to warn Mary ahead of time and she deflected to Kenning Hall in Norfolk to bide her time and make plans. To be fair, the plot has often been blamed only on Northumberland but it is almost certain that on his deathbed Edward was partly responsible for attempting to change the succession, persuading the Council to sign the 'devise' seeking to put Lady Jane Grey on the throne. The political power and the goodwill of the people relating to the dead King Henry VIII, however, was too strong. It was his will that his children should succeed him and indeed they did, Edward, Mary and Elizabeth in succession. Mary came to the throne with the goodwill of the whole country but her obsessive persecution of Protestants made her one of the most hated monarchs in history, earning her the nickname 'Bloody Mary'. She was also hated for her marriage in 1554 to Philip II of Spain, probably the foremost champion of the Roman Catholic faith in Europe. Mary had many Protestants burnt at the stake or otherwise executed. (In the end she died childless, sick, neglected by her husband and one of the saddest figures of the age). Andrew Huddleston, whose family owned Sawston Hall, suggested that Mary could stay the night there, which she did. John and Bridget Huddleston received the royal guest warmly. Still later that night they received information that Guildford Dudley was heading, with a force, towards Sawston, presumably to catch Mary. John woke the Queen and had her dressed as a milkmaid and smuggled out of the house to safety. Dudley was so furious at having missed Mary that he had the house burned down. But Mary promised, and kept her promise, to restore the Hall to glory as a reward for the Huddlestons' loyalty.

Mary is alleged to haunt the Tapestry Room in Sawston Hall, which contains what is known as Queen Mary's bed – the four-poster in which she slept that night. Why she should haunt the Hall is unclear; it represented a sanctuary in her time of trouble. There she was among an ardent Catholic family that supported her strongly. If her 'presence' is truly there it may still be seeking the sanctuary it sought in life. Perhaps, however, there is a certain amount of wishful thinking on the part of those staying in the Tapestry room, knowing of its close association with Queen Mary.

Many people sleeping overnight at Sawston Hall have heard a knocking at their bedroom doors and the rattling of latches. Several of those witnesses believe that the ghost is protective, one believing that the ghost was 'seeing if he was all right' and another that the ghost was 'checking up on people'. Tom Corbett, who stayed at the Hall, believes that the ghost might be a night-watchman whose job was to protect the family and continues to do so in death. He kept hearing a name which he thought sounded like Cutlass, but this meant absolutely nothing to the Huddleston family then in residence. However, they discovered that there is a local family in the village called Cutriss, and believe this could be the explanation; perhaps a Cutriss in former years was a night-watchman at the Hall.

Several people at the Hall have also heard spinet music though no such instrument exists in the house, for example, Mrs Clare Huddleston who, as a bride, first came to the Hall in 1930 and heard the music. Her husband was more sceptical but over time heard so many stories of other people hearing it that he came to believe in it. 'I'm perfectly certain that an influence exists which some people feel and others don't,' he said. The music was described as light and enjoyable and never frightening.

WHILE YOU'RE THERE:

- A short trip along the A505 will bring you to Royston, and the Royston Cave. The cave is beneath Melbourn Street and represents the junction of the haunted Icknield Way and Ermine Street. It is believed that the cave was the oratory of a hermit, who probably carved it out. It is thirty feet high and twenty feet across, cut into the chalk. The cave is covered in some elaborate carvings representing Christian imagery.

The Treasurer's House
(Minster Yard, York, North Yorkshire)

No collection of ghosts would be complete without a mention of one of the most famous Roman ghosts in the world. The Treasurer's House literature includes the following: 'While other towns may challenge the claim of York to be the most haunted town in Britain, Treasurer's House is the most haunted house in the city and its ghosts are the oldest in the country. For almost two thousand years there has been a building on the site of Treasurer's House. Radulphus, first Treasurer or York Minster, was appointed *c.* 1091 and he took up residence in his new house about 1100. That house was destroyed in the great fire of York in 1137 that razed the Minster and most of the town, but in the reign of Edward I a new house was built incorporating parts of previous buildings. It was largely rebuilt in the sixteenth and seventeenth centuries. During the eight hundred years of its history Treasurer's House has been the home of many interesting characters, so it is hardly surprising that succeeding generations have felt that the presence of some of them still remains'.

A great many people have seen ghosts of Romans and Roman armies in the Treasurer's House; the most famous first-hand account is that of of Harry Martindale. Tall, solid, dependable, a retired policeman, Martindale impresses everyone with his down-to-earth stability. All the more reason, then, to take note of his account of his sighting which arose when, in 1953, at the age of eighteen, he was an apprentice plumber installing central heating in the cellars of the Treasurer's House. Martindale first heard a trumpet call and then saw the top of a soldier's helmet emerging through the wall he was working on. Surprised, he fell off the short ladder he was standing on and 'scuttled back into the corner of the cellar'. If that shocked Martindale, what was to follow must have done so even more. The soldier fully emerged through the wall, carrying the trumpet, marched across the cellar and disappeared into the opposite wall. Following him a huge carthorse emerged, and then at least twenty soldiers in double file, all in procession. Martindale noted that they were all at a lower level than himself, their knees at floor level. The soldiers were carrying lances, round shields and short swords.

Throughout the whole experience Martindale heard the trumpet blowing, even though the trumpeter had long disappeared into the opposite wall. What impressed Martindale particularly was that the soldiers did not look like the sort of military formation he had been used to seeing in films. These soldiers were not marching formally but were simply walking two abreast, dishevelled and unshaven. Martindale remembers them looking 'extremely tired'. Martindale left the cellar at a pace, first running to the museum's curator. Martindale's face must have told it all, because the curator's first comment was: 'By the look of you, you've seen the Romans, haven't you?'

For some years there were questions about the round shields; it was believed that the Roman infantry carried rectangular, rather than circular, shields. However, records indicated that during the fourth century the Sixth Legion was withdrawn from York and reinforced by auxiliary troops who did use round shields.

Martindale had become the latest in a line of witnesses to the Romans at the Treasurer's House. In 1946 a previous curator had had a similar experience and in the 1930s an American professor visiting the House had reported the same. In the 1920s the Treasurer's House had been privately owned by Frank Green and he had thrown a fancy-dress party there. A young lady attending the party went down into the cellars but found her way barred by a man dressed as a Roman soldier who prevented her passing along the passageway by placing his spear across the way. She assumed he was one of the fancy-dress partygoers but her host was adamant that there was no one so dressed.

Another account of the Romans comes from a Mrs Joan Mawson, who worked as caretaker at the Treasurer's House in the 1950s, following Harry Martindale's sighting. In 1957, while she was walking through a low tunnel towards the cellars, the bull terrier she habitually took with her stopped and turned tail. Mrs Mawson could hear the sound of horses and, petrified, huddled against the wall. Like Martindale she saw a troop of Roman soldiers just a couple of feet away from her and again only from the thighs upwards. Yet they looked completely solid. She also described the soldiers looking tired, dishevelled and dirty. In fact Mrs Mawson had the experience on further occasions and noted on each occasion how dirty and mud-splashed the troop was. On a third occasion she saw mounted soldiers apparently so tired they were almost resting on their horses' necks from exhaustion. Curiously Mrs Mawson did not hear the trumpet, though it turned out that others in the house at the time had heard such sounds but had never, despite many trips to the cellars, seen the Roman troops.

Perhaps most importantly for the verification of the sighting, excavation of the site by archaeologists such as Peter Wenham discovered a Roman road known as the Via Decumana, which led from the north-eastern gate of York to the legion headquarters and was sighted some eighteen inches below the floor level of the cellar of the Treasurer's House. This could well account for the sighting of the Romans from the knees or thighs upwards if their feet were actually positioned on the old Roman road. The road precisely follows the description of the direction given by Mrs Mawson. Harry Martindale's sighting was also corroborative on this point; the excavations had already begun at the time he was there and there was one part where the road level had been exposed; it is here that he actually saw the sandals of the soldiers, and in another area where excavation had gone down below the road level the soldiers seemed to be walking on air. Martindale's sighting of the soldiers was not along the same line and indeed those he witnessed seemed to be moving at right angles to the ones seen by Mrs Mawson. If the speculated plan of Roman York is correct, then those sighted by Martindale seemed to have been coming from the barracks.

In 1663 the Treasurer's House was bought by George Aislabie. In January 1674 the Aislabies attended a ball given at the home of the Duke of Buckingham in Skeldergate. They took with them Mary Mallorie, then engaged to one Jonathan Jennings. Having failed to awaken anyone at the Treasurer's House when they returned there late in the evening, Mary spent the night with a relative of Jonathan. The possible disgrace led to a bitter argument between Jonathan and George Aislabie. The following day the two fought a duel at Penley Crofts, just outside the city walls. Fatally wounded, Aislabie was brought back to the Treasurer's House to die. He was laid to rest in the Minster but there are many who believe that his ghost haunts the Treasurer's House. Many witnesses have reported a 'threatening presence' at the door of the Treasurer's House in Chapter House Street; some believe that it is George Aislabie.

Other ghostly apparitions seen within the Treasurer's House include that of Lady Beaumont, who is said to have appeared in the Drawing Room. Visitors recognize her from her picture, which is displayed on the staircase. Another apparition reported is that of 'a tall young man with long, fair hair tied back at the nape of the neck, wearing a scarlet tunic trimmed with gold, black trousers and buckled shoes'. His shade appears in the Lower Hall.

SEE ALSO:
- Sheriff Hutton.
- National Railway Museum, York.
- Theatre Royal, York.

Washington Old Hall
(Washington, Tyne and Wear)

Washington Old Hall was rebuilt on twelfth-century foundations in the early seventeenth century. The rebuilding was moderate and un-ornamental. Despite this, the building is the ancestral home of the first president of the USA, George Washington. His direct ancestors had lived there for five generations and the property remained in the family until 1613. Open to the public, and administered by the National Trust, there are many reminders of the American connection throughout the house: a portrait of George Washington on drum parchment, a letter from the second Duke of Northumberland, a lottery ticket signed by Washington, and a uniform of the Washington Greys. The American connection has been maintained and in 1977 President Jimmy Carter visited the house and presented it with a print of Mount Vernon. Indeed the house is in its present condition due to American gifts. It had fallen into disrepair in the nineteenth century and was considered for demolition in the 1930s. However, contributions and gifts from the USA enabled a full and proper restoration to take place. The National Trust took it over in 1956.

Tourists visiting the house have often reported a 'lady in a long grey dress' in an upstairs corridor. Americans in particular are keen to associate the lady with the Washington family, though such connection is speculative; no origin or identity for the ghost has been presented.

WHILE YOU'RE THERE:
- Almost as if catering to the many American tourists visiting George Washington's ancestral home, the ghost in the cathedral church of St Nicholas in nearby Newcastle upon Tyne could not be more 'classical'. He is a knight in full armour, heard clanking his way down the aisle near the tomb of a crusader.

Windsor Castle
(Windsor, Berkshire)

In 1897 Carr Glynn, Officer of the Guard, often visited the Royal Library. During one visit he heard the sound of clicking heels and saw the shade of a tall woman dressed in black walking towards and close to him. She reminded him of portraits of Queen Elizabeth I. Glynn saw her walk to a corner of the room and disappear from view into, he thought, an adjacent room. However, he discovered that there was no room there, though in Queen Elizabeth's time a flight of steps at that point had led from the library to the terrace and was believed to be a favourite walk of the Queen. There have been several other reports of the same ghost, not least the one by the Empress of Russia, Princess Victoria, Queen Victoria's daughter.

During the last years of his life, blind and insane, George III stayed at Windsor and was seen shortly after his death by a patrol of guards. His body was lying in state, and as the patrol passed the King's window the commander saw George III standing there; automatically he gave the command 'Eyes right' and the ghostly King saluted.

Another haunting associated with Windsor Castle is that of Sir George Villiers. His son, the Duke of Buckingham, was very unpopular and there is a report that several times the ghost of his father appeared to an officer in Windsor Castle, instructing him to warn his son of insurgence against him unless he took steps to relieve his unpopularity. It took three appearances before the officer decided to pass on the message and after that the ghost was not seen again. The message went unheeded, incidentally, and the Duke was murdered later that year, 1628.

Henry VIII is held to haunt the cloisters near the Deanery; many have heard the sounds of pain and dragging footsteps, indicating the possibility of someone suffering from gout as Henry did in his later years.

SEE ALSO:
• Bisham Abbey.

WHILE YOU'RE THERE:
• There is a persistent and famous story of a haunting by Herne the Hunter in the nearby Park. However, this story is more legend than witness report.

Woburn Abbey
(Woburn, Bedfordshire)

Built in 1744 on the site of an earlier Cistercian building, Woburn Abbey has many tales of hauntings. Several people, including the Duchess of Bedford, visitors, employees and workmen have seen what appears to be a monk in a brown habit in the crypt, and a similar figure was seen in the sculpture gallery in 1971. The figure was 'standing between the entrance pillars with his back to the room. Then he just glided through the door'. The assumption has been made that this may have been the abbot who was hanged in the grounds of Woburn Abbey for voicing his opposition to Henry VIII's marriage to Anne Boleyn. The *Bedfordshire and Buckinghamshire Observer* reported that on one occasion there was 'an icy blast' when the monk was seen.

In the Antiques Centre a ghostly figure in old-fashioned costume and a top hat was seen by several members of staff, visitors and workmen.

Perhaps most famously, there are many stories of guests staying in Woburn Abbey finding doors opening and closing on their own and being disturbed by such movements at night.

SEE ALSO:
- Bedford.
- Cecil Higgins Art Gallery.

WHILE YOU'RE THERE:
- A short journey across the Bedfordshire/Buckinghamshire border will bring you to Loughton, near Milton Keynes. It is said that three times a year Dick Turpin's ghost is seen riding up Trap's Hill, the site of some of his highway robberies.

CHAPTER 4

~

HAUNTED THEATRES

Adelphi Theatre
(London)

Like other theatres, the Adelphi is reputed to have a string of hauntings, as the stage manager of the theatre confirmed when we spoke to him in 1997. The most famous of all is the alleged ghost of William Terriss. Terriss was the leading man in many productions at the Adelphi during the latter part of the nineteenth century. He has been described as the first matinée idol and was praised by audience and critics alike. However, he became the object of envy by at least one bit player, Richard Prince. On 16 December 1897 Prince stabbed Terriss in the chest as Terriss was approaching the stage door. Terriss died in the arms of his then leading lady, Jessie Milward, and promised her, 'I shall come back'.

An eye-witness to the murder was quoted in the *Daily Telegraph* of 17 December 1897. 'I was standing near the front of the Adelphi Theatre, shortly before half past seven this evening, and I observed a man who is very familiar to frequenters of that path. He wore a soft felt hat with a sort of ulster with a case to it . . . Mr Terriss came along and went to the private door of the theatre. He stopped in front of the door for an instant, started to take out his keys from his pocket. The man I have described, who I noticed had a sort of wild look in his eyes . . . walked up to Terriss and quickly stabbed him with a knife. Terriss was heard to cry out: 'You have stabbed me! Arrest him!' But before the assailant could be seen he had aimed another determined blow at Mr Terriss – a blow which appeared to have completed its dreadful work. The actor staggered and reeled, and a few minutes afterwards he was heard groaning in the agony of death.' It appeared that Prince, the murderer, had two months earlier been sacked from his touring company in Newcastle and had shadowed Terriss for some six weeks in his anger.

In the years since there have been many reports of strange noises and lights coming from Terriss's old dressing-room; his apparition has been seen in the theatre and, unique in theatre ghosts we believe, he has also been reported in the London Underground at the site of where he would in life catch his train home. He is consistently reported as wearing a frock coat, top hat and holding a walking stick, all very much a description of Terriss. On being approached or spoken to the ghost disappears immediately.

There is an account in the 'Sunday Dispatch' of 15 January 1956. The newspaper wanted to know who was 'the ghost of Covent Garden Underground Station'. The article went on to say: 'A four page report has been sent to the London Transport Executive Divisional Head-quarters. And this question has been put to officials: *Is the statuesque figure wearing white gloves and seen by members of the station staff, the spectre of William Terriss, the actor stabbed to death at the Adelphi Theatre by a maniac 59 years ago?*' Several members of the station staff had seen the figure, including Victor Locker, who applied for and was granted transfer to another station because he could not work after having seen the ghost, and Jack Hayden, who saw the figure after the last passengers had left and who it seems he thought might have been evading fares. He phoned the booking clerk to 'catch the man coming up the emergency stairs' but no one appeared. Hayden saw the figure again and described it as 'wearing a grey suit, funny old collar and white gloves, looking at me from the ante-room'. Hayden asked if the man was looking for the cloakroom and the thing disappeared. Both Locker and Hayden when shown pictures of William Terriss, identified the figure immediately.

Many accounts of Terriss's appearance have him materializing out of a green light. For example, one actress in 1928 was in her dressing-room reclining on her chaise-longe and felt it shaking and bucking as if someone was kicking it underneath, though she could see no reason for this. When she lay down again she felt her arms were being gripped and hit and then saw a green light above her dressing-table mirror. She heard two raps and then the light vanished. The actress later learned that she had been in Jessie Milward's dressing-room and that Terriss always gave two taps with his cane when he passed her door. In 1962 the same green light was seen by two workmen in the auditorium, who saw it take the shape of a body that then floated across the stage.

During a visit to the Adelphi Theatre, ghost-hunter Eddie Burks also seems to have contacted the ghost of Jessie Matthews, an experience he found light and cheerful. It seems the ghost was enjoying the play in production, *Sunset Boulevard*, and wished she was dancing in it.

During Eddie Burks's visit to the Adelphi he caused consternation in the administration by assisting the ghost of William Terriss to 'move on' so that he would no longer haunt the theatre. Burks was perhaps more concerned for the disturbed spirit than for the theatre, which, like most theatres, jealously protects its ghosts.

SEE ALSO:
• London's various locations; mainly palaces and theatres.

WHILE YOU'RE THERE:
• Take the train. You never know who you might meet!
• And while you're down there check if you feel anyone tap you on the shoulder. Philip Atkins of the National Railway Museum in York told us that when the Victoria Underground line was being built in the 1960s there were several reports of workmen being tapped on the shoulder but finding no one there. Rumour was that they were, at the time, digging their way through an old burial pit from the Great Plague.

Haymarket Theatre
((Theatre Royal, Haymarket), London)

The Theatre Royal, Haymarket, was managed by John Buckstone (following a period performing in the theatre as a comedian) until his death in 1879. Just the following year his ghost was seen watching performances from the Royal Box. His ghost has been seen by many, including the actress Dame Margaret Rutherford. It is said that his ghost is pleasant and harmless, though with a penchant for startling people – perhaps harking back to his days as a comedian.

In 1961 Dame Margaret Rutherford and her husband slept at the theatre in her dressing-room as a result of a rail strike which prevented them returning home. In the room was a cupboard next to a bricked-up entrance to the stage. Rutherford dreamed that on going to the cupboard she could not close the door because of the billowing skirts of eighteenth-century costumes. While trying to close the door she dreamed she saw a man's leg and a glimpse of Buckstone's face, which she recognized from a portrait she had seen. At the time she did not know of Buckstone's association with that particular theatre. We might therefore suppose that even though the impression of Buckstone came in a dream it might have been a dream inspired by a presence or telepathic imprint.

In 1963 there was an account in the *Daily Telegraph* of Buckstone's ghost being seen. The production on stage at the time was *At The Drop Of Another Hat*, featuring Michael Flanders and Donald Swann. During a piano performance the assistant stage manager, Olga Bennett, saw someone standing behind Michael Flanders's wheelchair. She assumed it was a stage-hand and was very angry, but when she realized that the figure was wearing a long black frock-coat she was somewhat confused. It was later that she discovered that her description 'exactly fitted the ghost of J.B. Buckstone'.

Like so many theatre ghosts, a sighting of John Buckstone is thought to herald a successful production.

Donald Sinden saw John Buckstone's ghost in 1949 when performing in *The Heiress*. He had passed Sir Ralph Richardson's dressing-room and, seeing a black frock-coated figure at the window looking out into the street, he called 'Good evening' to it. The figure did not reply. Some way further on Sinden realized that Richardson was on stage at the time and went back to the dressing-room to see who was there. The figure had disappeared. Sinden was sure that no other member of the cast could have been there at that time either.

SEE ALSO:
- London's various locations; mainly palaces and theatres.

WHILE YOU'RE THERE:
- Follow up your evening at the theatre with another reminder of Britain's cultural heritage. Take a walk towards Holborn and Clerkenwell to 48 Doughty Street. This was one of the homes of Charles Dickens; his ghost has sometimes been reported standing outside.

Lyceum
(Crewe, Cheshire)

The Lyceum in Crewe stands on the site of an old Roman Catholic church and graveyard and first became a theatre in 1887. The original building was destroyed in 1910 by a fire and the present building was built to replace it.

Three ghosts have particularly been seen in the theatre: a sad and apparently guilty-looking monk, a distraught ballet dancer who it is said hanged herself in a dressing-room in the theatre, and an actor who haunts the area around the stage door. In the late 1800s a service of exorcism was performed to eradicate the ghosts but there have been sightings in more modern times, suggesting that this was not successful. On one occasion the ghost of the actor was seen at the back of the stage together with the ghost of the ballet dancer! Sightings have been made by actors, theatre staff and guests.

SEE ALSO:

- Tarporley, Cheshire.

WHILE YOU'RE THERE:

- Visit nearby Barthomley, close to junction 16 of the M6. There are reports of a White Lady ghost in the church field, and a spectral dog on the road near the same location.

Lyceum
(Wellington Street, off the Strand, London)

The Lyceum was refurbished to its former glory in 1996 and opened again as a prominent theatre in London's theatreland. A century ago it was a marvellous venue, though in the intervening years it had been a somewhat run-down dance hall and ballroom.

This story derives from the 1880s and is particularly grisly, though frankly it has the air of Victorian melodrama about it. The story has it that a husband and wife were sitting in one of the boxes watching the show when the wife saw a woman sitting in the stalls with a man's severed head in her lap. The lights went down and the couple waited until the interval to confirm their sighting, which the husband had also caught a glimpse of. However, during the interval the object in the woman's lap was covered by a shawl. At the end of the performance the woman left the theatre so quickly that the couple, even though they attempted to pursue, could not reach her amid the crowds. This experience stayed with the husband for many years, and at some time later he saw a portrait which he was sure was the man whose head he had seen in the woman's lap. The man, he was told, was a member of the family that owned the land on which the Lyceum had been built in 1772 and he had been beheaded on the orders of Oliver Cromwell.

This does not quite fit historical facts, though of course Cromwell was responsible for a number of beheadings and the person could have been a more distant relative of the family. Alternatively it could have been the head of Henry Courtenay. He was executed in 1538 when 1st

Marquess of Exeter; the Lyceum was built on part of the grounds of Exeter House.

Nevertheless, it seems an unlikely story overall. If the couple were unsure whether or not the object in the woman's lap was a head then they could hardly have identified it so accurately as to be able to recognize the features on a portrait. On the other hand, if they were that certain that it was a severed head then it seems hardly likely that they would have sat through an interval without asking someone to investigate further.

Perhaps the answer will unfold to a new generation of theatregoers now that the Lyceum has returned to its former grandeur.

SEE ALSO:
- London's various locations; mainly palaces and theatres.

WHILE YOU'RE THERE:
- A walk along the Strand, Fleet Street and Ludgate Hill will bring you to the magnificent St Paul's Cathedral, arguably Wren's greatest legacy. It has a ghost, a clergyman who has been seen in All Soul's Chapel (now the Kitchener Memorial Chapel) by the visitors' entrance. Several vergers have reported the same apparition and all have commented on one other aspect – a high-pitched whistling noise associated with the sighting.

Old Vic
(London)

The Old Vic opened in 1818, when it was known as the Royal Coburg Theatre. In 1843 it was renamed the Royal Victoria Theatre and in 1880 the building was purchased by the British social reformer Emma Cons, who intended it to be used for the presentations of lectures, concerts and so on, designed to bring moral and spiritual enlightenment. In 1898 Cons brought her niece, Lilian Mary Baylis, into the management. In 1914 Baylis began productions of Shakespeare plays and English opera.

The Old Vic was very badly damaged during Second World War bombing and was rebuilt and re-opened in 1950. For a time it housed the National Theatre of Great Britain, and when the company moved to its own headquarters in 1976 the Old Vic was closed. After refurbishment it re-opened in 1983.

The hauntings apparently date from the days of Baylis and Cons. We spoke to an administrator of the Old Vic in 1997, who explained that he understood Emma Cons to have been 'a very stroppy woman' who 'bullied God', shouting at the Lord to make productions a success. Her niece apparently had the same strength of character. There have been several reports of the ghost of Lilian Baylis in the theatre, displaying her customary fiery characteristics. As with so many theatre ghosts, the apparition of Lilian Baylis is held to be a portent that the production under development at that time will be a success.

SEE ALSO:
- London's various locations; mainly palaces and theatres.

WHILE YOU'RE THERE:
- A short stroll will bring you to Westminster Bridge. Keep a careful eye on the boats that pass underneath it – there is a belief that a ghost boat is seen on that part of the Thames and that it goes under one side of Westminster Bridge but does not re-emerge on the other side.

Theatre Royal
(Bath, Somerset)

The Theatre Royal, Bath, was built in 1805 and fully restored to its former glory only a few years ago.

Its most common ghost is a Grey Lady. Like so many ghosts she appears in monotones – a long grey dress, grey feathers in her hair. Witnesses report a strong smell of jasmine perfume in association with her sighting. She is believed by many to be an actress from the eighteenth century, though she has not been specifically identified.

The legend is that she performed regularly at the Theatre Royal but committed suicide in the nearby hotel, the Garrick's Head. Although married, she had a lover, and when her husband discovered her liaison he challenged his rival to a duel and killed him. On learning that her lover was dead she hanged herself. Her ghost now haunts the Theatre Royal, scene of her many triumphs, perhaps looking for her lover.

The Grey Lady has been seen many times, for example reported two or three times by Dame Anna Neagle. Most recently, in the early 1990s, the Grey Lady made an entrance during the Saturday afternoon perform-ance of a play called *A Moment Of Weakness*. According to researchers Tony Wells and Melanie Warren, both stars of the play, Liza Goddard and Christopher Timothy, saw the Grey Lady sitting in a box which they knew was not occupied during afternoon performances. They felt a cold atmosphere and although they did not allow it to disturb their performance – the show must go on! – they admitted afterwards to being somewhat shaken by the experience. The sighting also matched part of the legend: the particular box the lady was sitting in is the one that her lover is supposed to have sat in and from where he threw trinkets to her on the stage.

The Theatre Royal in Bath is also the location of a rare ghost: that of a butterfly. The origin of the butterfly would seem to come from a pantomime held at Christmas 1948. Butterflies were the theme. It included a butterfly ballet, where dancers dressed as tortoiseshell butterflies surrounded by a large illuminated butterfly on the stage. Then a real tortoiseshell butterfly was seen, or at least it was supposed to be real but given the time of the year it was certainly out of season. It is alleged that at every Christmas pantomime since – bar one – a ghostly butterfly – or the same ghostly butterfly – appears.

In 1963 another paranormal incident occurred at the theatre. At precisely three o'clock a stage clock struck three o'clock. This would not be all that surprising were it not for the fact that the clock mechanisms had been removed. At a later performance of the same play all the lights dimmed at precisely three o'clock apparently without explanation.

SEE ALSO:

- Farleigh Hungerford, near Trowbridge.
- Frome.
- Warminster.
- Theatre Royal, Bristol.

WHILE YOU'RE THERE:

- Talk a walk down Grosvenor Place. It is said that at least one building in the street is haunted by the spectre of a woman in old-fashioned clothes, including a bonnet.

Theatre Royal
(Bristol)

The ghost of the Old Vic, as the Theatre Royal, Bristol, is known, is a Victorian lady thought to be the actress Sara McReady. Her association with the Old Vic appears to stem from the time when, on the death of her husband who had been manager of the Old Vic, she took over the job. To manage a boisterous theatre in Victorian times would not be an easy task, least of all for a woman, though it seems that Sara was a tough and eccentric woman who performed the job admirably. She died in 1853 after over thirty years as manager of the Old Vic and must have had a loving association with it.

The ghost seen is said to be dressed in black with a high collar, hair parted in the middle in Victorian style. She is often accompanied by a cold atmosphere and the smell of perfume. Occasionally people have reported something brushing past them but have been unable to see anything. Whether it was Sara or not, one night-watchman became quite terrified when, working in the theatre alone, he heard a woman's voice shout at him to 'get out'. Other people in the theatre have also heard whispering sounds.

Interestingly, the senior scenic artist at the theatre, Jane Cooke, has kept a record of Sara's appearances and noted that she is only seen in those areas of the theatre which existed during her life; she does not appear in the recent extensions.

Sara has been reported sitting in a box, usually for short moments but sometimes long enough for the sighter to get a good look. The late comedian Michael Bentine, who had a lifelong interest in the psychic, was on stage at the Old Vic and instantly pointed out the box in which she has been seen, stating that he thought 'something was there'.

SEE ALSO:
- Theatre Royal, Bath.

WHILE YOU'RE THERE:
- Visit St Anne's Well in St Anne's Park, Bristol, which is said to have curative powers (as have, of course, the waters of nearby Bath). Henry VII and his wife used to patronize it.

The Theatre Royal
(Drury Lane, London)

The Theatre Royal, Drury Lane, has several ghost stories associated with it. The ghost of Charles II and some of his attendants were seen during a performance in 1948. During his life Charles II was a regular theatregoer and lover of the theatre.

Another ghost is seen during the daytime and never at night, frequently during matinée performances. He is known as the Man in Grey and is thought to be the ghost of a murder victim dating from the seventeenth century. Support for this arises from a skeleton discovered in the theatre in 1848. A dagger was found between its ribs. The small room where the skeleton was found is in the theatre's Upper Circle where the ghostly Man in Grey walks. There have been hundreds of witnesses, even in recent years. On one occasion the theatre historian W.J. McQueen Pope reported that seventy members of the cast of a play during a rehearsal saw the ghost. (On one occasion McQueen Pope saw him when conducting a troop of sightseers around the theatre.) The Man in Grey appears to be a recordings ghost, making no sound and always being seen walking in the same direction. His route would appear to be through a wall in the upper circle, across the seating area, up the stairs, around the back and down the stairs on the other side, through a door and then through a wall opposite his starting place, which is near where the skeleton was found. The Man in Grey is described as having a tricorne hat, a long riding cloak, ruffled sleeves and carrying a sword. He is described as being of average height with a strong, handsome, clean-cut face. There is nothing shadowy about his appearance, he appears solid, and has convinced several people that he is in fact an actor in costume. If his walk is disturbed by someone standing in the way it is said he 'dissolves' and then reappears beyond them. One suggestion for the origin, if not of the ghost at least of the skeleton, is that he was the murder victim of the bad man of 'Old Drury', Christopher Ricks, who was the theatre manager at the time of Queen Anne and known for his bad temper and violence. The skeleton itself was given a pauper's burial in a nearby graveyard though the ghost has continued to walk to the present time.

Appearances of the Man in Grey are not apparently dependent on tranquillity; during the Second World War a fire-watcher apparently saw the ghost during the peak of activity of an air raid.

The fact that the ghost was frequently seen during sightseeing tours conducted by McQueen Pope, particularly in the period from the 1930s to his death in 1960, has raised the question of whether or not McQueen Pope had whatever special faculty it was that enabled the ghost to appear. It has often been suggested that those who see ghosts have certain qualities in their own mind but this would be one stage further: to have a quality which allows for a manifestation that many other people can see. The uncharitable suggestion that the Man in Grey was indeed an actor hired by Pope to spice up his sightseeing tours clearly does not reflect the facts; for example in 1977 there was a sighting quite consistent with all the previous sightings, seventeen years after Pope's death.

In addition to McQueen Pope and several actors and actresses who have seen him several times, he has been seen by the Broadcasting Officer for the Entertainments National Services Association, Stephen Williams, and the ghost-researcher James Wentworth Day.

The Man in Grey has been seen for some 200 years, since the early eighteenth century. Sightings of the Man in Grey are believed to be a good omen, suggesting that the play in rehearsal or underway at the time will be a success. Having been seen just before the opening nights of *Oklahoma!*, *Carousel*, *South Pacific*, *The King and I*, *42nd Street* and *My Fair Lady*, the Man in Grey certainly seems to have an eye for a good production.

The theatre has other ghosts; one that perhaps leaves little to chance when aiding new productions. During the rehearsals for *Oklahoma!* the actress Betty Jo Jones not only saw a man in grey but also, when the show opened and was not going terribly well, apparently felt herself pushed around the stage by an invisible hand; after a few performances, when she felt her stage performance had improved, she received 'a ghostly pat on the back'. Doreen Duke was also guided around the stage during *The King and I*. McQueen Pope believed that the ghost was that of Joe Grimaldi, who often performed at the theatre and was known for his willingness to help young performers.

It has been said that the Theatre Royal, Drury Lane, has 500 ghosts, at least according to Nina Smirnoff who conducted public tours of the theatre; they include a Victorian pantomime dame, the actor Edmund Kean and the actor Dan Leno, who was recognized by the actor Stanley Lupino. Another ghost is allegedly that of Charles Macklin, a stern and aggressive figure that is seen on the stage just before the curtain is raised. Macklin was an Irish actor who in 1735 killed a fellow actor when he struck him in the eye with a walking stick. Though in this case it is the ghost of the perpetrator rather than the victim that is allegedly appearing.

A highly successful psychic, Eddie Burks, visited the Theatre Royal, Drury Lane, in June 1994. Burks picked up the echo of a man who had been injured in the theatre; his lower ribs had been broken, apparently in a fall to his death. It was 1930; he was a tall muscular man in his late twenties or early thirties wearing the outfit of a workman. Curiously enough, during a performance of *Miss Saigon*, as reported in *The Times* of 19 November 1991, the Theatre Royal had been fined when an electrician had fallen head first through a trap door and had broken an arm and wrist. As Burks writes in his book *Ghost Hunter*, co-authored with Gillian Cribbs, 'there are many instances where a terrible accident or murder leaves a psychic imprint on a place, and if this is not cleared, it will tend to build up an energy which can attract repeats of the original accident'.

SEE ALSO:

• London's various locations; mainly palaces and theatres.

WHILE YOU'RE THERE:

• Nearby Somerset House is a building of great splendour designed by Sir William Chambers in 1776. It is on the site of a previous magnificent building: a Tudor palace built by the Duke of Somerset, which later became a royal palace. The new building was designed to house Departments of State, and specifically the Admiralty, so it is appropriate that the ghost of none other than Lord Nelson himself has been seen here, striding across the Quadrangle. Visitors here today may sense an atmosphere of depressing gloom but that is nothing paranormal; the building presently houses the Inland Revenue!

Theatre Royal
(Norwich, Norfolk)

As the clock chimed to celebrate the new year when 1978 became 1979, Bob Piacentini and his girlfriend of the time, Patricia, were embracing in the street outside the Theatre Royal in Norwich. Patricia was a dancer who was appearing in pantomime in the theatre.

He told us: 'We heard the clock strike twelve and as I looked round there was a character in a black top hat and tails. He was wearing very tight trousers and weird, old-fashioned shoes. As his jacket flapped open you could see the white lines of ribs on a tight, white shape underneath. When we looked at his face, as he approached us, he had a skeleton-type face. Not actually a skull, but like stretched, tight, skin. Both of us looked at each other; we just couldn't believe it. We thought it was someone in a pantomime costume or fancy-dress costume. He gave us this weird look, staring eyes as he walked past. Then he walked out on to the street and turned left. Patricia said, "Wow, that was unbelievable." I said, "I can't believe it. This is untrue." He had only just turned out of the road, maybe fifteen to twenty yards, so I followed him. I really walked quickly, then looked down the road both ways. But he was gone, completely gone. It was as if he had disappeared into thin air. It was definitely some sort of haunting. I believe that it was an experience that happens only at that time, but perhaps regularly. Maybe if you went there another year at that same time you'd see the same thing. I've often said to myself, one day when I've got spare time, I'd love to go there again and just see if the apparition comes back. If it was an apparition. Perhaps it was an old actor who had died in the theatre, still in costume. But it had to be a haunting simply because of the way he disappeared into thin air.'

SEE ALSO:

• Blickling Hall.

WHILE YOU'RE THERE:

• Visit Norwich Castle, which once housed the county jail. There is an interesting record of a manifestation of some sort which appeared to three men jailed there in 1820, awaiting transportation. None of them could describe the thing that scared them so much, but their story must have been sufficiently credible for the jailers to record it in their logs which the magistrates would inspect. There are also more recent reports by museum staff of the ghost of a lady in a black Victorian dress being seen.

Theatre Royal
(York)

This theatre stems from 1744. Like its Bath counterpart, the Theatre Royal in York is frequented by a ghostly Grey Lady. She has been seen by a number of theatre directors, actors and actresses, including the actress Evelyn Laye in 1975. The theatre is also haunted by inexplicable sounds of chanting which are believed to be an echo of a thirteenth-century hospital which once stood on the site and which was administered by nuns.

One ghost said to haunt the Theatre Royal is an actor who died in a duel in Blake Street. An understudy on stage in the theatre had the unexpected pleasure of seeing the ghost staggering in his death throes in the wings.

The Grey Lady of the Theatre Royal, York, is the most famous of their ghosts. She is thought to be the spirit of a nun who worked in St Leonard's Hospital, which once stood on the site. She broke her vows by falling in love with a local man and as punishment was bricked up alive. Her ghost now haunts the theatre built on the site of her entombment. Rather like the Man in Grey who haunts the Theatre Royal in Drury Lane, sightings of the Grey Lady at the Theatre Royal,

York, are supposed to herald a successful production. The Grey Lady's most frequent appearances are in the dress circle during technical or dress rehearsals.

Sightings of the Grey Lady are somewhat unclear, and indeed it is only association and perhaps expectation which has her described as a nun from the thirteenth century. Generally her appearance is simply that of a misty grey accompanied by a cold atmosphere, as attested to by several members of the staff of the Theatre Royal. In August 1975 Evelyn Laye was rehearsing for *Dear Octopus*. She sat down at the piano and 'began softly to recall Days Gone By' when the Grey Lady put in an appearance. To quote *The Ghosts of The Theatre Royal*, which the theatre publishes: 'A white/grey mist began to move slowly across the middle of the Dress Circle. The doors to the foyer were locked, there was no one in the Dress Circle and no one was smoking . . . There was no obvious natural explanation for the manifestation that the wide-eyed cast were witnessing'. Miss Laye stopped singing and together with her colleagues she watched the mist contract into a tiny ball and disappear. When she recommenced singing the mist reappeared. *Dear Octopus* was a great success.

The Grey Lady is also held to haunt the dressing-rooms and particularly likes to frequent costume plays.

SEE ALSO:
- Treasurer's House, York.
- National Railway Museum, York.

WHILE YOU'RE THERE:
- You are in a city that is a candidate for the most haunted in Britain, and the choice for the ghostwatcher is one of an embarrassment of riches. Perhaps visit Trinity Church, Micklegate, which is believed to sport a family of three ghosts, a relatively unusual claim.

GHOSTS
CUT OFF IN
THEIR PRIME

Why should sites of murder and execution, of death and suffering, create more ghosts than sites of happy, playful experiences? The cases in this section are examples of ghosts reported at scenes of murders and executions, and ghosts of wartime. Ghosts 'created' by unhappy events are typical, yet there are reports of playful groups of children being seen, of contented people sitting in their favourite armchairs, and so on. So we might conclude that whatever the factors that create such ghosts, they are not exclusively 'death and suffering'. We have to take into account, however, that ghosts of death and suffering outweigh those of obvious happiness.

What might those factors be? In addition to the atmosphere and geology speculated in the previous section, we must further consider the possibility that emotion plays a part in creating ghosts: whether 'recordings' or actual returns of 'personality'. Those who have been murdered or killed in accidents may well feel 'cut off in their prime'; they may have unfinished business; perhaps such desires can bring about a 'return'. They might also feel cheated, or a sense of injustice – true, perhaps, of some of those executed – and this might play a part. So emotion might be a factor in creating ghosts, and perhaps negative emotions are stronger, or of a nature to impress lastingly, hence a disproportionate number of ghosts of death and suffering.

There are cases where the 'unfinished business' is to bring retribution on those who killed them; haunting them or even exposing their crimes. In our *Encyclopedia of Ghosts and Spirits* we outlined the case of Richard Tarwell, whose ghost literally led to the discovery of his own murdered body and the conviction of those who had killed him; in Chapter 5 there are cases of ghosts seemingly performing similar 'missions'.

There is another possibility: perhaps ghosts are created not by the dead but by the living. Perhaps the images are created by the sighter projecting something on to the scene. If so, then why? Is knowledge of a violent past a trigger for the psyche to activate something? If we are standing in a old castle knowing that it was used for war, is it a trigger for us to envisage images of war and killing? Perhaps, but that alone would not explain cases where witnesses with no knowledge of the locality report exactly the same thing as others have done. Perhaps the dead leave behind not a ghost but a trace that can be telepathically connected with – perhaps the right mind in the right place can pick up on it and create the image from the telepathic impression.

One other factor: if emotion embeds recordings or other forms of ghosts then why do we not impress images in our lifetimes that are seen while we are still alive? If we perceive a sense of terrible injustice, or are unable to complete a task not because of our own deaths but because of the deaths of others, for example, then why are we not seen as ghosts when we are still alive? The answer, surprisingly, is that we are. A great many so-called ghosts are actually alive at the time they are seen. And often the reason for these 'bilocations' or 'projections' is unclear. For example, in Chapter 17, in the entry for the George and Dragon Hotel in West Wycombe, there is an account of the 'ghost' of the landlady who still works there today. And when the battle of Edge Hill was first 'replayed' as a sky vision (see October anniversaries in Chapter 15), many of the participants who could be seen were still alive.

All interesting but speculative possibilities, and certainly a long way from being proven in any scientific way. But the nature of ghost research includes monitoring of the environment and the witnesses to find out just what the varied mix of characteristics might be. Then, perhaps, one day we shall be able to predict or even create a ghost under 'laboratory conditions'. That would be a major breakthrough in understanding – perhaps of the dead, but mostly of the living.

Probably the ghosts reported from modern warfare are merely more modern versions of accounts of ghosts of ancient wars. Yet there are factors relating to modern wars that might be relevant when considering the high numbers of reports of soldiers, sailors and airmen that have been reported around the world in private as well as public places.

The sense of injustice and an incomplete life is clear; few of those who went to war wanted to do so even if they understood that it was a necessary act. It is said that no one hates war more than a soldier. And many of those people were young, teenage or not much older. Their lives were cut off in youth and this might well create a sense of not wishing to give up this world. In addition, they were fighting to make this world a better one; all the more poignant to have succeeded and then not be able to take part in it.

What is of interest and shown in these cases is that it is not just the people that manifest, but often machinery such as aircraft. (Actually this is true of virtually all ghosts; they manifest their clothing, or their horse-drawn carriages, and so on.) So perhaps the ghost is a shell constructed to represent the figure as it was in life, or at the time of death. Constructed by the dead? Or the living?

The living might play their part in projecting ghosts. If so, then we must consider the irrational, but real, guilt in surviving where others died. Perhaps the ghost is the result of a concentration on their misfortune and your good fortune, even the emotion of a sort of penance being paid.

The wars are still very much a living history. Perhaps that very concentration, that perspective, helps to create the ghosts by whatever factors are involved.

CHAPTER 5

~

SITES OF MURDER AND EXECUTION

Bedford
(Bedfordshire)

Black Tom was a highwayman who frequented the highways and byways of Bedfordshire and surrounding areas. In 1607 he was hanged on the public gallows in Bedford. The location of the former gallows is near Union Street in Bedford, in a parking area near the main shopping thoroughfare. Several people, particularly late in the evening returning to their cars, have seen what is believed to be the ghost of Black Tom 'wavering about as if drunk with its head lolling on one side like a loose puppet' – as described by one witness in 1963. No one has got very close to the apparition; those who try find it disappears in front of them.

SEE ALSO:

- Woburn Abbey.
- A5 at Markyate.

WHILE YOU'RE THERE:

- The town contains the headquarters of the Panacea Society. They are custodians of the Box, left by the prophetess Joanna Southcott who died in 1814. The Box is alleged to contain the answer to all the world's ills – war, disease and crime – all of which will increase until the Box is opened. But, according to Southcott's will, it must be opened in the presence of twenty-four bishops, who have not yet agreed to cooperate. However, an X-ray of the box shows that it contains what appears to be a gun, and another Box also said to be hers and opened in 1927 contained only a night-cap and a lottery ticket.

Black Abbey
(Accrington, Lancashire)

The site of the former Black Abbey – now known as Black Abbey Road – has been reported by many witnesses to be haunted by a beautiful young blonde girl, her face showing deep sadness. She appears dressed in white and, most horrifically, her right arm is withered and scarred as if the skin has been burned off. Her piercing screams terrify any witnesses, and then she disappears.

Inevitably there is local legend to explain this haunting, and it is a story the like of which arises widely around Britain. The Black Abbey was once a thriving monastery actively run by the monks. One monk is said to have fallen in love with the girl but of course kept their affair a secret to avoid punishment. The monk and the girl met in secret in one of the towers of the abbey. One evening, it is said, the girl's father guessed what was happening and sought to confront the pair. As he approached the room the monk hid the girl in a secret passageway and faced down her father, denying her presence. The father, perhaps with the aid of outraged monks, chained up the errant brother, sealed the room and set fire to the tower. The girl emerged from the passageway into the burning room to try to release her lover. In the morning their incinerated remains were found locked in embrace.

Such a story must be embroidered; how could we know what happened in a room where the only two people ended up dead? The ways in which 'explanations' for ghost sightings develop from local stories are often varied, and rich with fantasy. But never forget that there are still frightening sightings of a screaming blonde girl, whatever the truth of her origins.

SEE ALSO:
- Samlesbury Hall.

WHILE YOU'RE THERE, OTHER ACCRINGTON GHOSTS INCLUDE:
- At 38 Pendle Street, in 1965, young Carole Mackey encountered an amorphous, amoeba-like, vaguely humanoid evil presence which seemed to trigger off scratching and banging noises that lasted at least a year and were heard by Carole's younger brother Gary also. Gary also admitted he had seen an amorphous blue light phenomena in the house. Pendle Street takes its name from Pendle Forest, one of Britain's now lost forest areas but one which was associated in the 1600s with witchcraft. During witchcraft purges nine witches were executed there

in 1612 and seventeen further sentenced to death in 1633 were reprieved after a series of prolonged tortures.

Bosley
(Macclesfield, Cheshire)

The stiles on the field borders around Bosley are made from the wood of a gibbet which stood on nearby Gun Hill until the 1880s. Locally it is believed that the stiles are haunted by the ghost of John Naden, a vicious and menacing figure that approaches people out of the darkness, reeling and gesturing as if drunk and aggressive.

Naden's story is that he murdered his employer, Robert Brough, while in cahoots with Brough's wife. Whether Naden and Brough's wife were having a liaison or whether Naden was paid for the deed is uncertain. Certainly murder could not have come naturally to Naden, as he apparently had to bolster his courage with excessive drink – hence presumably the reason his ghost is seen weaving drunkenly. Naden reported to Brough's wife that the deed was done, and she emptied her dead husband's pockets to create the appearance that he had been murdered by thieves. However, Naden had left his knife at the scene of the crime beside the body and neither of them noticed. Naden was prosecuted on the strength of the knife and lack of an alibi and executed just outside Brough's house. His body was hung in chains on the gallows on Gun Hill, a decomposing reminder to all of the penalty for murder.

SEE ALSO:

- Lyme Park.
- Whaley Bridge.

WHILE YOU'RE THERE:

- Stoke on Trent was the centre of a UFO wave (a period of frequent sightings) during the months of August to November 1967. One object was reported landing in a field off Wendline Close. The police were called, but before they arrived children who had been going towards the UFO reported that it 'hedge-hopped' and then disappeared.

Haddenham
(near Aylesbury, Buckinghamshire)

There is a grisly apparition allegedly forewarning of danger at the junction of the A418 and the tiny road leading to the village of

Haddenham. As a somewhat dramatic way of warning witnesses of impending danger, the apparition appears as a man staggering, clutching a bleeding hole in his chest.

He is the victim of a murder in 1828, whose first reappearance as a ghost was to his unfortunate wife. He was a farmer and he had been to Thame market and was returning home. As it was very late his wife had become concerned; she went to the farmhouse door to look for him. Horrifyingly, he appeared – slowly materializing before her eyes – holding his bleeding chest from which could she could see the shaft of a hammer protruding. When she rushed into the road she found the physical body of her husband lying on the roadside with wounds precisely matching those she had seen on the apparition. He had been murdered by two sheep stealers, Tylor and Sewell, in an attempt to cover up their crimes and prevent the dreaded punishment of transportation to Australia. They were tried, convicted and publicly hanged on 8 March 1830 at Aylesbury Prison.

WHILE YOU'RE THERE:

- Tring, on the other side of Aylesbury, is haunted by a black dog that is said to be the spirit of a murderer hanged in 1751 for the murder of a local witch.

The Heddon Oak
(Stogumber, Somerset)

To the north-west of Taunton in Somerset, a turning off the A358 runs between the villages of Stogumber and Crowcombe. On this road stands the Heddon Oak. It is a famous local tree with a long history. It dominates the road, and a huge branch which reaches out across the road is the one on which several of Monmouth's soldiers were hanged. The Duke of Monmouth had led a rebellion against King James II, who had come to the throne in 1685. Monmouth was defeated but he and his followers were so cruelly treated at the Bloody Assizes by Judge Geoffrey that public opinion turned against the King. Many locals believe that when passing the Oak the hanging sounds are re-enacted; heavy breathing and strangling noises have been reported. Local people have declared that there is also a 'choking sensation' felt when passing the tree.

The area is also supposedly haunted by the Wild Hunt, which rides through the streets of Stogumber to the sounds of crying hounds, horses' hooves and jingling of horse bridles. It is thought to be a portent of doom to see the hunt and many locals, aware of the superstition, say that even though they hear it they would not look out of their windows to see it.

SEE ALSO:

- Sedgemoor.

WHILE YOU'RE THERE:

- Take care walking around on the nearby Quantock Hills. In 1988 Anthony Burfield was sitting on the hills taking photographs of the scenery when he saw a 'bat-like' UFO approaching him. He suffered years of illness as a result of the close encounter.

Holyrood House
(City of Edinburgh, Scotland)

This imposing palace within the City of Edinburgh was the scene of a particularly brutal murder on 9 March 1566. Mary, Queen of Scots was resident at Holyrood House and had incurred the jealousy of her husband, Lord Darnley, by appointing a musician, David Rizzio, as her secretary. On the night in question the Queen, Rizzio and four other guests were dining in Mary's apartments when a number of armed guards, almost certainly with Darnley's approval or at his behest, grabbed Rizzio, accused him of adultery with the Queen, and while dragging him out to the main staircase stabbed him more than fifty times. Many visitors to the house have felt oppressive presences and strange cold spots in the area believed to be the scene of the crime. Visitors to the 'Rizzio room' find it has a frighteningly oppressive atmosphere and is difficult to stay in. On other occasions a Lady in Grey has been seen standing in Mary's audience chamber near the scene of the brutal murder.

SEE ALSO:

- Drem airfield.

WHILE YOU'RE THERE:

- Visit Edinburgh Castle, dominating the skyline of the city. It has a phantom drummer, reported since the mid-seventeenth century.

Ringstead
(near Raunds, Northamptonshire)

A murder victim is thought to be the spectre seen in the lanes around Ringstead in Northamptonshire and reported frequently between 1850 and 1865 – also seen, though more rarely, in the years since.

Lydia Attley had been in love with a landowner and butcher known as Weekley Ball. At some point, perhaps in the normal course of relationships, Ball ditched Lydia but by then she believed she was pregnant with his child. She threatened to expose his infidelities and demanded money. An arrangement was made to meet in Ball's orchard and the meeting was overheard by a labourer walking home, who heard their argument and Lydia exclaiming: 'You plan to be rid of me tonight, Weekley Ball'. Lydia disappeared that night and nothing more was heard of her. Fifteen years later a skeleton was found in a ditch, the bones and teeth of which seemed to match those of Lydia Attley. Ball was arrested and charged with murder but acquitted on the basis that the evidence was inconclusive. However, Ball was ostracized and eventually left the area.

Lydia's ghost is said to walk from the orchard to the location where her body was found and also walks to the church gates, then returning to the orchard where the apparition fades away.

SEE ALSO:

- Grosvenor Centre, Northampton.

WHILE YOU'RE THERE:

- Travel north to Oundle, where you will find a well in Drumming Well Lane by the side of a Methodist chapel. It is said that the Drumming Well beats a tattoo before any important event.

Sizergh Castle
(near Kendal, Cumbria)

Sizergh Castle is the scene of ancient tragedy which has resulted in a reported haunting. During its medieval history a warrior-baron insisted that his servants keep his wife locked up in a room during his absence warring in Scotland. His love for her was apparently matched by his distrust. The baron was unclear in his orders, and the servants decided that he meant them to ignore her completely. They ignored her cries until she starved to death – and her ghost is said still to be heard screaming for release. Henry VIII's last wife, Catherine Parr, often stayed at Sizergh Castle; her ghost is also said to haunt the structure.

SEE ALSO:
- Tebay.
- Cark Hall / Holker Hall, near Cartmel.
- Reston House, near Ings.
- Rydal Mount.

WHILE YOU'RE THERE:
- Gaythorne Hall is situated between Tebay and Appleton and dates from the Middle Ages. Like the legends of Glamis, Gaythorne has a 'deformity' legend. There is a small cell known as the 'Dungeon of the Hairy Man'. Legend has it that a child was incarcerated in the dungeon to emerge as a wild and crazy adult in later years. It is similar to the so-called Monster of Glamis, and if there is any truth in the legend it may relate to some form of suppression of title or child born out of wedlock. Another version of the legend is that in the sixteenth century a child was born to parents of mixed religious background: Protestant and Catholic. Unable to decide on which religion to raise the child, the child was incarcerated. A further telling of the same legend says that when he was seventeen years old he was rescued by someone who brought him up and that eventually he became the Mayor of Appleby.

Town Museum
(Poole, Dorset)

Poole Town Museum occupies a fifteenth-century haunted building, Scaplens Court. The principal ghost reported there is thought to be that of Agnes Beard.

The story is as follows: Agnes was a maid to Alice Greene. When Alice's husband William died he left a large sum of money to his widow, £200, which in 1598 was a substantial sum. Three local villains, Gowin Spencer, Robert Hill and Richard Parmiter, decided to steal the money. They broke into the house and first came across Agnes Beard in the kitchen where she was eating. She was brutally murdered by a hatchet blow to the head. The robbers moved on and, locating Alice Greene, murdered her also, then stole her inheritance. In fact the robbers were very soon caught and Robert Hill was hanged the following year.

Agnes Beard is held to haunt Scaplens Court, though no one has reported a sighting of the ghost of Alice Green.

In addition to Agnes another ghostly apparition has been seen. Several times within a short period the form of a man draped in a cloak, sporting a white beard, has been seen in Scaplens Court. One witness, Mrs Joan Patch, has described him as 'rather lonely, but not in the least frightening'.

SEE ALSO:
- Clouds Hill.
- Corfe Castle.
- Wool.

WHILE YOU'RE THERE:
- A short trip north will bring you to Badbury Rings. This is an outstanding Iron Age hill fort in the care of the National Trust. It consists of three tiers of concentric ramparts and contains several burial mounds.

Wycoller
(near Colne, Lancashire)

This is really a story of 'ghosts of the open roads' and relates more to the village of Wycoller than to any specific building. But it is a fascinating story and involves possibly two separate ghosts.

Wycoller is almost a hidden village, the only place reached down a small road off the A6068 just north-east of Burnley. Wycoller Old Hall was once the dominating residence of the village originally built in the sixteenth century.

The story associated with the ghosts is as follows. An early member of the Cunliffe family, who took over the Hall, is shortly afterwards alleged to have discovered that his wife had taken a lover and rode to the hall to murder her. The legend has it that this scene is played out by the ghosts. Once a year when the wind and rain are howling as they were at the original time, villagers hear the clattering of hooves and see a rider wearing a cape and hood gallop through the village, cross the twin-arched packhorse bridge over the river, and stop at the front porch of the Hall. From there he enters the building, runs to a bedroom, and the sounds are heard of a woman being beaten. Then the ghostly rider reappears, leaps on the horse and rides off into the night.

In addition is the story of Old Beth, who is said to be the ghost of the murdered wife. She is seen walking around the grounds and disappears if approached by witnesses. There are those who say that she cursed the Cunliffes while she was dying and that perhaps she lingers around to make sure that the family does not return to the hall.

SEE ALSO:

- Black Abbey, Accrington.

WHILE YOU'RE THERE:

- Cottingley, near Bradford, over the border into Yorkshire, is the scene of the world's most famous fairy photographs. Two children, Elsie Wright and Frances Griffiths, claimed they had photographed fairies. The pictures were sent to Arthur Conan Doyle, who believed that they were genuine. The first pictures were taken in 1917. Further photographs were taken in 1920. Criticism of the pictures was that the fairies were dressed in contemporary clothing. In 1977, researcher Fred Gettings found pictures of fairies in *Princess Mary's Gift Book*, published in 1914, which looked very similar to the ones photographed by the girls. In 1981 Frances admitted that the photographs were faked but she always insisted the fairies were real, the fake photos being produced only to satisfy the grown-ups!

CHAPTER 6

~

WORLD WAR GHOSTS

Berechurch Hall Road
(Colchester, Essex)

Essex Ghosts and Hauntings No. 6 lists two sightings of a ghostly horseman in the sky. A family driving to visit a relative in Colchester Hospital were driving along a lane near the Military Corrective Training Camp when they saw a grey shape fifty yards ahead of them. It appeared to be a leaping horse, with its rider dressed in the livery of a First World War soldier. He was wearing a grey uniform with sash and chest belt and wore a large pack on his back. His hat was Australian style, turned up at the left and pinned by a badge. In his right hand he held a staff from which a pennant blew in the wind. Tall and upright in the saddle, he seemed to be staring straight ahead. Perhaps more amazingly, the apparition was some forty feet in the air and apparently leaping over the tree-tops.

As reported in the magazine, researchers discovered that during the early days of the First World War many Australian horsemen were stationed at Colchester. They were Australian criminals who had been given the option of serving their sentences or joining up in the Australian army to serve in Europe. They had to break their own horses in, and it was apparently a familiar sight to see a hundred soldiers riding through the lanes and competing with each other to clear the high hedges. The magazine speculates: 'Could this apparition possibly be a re-enactment of those days or maybe one of the 'Riders' had failed to clear a hedge and had been killed?'

However, the magazine also reveals that there was a sequel to the story. They received the account of an employee from the Military Corrective Training Centre who, one morning when cycling to work before 4 a.m., was in the same area when he suddenly saw a horse and rider jump over a hedge in front of him, gallop down the road and disappear over a hedge on the opposite side of the road. Throughout the whole sighting he heard no sound whatsoever. It is speculated that the same or a similar ghostly horseman had been seen. Though the second report was of a slightly different uniform, bluish with three-cornered hat and cape and perhaps more reminiscent of highwaymen or cavalier, either or both of the witnesses could, in the circumstances, have been inaccurate in some of their description. Alternatively, perhaps they are two different riders from two different time periods, in which case the question must be asked as to why so similar an apparition should be seen in the same place. Is there something about the locality which is particularly respondent to that type of ghostly form?

SEE ALSO:

- Mersea Island.
- Langenhoe Church (site).

WHILE YOU'RE THERE:

- Take a trip to Saffron Walden, where you will find the largest turf labyrinth in Britain, 150 feet across. This maze is situated on the east side of the common. There is also a more modern hedge maze nearby.

Bircham Newton Airfield
(near Hunstanton, Norfolk)

Built in 1914, this airfield was, for a time, derelict and recommissioned for the Second World War. The modern training centre on the site has a reputedly haunted squash court where the ghost of a man in RAF uniform has been seen on the walkway overlooking the court. A tape recorder left running overnight recorded the sounds of an active airfield, machinery, aircraft in flight, male and female voices and strange groaning sounds. Equipment failure – reported in many ghost hunts – is frequently the case on this site and even affected a BBC *Nationwide* television crew who stayed there overnight. There are a number of other associated ghost and poltergeist reports from the old airfield.

SEE ALSO:

- Castle Rising Castle.
- Sandringham.

WHILE YOU'RE THERE:

- South of Bircham Newton is Houghton Hall, which is open to the public. It is situated off the B213 between Great Bircham and West

Rudham. A ghostly figure there, seen by the Prince Regent in the State Bedroom, produced the exclamation, 'I have seen what I hope to God I may never see again'.

Burtonwood
(near Warrington, Cheshire)

Burtonwood airfield was used during the Second World War to receive the bombers flown in from America. It is said to be haunted by the ghost of a headless airman. The origin of the ghost is thought to be a pilot whose plane was crashing; the airman attempted to jump out before the fatal moment but was decapitated by his own canopy.

Inside the airfield there is a museum in one of the hangars and a bus is displayed where it has been said that the ghost of an old gamekeeper has been seen. Apparently he lived in the bus after it was withdrawn from service and has apparently not left it despite his demise.

SEE ALSO:
- Golborne.

WHILE YOU'RE THERE:
- Should you find yourself in the police jail in Liverpool, cell G2 is said to be occupied by the ghost of William Kennedy, who was incarcerated there prior to his execution for the murder of a police officer in 1927.

RAF Cosford
(Shropshire)

RAF Cosford contains a Second World War Avro Lincoln bomber. There are several reports of crewmen being seen inside the aircraft, of spectral voices of the crew talking being heard, of the sounds of the engines turning over, and of poltergeistery such as hangar doors opening and closing spontaneously.

East Cowes
(Isle of Wight)

An airman, who some say is headless, is seen parachuting to earth here, presumably a replay of a dramatic wartime incident but not one specifically identified.

SEE ALSO:
- Beaulieu, Hampshire.

WHILE YOU'RE THERE:
- At Mottistone is a standing stone thirteen feet high. Druids are said to have sacrificed a white bull there.

Frome
(Somerset)

Photographer Reginald Wickens took a picture outside Morton House which appears to show the spectre of a motorcyclist banking in a curve. It looks as if it could be a reflection of the photographer, or of someone else, in glass but it is held that the sun was directly overhead when the photograph was taken and the shadows would not have been as suggested in that photograph. Morton House was the headquarters of Field Marshal Bernard Montgomery from June 1940. During the Second World War three dispatch riders were killed there and it is thought possible that the photograph has caught the image of a spectre of one of those victims.

SEE ALSO:
- Warminster.
- Longleat House.
- Farleigh Hungerford.

WHILE YOU'RE THERE:
- It was in an oat-field owned by John Scull at Westbury, to the east of Frome, that the crop-circle appeared which effectively 'launched' the whole phenomena. It was probably not the first crop-circle, but it was the first to achieve public attention, and arose in the summer of 1980. It was reported in the August 1980 edition of the *Wiltshire Times*. Although early researchers suggested a meteorological origin for the circle, they quickly became associated with the UFO phenomenon, partly due to the proximity of the majority of sightings to the Warminster area, which itself had been the centre of UFO activity in England a decade and a half earlier.

Lincolnshire Aviation Heritage Centre
(East Kirkby, Lincolnshire)

At seventeen Christopher Panton became a flight engineer with a pathfinder crew based in Yorkshire. In 1944 he was promoted to Pilot Officer. On the night of 30–31 March 1944 his aircraft, a Halifax bomber, was hit over Nuremberg and all seven crew died in the resultant crash. It had been just that morning that his family had been told of his promotion. His brothers Fred and Harold were too young at just fourteen and ten to join the services, but they have obviously felt the loss of their brother in the years since.

In 1981 the Ministry Of Defence offered the airfield at East Kirby for sale. It was where the brothers had watched the bombers leaving and returning during the war. Fred and Harold bought it to convert to a museum, also to be a memorial to their brother Christopher.

The Lincolnshire Aviation Heritage Centre is popular with visitors and contains a great deal of memorabilia and aircraft from the Second World War. But some visitors have seen more than they expected: a phantom pilot has been seen near a hangar, sometimes described as trailing a parachute.

Fred has heard visitors report some strange happenings in the tower, where he himself had a strange encounter while alone. Fred's son David has seen the figure walk between the hangar and the control tower. The airman is thought to be someone who was once directly associated with the airfield, perhaps flying from or to it. Around the airfield are thought to be many buried, crashed airplanes – there are many around the east coast of England – and they are not disturbed if they are believed to contain bodies. Some of those that have been recovered are being reconstructed at the Centre.

These events caused the owners to contact medium Eddie Burks, through whom a message was given from Christopher Panton. Eddie also contacted other airmen who were haunting the site.

We visited the museum and spoke to Peter Parnham, who promotes the Centre. He told us of his own experience in the control tower. Although he did not see the ghost others had reported, his experience was very startling: Mr Parnham and a companion entered the building and stayed a while both feeling 'quite jolly'. In an instant the atmosphere changed and Mr Parnham became so frightened he ran at a pace outside. His friend had also felt the change but she somehow felt herself 'stuck' where she was, calling for help and not realizing that Mr Parnham had left. The experience was so disturbing it was years before Mr Parnham would enter the building again. Now, when he takes visitors on tours, he will suggest that if you feel something strange you should leave the building. Eddie Burks also reports in his book *Ghosthunter* (co-written with Gillian Cribbs) that this is the location where Fred had 'a bad time' when painting the stairs. Fred told Eddie that as it fell dark he experienced a strange silence. 'A voice in his head' told him to get out – NOW! Fred actually shouted back that no one was going to force him out until he had finished. But he had trouble finishing, and then found that somehow the step below where he was standing was already wet with paint. 'Someone had painted it,' he said. At that point he collected up his tools and ran.

WHILE YOU'RE THERE:

- Nearby Bolingbroke Castle is haunted by a witch who has taken the form of a hare. It is said that dogs see and chase the spectral animal, only to become alarmed when it disappears.

Montrose Airfield
(Angus, Scotland)

Montrose Airfield has a well-known ghost of a First World War aircraft and pilot. Sir Peter Masefield, former Director-General of the Ministry of Civil Aviation, saw the apparition in 1963. It is held to be the ghost of an aircraft and pilot that crashed at the airfield in 1913.

Montrose Airfield also sports the ghost of a Second World War officer who similarly died in a plane crash at the airfield.

SEE ALSO:

- Letham.
- Dunnottar Castle.

WHILE YOU'RE THERE:

- The Loch of Forfar, to the west of the town of Forfar, is said to be haunted by various ghosts whenever it freezes over, all half submerged in the ice. They are the ghosts of those who drowned after the murder of King Malcolm II.

Northern Moors
(Peak District)

The Second World War had already ended in Europe by 18 May 1945. Captain Anthony Clifford, known as 'Sonny', and his crew of a

Lancaster bomber known as 'Vicky the vicious Virgin' had seen three active years over Germany and had completed a final mission targeting Hitler's Eagle's Nest hideaway at Berchtesgaden. Now the Canadian Air Force crew were on a routine, and boring, training flight. They detoured, and got lost over the hills and valleys of the northern moors of the Peak District between Sheffield and Manchester. The hills were covered in cloud, and perhaps the crew failed to see the 'Dark Peak' until it was too late. The plane crashed and exploded, killing the crew of six.

But the Lancaster has not, it seems, given up flying. One moonlit night in October 1982 David and Helen Shaw were parked by the side of the Ladybower Reservoir when Mr Shaw saw a plane in the air. 'I was just turning away from the reservoir when, out of the corner of my eye, I caught sight of something flying over the water towards me,' he said. They could not make out the shape at first but by the time it was just four hundred yards away and illuminated by bright moonlight they could see quite clearly that it was a Lancaster Bomber, Second World War vintage.

In March 1997, Mariafrance Tattersfield and a companion were on the moors at around ten o'clock in the evening to get an unimpeded 'light pollution free' view of the Hale–Bopp comet, visible for a few months around that time and one of the more spectacular comets of recent times. They saw a plane flying very low, almost at ground level. A nearby farmer also saw it and instinctively ducked. And shortly there-after a gamekeeper and his wife heard an impact and explosion and saw the orange blast light up the sky. The emergency services were alerted and over fifteen hours were spent in a search for a crashed plane involving two helicopters, over 140 mountain rescue personnel, 100 police officers and tracker dogs. Nothing was found and there were no reports of an aircraft missing.

The belief locally is that the crashed plane has been seen in spectral form flying again. Whether it was the 'Vicious Virgin' is a moot point; it is believed that there have been at least fifty-five crashes in the area, several in wartime due to the terrain and the relative inexperience of many of the fliers.

Another crash that is believed to be represented by a 'ghost flier' is that of a USAF Dakota which crashed only 100 yards or so from the Vicious Virgin's final resting place, and only two months later on 24 July 1945. Flight Lieutenant George Johnson, a five-man crew and two other personnel all died in the Dakota. In 1995 postman Tom Ingle, walking in the area, saw what seemed to be a plane flying low, trying to gain height. Although he could see the propellers turning, he could hear no sound of engines. It banked, and seemed to crash. Ingle ran to the field to see if he could assist, but found nothing except a peaceful area scattered with a few sheep. The ghost plane was also seen by visitor to the area John O'Neill, who saw the plane flying so slowly it seemed almost stationary. It disappeared as he looked for it. Another local couple, Steve and Barbara Morgan, saw the plane seemingly about to hit the hillside; but the explosion they expected never happened.

SEE ALSO:
- Whaley Bridge.

WHILE YOU'RE THERE:
- On the road between Whaley Bridge and Disley a man travelling home, William Wood, was waylaid and murdered in 1823. His skull was crushed and pressed into the ground. Wood was buried, and a stone monument erected at the roadside to commemorate the crime. However, the hole which his skull had pushed into the earth was said to be impossible to fill, and no grass would grow in it. In 1859 Alfred Fryer, author of *Wilmslow Graves*, tried filling the hole with stones but always found them scattered around shortly afterwards. Other local people tried the same thing, with the same result.

Rougham Field USAAF Base (Suffolk)

Rather than a tale of the war this is a tale from the war, as related in issue 13 of *Ghosts and Hauntings* by the long-standing ghost-researcher Wesley Downes. On 5 January 1944 a B17 Flying Fortress, serial number 42–30112, nicknamed L'il Butch, was part of a flight that undertook a bombing raid deep into German territory. The plane had survived twenty-seven missions and had succeeding in shooting down two German fighters during the course of her missions. She was lovingly tended by engineer 'Pappy' Cordes.

But L'il Butch did not return; she was one of four planes that did not make it back. Some months later the base was empty, all planes out on a mission bar a couple that had developed faults. Pappy's job was to get these two remaining aircraft airborne as soon as possible. Driving across the airfield he saw, standing on the tarmac, L'il Butch. He drove up to her and checked out her serial number; it matched. But the 'A' on the tail stabilizer was missing. He could hear the crepitations of a cooling engine, so presumably the plane had only just landed, yet he could see no sign of the crew at the plane or on the airfield. He approached with a feeling of great apprehension and uneasiness. He felt he was being watched from within the plane, and it was not a pleasant feeling. The plane did not seem right; it neither looked nor felt quite like the L'il Butch he'd known. He decided to get aboard and check the flight log.

When he opened the hatch he saw an individual standing within looking at him: 'one of the meanest, coldest, looking individuals that Pappy had ever seen . . .' The man's hand rested on a revolver and in a gruff voice he said, 'Wot t'hell y'want?' Pappy hi-tailed it back to the operations room in his jeep.

He told his story to his senior officer, and together they went out to examine the plane. But there was no plane there.

WHILE YOU'RE THERE:
- Take a walk around Kingshill Street and Gypsy Lane, in Rougham. Both are reputedly haunted. Shadowy forms of people have been seen in Kingshill Street and horses have often refused to go down Gypsy Lane. Other reports have included a galloping white horse and a hooded monk.

GHOSTS
IN THE
OPEN AIR

There are many types of haunting phenomena recorded in the open air of the countryside. Sky visions of battles, wartime ghosts (examples of both are included in other chapters in this book), nuns walking through fields, eerie balls of light, and so on. It is unlikely that they all have the same origin.

Of the various clear sightings, they would seem to be no different from sightings in buildings, except that the events took place outside rather than inside buildings in the first place. In a few rarer cases ghosts may still appear where buildings used to be. Of the balls of light, there is an impressive body of research by people such as Paul Devereux (as published in books such as *Earthlights* and *Earthlights Revelation*) stating that there are natural luminous energies which can become visible in the atmosphere as a result of geological action or stresses. These not only might explain modern, vague, sightings of shapes in fields and so on, but may be the origin of many legends of floating white ladies and the like.

One other factor that is of interest when dealing with open-air ghosts is that they seem for the most part to be more unexpected. The 'Hollywood' image of ghosts in old, run-down castles on stormy nights was never particularly accurate, nor does it account for ghosts in modern buildings, brightly lit shops, and so on. But the image is a strong one; walking into a gloomy old castle at night undoubtedly gets the senses on edge, and perhaps a touch of the imagination also. Walking about in the open air simply does not have the 'classical' image of a place where you expect to see ghosts, and it can be all the more surprising when you do. One case we recall was of a woman passing another on a gravel drive, thinking nothing of it, then glancing back and finding the figure had disappeared. Only then did the sighter realize that she had not heard the sound of the crunching of footsteps by the other party, as would have been expected. Ghosts are often appreciated in this 'delayed' way, and open-air ghosts perhaps more so.

Phantom hitch-hiker reports are a very special category of 'open-air' ghosts however. Phantom hitch-hikers are a form of ghost that falls between witness-accounts and urban legend. First-hand witnesses are sincere, and they seem to be reporting ghost-sightings as they perceive them. But there are also a whole batch of stories that seem to have been elaborated on over time, and often from 'a-friend-of-a-friend' in nature. The case of the Blackwall Tunnel Ghost (Chapter 8) is an example of one that has a 'tied up' ending – the identity of the ghost was found. This rarely happens with such clarity outside of 'hitch-hiker' reports.

Why such reports should be subject to urban legend might be related to the phenomenon known as the Cult of the Car – people today vest elements of their psyche into their cars – men perhaps more so than women. Cars are seen as extensions of the ego, as status symbols. They represent a protective shield from the world and perhaps there is a fear of 'invasion' through that shield. If an 'Englishman's home is his castle' then his car is certainly his 'fortress on wheels'. The phantom hitch-hikers are sometimes said to be a form of protecting ghost – warning people of the dangers of stretches of roads, according to one theory roads on which they were themselves killed. If so, then some of them have a strange way of demonstrating danger – as likely to cause crashes themselves by leaping out and frightening people. But even if we accept that this is their motive, why do we have a whole strata of this type of protective ghost and not ghosts that seek to prevent accidents in the home, accidents at sea, accidents in factories, and so on? There are reports of all of these of course, but nothing like the numbers of 'hitch-hiker' reports.

Lastly we should consider the special circumstances in which these ghosts are seen. Drivers at night are prone to 'highway hypnosis' or at least a tendency to 'switch off' and drive 'on automatic', particularly if somewhat sleepy. The fact that many hitch-hikers are seen 'just around bends' suggest that perhaps the drivers are being startled into full wakefulness by having to steer the car and that it is at that time that they see the apparitions. This fits with the facts of imagery and the hallucination which is known to form at the borders of sleep-into-wakefulness. Perhaps some element of the reports is hallucination caused by this.

But these circumstances do not seem to account for situations such as the reports from Blue Bell Hill, where several drivers have reported the same phenomenon, each knowing nothing of the history of reported hauntings. It does not explain so many reports that the police even suspect it's 'just the ghost again' when they hear the story yet again from another frightened and shocked driver. The phantom hitch-hikers have a legendary and mythological quality about them, but there is surely a reality in the reports that cannot be ignored.

The Cult of the Car represents a modern-day attitude towards the vehicle that has transformed the lives of everyone in the technological world, and arguably everyone on the planet. But trains also seem to have had that effect, again particularly on men (many of whom still hanker for a train set!), and particularly related to the 'Golden Age of Steam', as many would describe it. The steam trains have a nostalgia and a following. In other words, we seem to be seeing elements of a 'cult' around trains, which is perhaps why so many ghosts are reported relating to this form of transport. Most of the cases in Chapter 10, like the majority of cases in this genre, are from the steam age. There are reports from the London Underground, and of modern trains, of course, so we cannot make too much of this observation.

Another aspect of hauntings related to trains are the reports of people seeing ghost trains – generally steam trains – long after the steam trains have been taken out of service. The fact that something is amiss is obvious. Perhaps people also see phantoms of modern trains on rails where they still run, in which case they would probably pass by without being noticed, or thought of as special. The same is true of people of course; one ghost-researcher we know believes that the streets of London have many ghosts walking about in them every day and that people never realize it because they don't talk to each other and for the most part ignore each other. Certainly they might not notice them as ghosts if they were not in particularly old-style dress, say. We think that this belief is possibly a little extreme – there seems to be more to seeing ghosts than just passing them in their masses – but it does clarify the thought that ghosts not only have to be seen, but to be recognized as such. Perhaps 'modern' ghosts – of railways or anything else – are going unnoticed. Perhaps that is why the ghostly trains seem to be mostly of the majestic age of steam. One day, perhaps when we are running linear-engine trains, 'electric train ghosts' will be recognized for what they are!

There is little doubt that at least some element of expectation plays a part in the seeing of ghosts. Sceptics might say it triggers the imagination and that ghosts are imaginary. 'Believers' might argue that expectation opens up aspects of the mind that become receptive to images to which it was previously closed.

Perhaps some of the images seen are more vague than actually reported. If there is a vague sighting of a fast-moving black shape and it takes place near Blickling Hall, perhaps the sighter colours in some of the detail and creates the image of the coach and horses. But there was still something there in the first place for the sighter to see – it may not be a classical ghost, but it may have been paranormal in the sense of not being fully appreciated by science at the present time. We know of one case where the witness to a ghost reported 'clear, blue eyes', but when tested could not at that distance discern the colour of a 'real' person's eyes. Was he making up detail to fit the sighting? Or does a person actually 'see' in a different way to 'normal' in these circumstances of haunting? There is evidence in some cases we have studied that this can happen. Three witnesses of UFOs that we interviewed, all independent of each other, reported a strange effect where they saw an object at a distance and simultaneously very close up – and none of them could understand this 'divided vision'. Perhaps ghost-sighters occasionally have such perceptions. Perhaps there is an element of psychic vision involved.

Whatever the truth, understanding the reports of 'classical' ghost images will assist us in understanding the whole spectrum of hauntings, and perhaps a little about the workings of the mind.

CHAPTER 7

~

GHOSTS
AL FRESCO

Cadbury Castle
(near Yeovil, Somerset)

Just off the A303 north of Yeovil is Cadbury Castle, an Iron Age hill fort situated on a hill that, according to legend, is hollow. Local tradition claims that the hill was the site of King Arthur's court and that he and his soldiers sleep within Cadbury Hill, occasionally riding forth in full battle armour. It is said that when England is desperate with its back to the wall then Arthur and his troops will ride out to save the day. Cadbury Castle has been identified with Camelot since at least the fifteenth century and is held by many to be the inspiration for the stories of Lancelot and Guinevere. Whatever the truth of the Arthurian legend, archaeological evidence has confirmed that in the sixth century – the Arthurian era – the site was the fortification of a warrior chieftain believed by many to be Arthur himself. It is also true that no equivalent fortification has been found dating from the Arthurian period anywhere else in Britain.

Further legend has it that every seven years on Midsummer Eve a door in the hillside opens and the troop take their horses down to Sutton Montis church, where they drink at a spring. In the 1930s a schoolteacher reported seeing just such an apparition, though whether she was influenced by local legend is uncertain. Driving past the hill late one night with a friend, the two saw bright lights slowly moving down the hill. They stopped to inspect them and saw that they were torches attached to the lances of a troop of armed warriors on horseback. The troop galloped into the darkness and then disappeared.

The legends of Arthur have grown and become convoluted over the centuries and probably no idyllic and 'many-tower'd' Camelot ever existed, but it is highly likely that the true inspiration was the sixth-century warrior who fortified Cadbury Hill.

SEE ALSO:

• Sherborne Old and New Castles.

WHILE YOU'RE THERE:

• While you're in mystical mood, take a journey to the Bristol Channel. Legend has it that there are fairy islands somewhere there – invisible to human eyes normally – called the Green Meadows of Enchantment. The problem is that they are said to disappear from the view of anyone who actively seeks them, but perhaps a day in Arthur's realm will have put you in an acceptable frame of mind for the fairy folk.

Cark Hall / Holker Hall
(near Cartmel, Cumbria)

In 1809 a young servant boy was sent from Cark Hall to nearby Holker Hall to deliver newspapers. When he arrived back at Cark he fainted and eventually told the story of having been chased all the way by a 'dobbie'. The dobbie was a ball of fire that had chased him across the countryside. Eight years later a similar story was told of a bobbing light following another person in the countryside. It is believed that this would be the 'going fire', also known as the 'will-o'-the-wisp' or the 'jack-o'-lantern'; the spontaneously ignited marsh gas that can be seen in some areas.

Visitors to the area might look on Cartmel Fell, a remote area in the countryside. It is said that the ghost of a forlorn young girl sits there mourning for her lost lover who was killed by a lightning strike on the spot she now refuses to leave. She is said to have been sustained in life by friends bringing her food but to have died in the cold of winter, still crying out his name.

SEE ALSO:

• Tebay.
• Reston House, near Ings.
• Gaythorne Hall, Tebay.
• Rydal Mount.

WHILE YOU'RE THERE:

• To the north is Troutbeck Bridge. In the seventeenth century Calgarth Hall was owned by a JP, Myles Phillipson. He wanted the neighbouring farm and so invited the couple that owned it for a banquet, framed them for theft, presided at their trial and sentenced them to death, leaving himself clear to appropriate their property. The wronged pair laid a curse that he would live in poverty and his family line would die out. After they were executed two skulls appeared at the Hall which could not be disposed of. Despite smashing them and throwing them into nearby Lake Windermere, they always returned. The Phillipsons became poorer as time passed, and the family line died out. The Bishop of Llandaff performed a service of exorcism and the skulls were never seen again.

Cawthorpe
(near Louth, Lincolnshire)

To the south-east of Louth several small roads surround a farm near Cawthorpe. There are several ghostly manifestations reported around these particular roads. Perhaps the most interesting relates to a nun seen by Enid Borrill, the daughter of a local figure knowledgeable of the history of the area.

Enid was walking home one bright sunny day when she saw a nun walking ahead of her. It is a relatively isolated area and the nearest convent was some twenty miles away at Grimsby. As Enid watched the nun turned off the road and walked into the farm. There was no access way at that point; the nun had walked *through* the boundary fence. Enid found the experience upsetting and her father could not explain it, as his knowledge of local history indicated to him that there was no convent or nunnery nearby. In fact, however, his local history was incorrect and it turned out that there had indeed been a convent at Cawthorpe during the Middle Ages. It had been closed during Henry VIII's dissolution of the monasteries in 1539.

Did Enid see a replay of a nun walking to a nunnery as she had often done centuries ago? Did the nun leave an emotional imprint: perhaps her longing for her home after she was turned out by the dissolution? One thing seems important: Enid's household may well have rung with tales of local history but in this case her sighting was not in agreement with her father's understanding of the area and hardly seems likely to have been inspired by anything she would have heard around her house.

SEE ALSO:
• Louth.

WHILE YOU'RE THERE:
• Take a trip south to Burgh-le-Marsh for a somewhat romantic tale. In 1629 Captain Frohock was in difficulty on board the *Mary Rose*, being pushed towards the Lincolnshire coast by a harsh storm. Villagers of Burgh-le-Marsh were hoping to get rich by allowing the ship to run aground and then salvaging its cargo. The sexton of the church, however, refused to allow this, locked himself in the church and rang the tenor bell, which acted as a guide for Frohock to bring his ship to safety. When the angry villagers broke into the church they found the sexton dead from exhaustion. It is said that Frohock married the sexton's daughter.

Cheriton Cross
(Devon)

At around 7.30 one evening in October 1969, Ivor Potter was driving along the A30, near Cheriton Cross, heading to London, when in his headlights he saw a Great Dane, light-coloured, in his headlights standing in the middle of the road ahead of him. He tried to brake to avoid the animal but failed to do so and assumed he had hit it. He stopped the car and went to find it but discovered that it had vanished into thin air.

James Wentworth Day in *Ghosthunter's Game Book*, published in 1958, records another sighting of a spectral dog in the locality. Mrs Drummond of Budleigh Salterton saw a white dog while driving near Dartmoor in the 1930s.

SEE ALSO:
• Moretonhampstead.

Crier of Claife
(Lake Windermere, Cumbria)

In the National Trust woodlands bordering the side of Lake Windermere in the Lake District is Claife. There is a small hidden quarry there known as Crier of Claife. It was so called because in the eighteenth century it was the site of a screaming spirit not dissimilar to the Irish banshee. It is said to have terrorized the area with chilling screams until it was finally exorcized by a priest.

Local legend has it that the ghost is that of a monk from Furness

Abbey, who was rejected by a woman he had fallen for and who died in despair on the heights of Claife. Those wishing to visit this haunted site might stay at the nearby Sawrey Hotel, which commemorates the haunting in the name of the Claife Crier bar. The hotel literature recalls an account: 'On one occasion, his [the ghostly monk's] cry was mistaken by the ferryman for a call, and he went out for his fare. When he returned his hair had turned white and he never spoke again. Subsequently, the ghost was exorcized and his spirit confined to the quarry known as the Crier of Claife Quarry'.

SEE ALSO:

• Rydal Mount.
• Calgarth Hall, Lake Windermere.
• Sizergh Castle, near Kendal.

WHILE YOU'RE THERE:

• The churchyard of St Andrews contains what is said to be the grave of the fifth-century King of Cumbria, Ewan Caesarius, a giant. Two stone poles are supposed to mark the extremities of his grave – they stand fifteen feet apart!

Enfield Chase
(Greater London)

A ghostly red-cloaked knight is said to haunt the open spaces and footpaths that represent the old forest walks around Enfield Chase, though the Knight has also been seen in South Mimms and East Barnet. It is said that this is a special 'cyclical ghost' appearing every six years around Yuletide, the last appearance being in 1992. It is therefore due for a reappearance in 1998.

The ghost knight is said to be Sir Geoffrey de Mandeville, who died in 1144. He was Earl of Essex, one of the most powerful barons in England, holding land in Hertfordshire and Middlesex including Barnet, Monken Hadley, South Mimms and Enfield Chase. He was a major figure in the wars between King Stephen and the Empress Matilda, who fought each other for the English throne. Sir Geoffrey was fatally wounded fighting near Burwell, as noted by the chronicler Henry of Huntingdon: 'He made light of the wound, but he died of it in a few days, under excommunication. See here the just judgement of God, memorable through all ages!'

Sir Geoffrey gained the compassion of the Knights Templars who gently covered him in the habit of their order, the famous white with red cross, and arranged for a burial that would get round the limitations of excommunication. Eventually, due to the efforts of the Prior of Walden in Essex, a grant of absolution was obtained from Pope Alexander III and Sir Geoffrey's body became almost a religious relic. 'Both the Prior of Walden and the Templars contended for the honour of burying it.' It had been coffined in lead and hung in the branch of an apple tree in the Templar's preceptory at the Old Temple in London. Eventually the Templars buried Sir Geoffrey's body in the porch by the west door of their New Temple.

It is said, however, that Sir Geoffrey's spirit remains uneasy and walks his lands around Christmas. He has been seen in Trent Park near the earthwork known as Camlet Moat, held by many to be the site of the medieval de Mandeville Castle.

Probably the best known sighting of Sir Geoffrey's ghost took place on 17 December 1932 when he was seen from Oak Hill, East Barnet, approaching from the east. This inspired a vigil later in the month which was rewarded by a sighting of Sir Geoffrey's spectre. As described in *Tales of Old Hertfordshire* by Doris Jones-Baker: '. . . another group that kept vigil for Sir Geoffrey on Christmas Eve met at the junction of Brookside and Cat Hill in East Barnet, and walked slowly southward to the small wooden bridge over Pymms Brook, the ancient way from Church Path to Cockfosters. About midnight they heard the first "uncanny sounds", coming from the south, and after following Pymms Brook through the recreation ground they made a brief halt by Oak Hill. All being quiet again, however, the party went on towards the cemetery. At Monk Frith (Monks Wood) they saw at last the spectre that on most occasions heralds Sir Geoffrey's approach: his headless hound. Some minutes later there appeared the ghostly knight himself, dressed all in armour that shone silver in the moonlight, and wearing spurs and a large red cloak'.

As this was one of the most successful vigils we have heard of, we suggest that ghost-hunters 'stake out' the area, following the route described, in case Sir Geoffrey puts in an appearance in 1998 and 2004, as 'scheduled'.

WHILE YOU'RE THERE:
- A jet black phantom coach is reported to run down Bell Lane, but strangely six feet off the ground; usually on clear, moonless nights before Christmas.

Four Sisters Crossroads
(A12, Stratford St Mary, Suffolk)

Like many crossroads, 'Four Sisters' is a traditional burial place of suicides and murderers in ancient times. Such people were buried there to lay their ghosts which, if they rose, would not know which direction to take. Many were buried with a stake through their heart to prevent them rising.

This location, on the Essex/Suffolk border, is also known as an accident black spot. Whether that relates to the ten or more reports locally of ghosts and presences felt by drivers and hikers in the area is a matter for conjecture. One such witness is Irene Heath, who has had repeated experiences at the location. On the first occasion she was driving alone and became 'sure' that an evil and frightening presence was in the car. Despite turning round several times, and even turning on the car's interior light, she could see nothing. Two weeks later her car went out of control and crashed; her brakes seemed to have 'locked' for no reason. For obvious reasons Irene sought to avoid driving in that area after that, but was forced to use the road one night. At the crossroads she felt a claw-like hand poke her in the back. On yet another occasion she heard a loud banging from the back of the car for which she could offer no explanation.

SEE ALSO:
- Borley Church.
- Berechurch, Colchester.

WHILE YOU'RE THERE:
- On the other side of Ipswich is Rendlesham Fore , near the now-closed RAF/USAF airbase at Woodbridge. It was here in 1980 that an incident took place which involved a low-level or grounded UFO. The event has given birth to great controversy and a plethora of books in the years since.

Hickling Broad
(Norfolk)

There is a well-known manifestation seen on Hickling Broad: a woman dressed in white, standing in a punt, gliding across the broad. A couple holidaying on Hickling Broad in a cruiser encountered her late one evening when, following a series of delays, they were heading towards their berth in the dark. Regulations forbid vessels to move at night, but the couple were experienced enough to believe that they could deal with any circumstances and they ignored the rules. Half-way across the lake they encountered the punting woman. It appeared that they were going to run into her and the man on the cruiser shouted at her to move out of the way. He was ignored and became convinced that he had ploughed into the punt, but then he saw that the punt and the woman were on the other side of the vessel pooling off into the darkness, again completely ignoring his cruiser. Somewhat shaken by the experience, they berthed the cruiser and went to a local pub for the evening. There they heard the story of the punting woman. The landlord explained that she was a well-known local ghost who punted from a mill on one side of Hickling Broad to the other. Her origin is unknown, and so is the reason for her voyage. It could be that it was simply a common, even everyday, ride for her replayed at certain times. Or perhaps she was deep in concentration, perhaps swamped in emotion, at the time she made the original crossing ... we simply do not yet know what it takes to impress a ghostly recording nor indeed what it takes to cause it to replay.

SEE ALSO:

• Potter Heigham (anniversary ghosts).

WHILE YOU'RE THERE:

• Watch out for the skating soldier. There have been many sightings in the past 200 years or so of the figure of a soldier – dressed in the uniform of the time of the Napoleonic wars – skating across Hickling Broad as if it were frozen. Local legend has it that during the Napoleonic wars in the early nineteenth century the soldier was stationed in north Norfolk. He met a young local girl and they would get together when he was not on duty. In the year of his posting to Norfolk, the Broads were frozen to a great extent throughout the winter and the soldier would wear skates to skim across the frozen lake to meet his lover. Perhaps inevitably for the British climate, he crossed the lake in such a manner once too often. During the beginning of a thaw he set out across the ice but it cracked and he crashed through into the water below and drowned.

Irton Levels
(near Eskdale, Cumbria)

Jason Braithwaite of ASSAP interviewed a father and son who separately – thirty years apart – were driving along Irton Levels near a 'tunnel' of trees when they drove *through* a lady walking along the lanes.

On the lawn outside Irton Hall is a large hollow oak in which it is said King Henry VI slept after fleeing from the Battle of Hexham. (In 1460 Henry and his Queen, Margaret of Anjou, went into exile in Scotland, but in 1464 Henry returned to take part in a rebellion against Edward IV. He was eventually captured in 1465 and imprisoned in the Tower of London.)

The owner of Irton Hall is said to have refused the King refuge, hence his taking shelter in the tree. The owner's wife, Lady Anne Lamplugh, took bread and water to the King, her husband saw this and held her prisoner as punishment. The ghost wandering the lanes is believed to be Lady Anne.

If you follow the footpath round Irton Hall you can see the hollow oak, still standing.

SEE ALSO:
• Rydal Mount.

Lane End
(High Wycombe, Buckinghamshire)

During the UFO conference at Lane End in 1983 many local enthusiasts were also keen to share stories of local hauntings. One story which arose from several people was that of the ghost of a young girl seen in the country lanes around Lane End. In the early part of the century the ghost of the woman dressed in a dark red dress had been seen around the locality of Wheeler End Common. However, just after the war there were some thirty reports by different individuals of the same apparition, suggesting that something had triggered the 'replay' of the apparitional figure. What would seem to be the same figure had been seen in December 1961 in a field near Hanover Hill, and a similar report was received in December 1962. Local legend has it that the apparition is of Anna, a young girl who died in the locality and who used to frequent the area around Wheeler End Common and Hanover Hill during her courtship in the nineteenth century. She particularly liked wearing a dark red dress. She died before she was able to marry her suitor.

SEE ALSO:

- Bisham Abbey.

The Lanes
(Brighton, East Sussex)

Near the seafront area of Brighton is a small section of the town consisting of very narrow, windy throughways and known as the Lanes. They are far too narrow for vehicular traffic and are today a colourful collection of cafés, novelty shops and wine bars. In Meetinghouse Lane there is a bricked-up doorway in a wall, sealed up during the nineteenth century. In the twelfth century this was the doorway to the Priory of St Bartholomew, and there is a tale of broken vows and a ghostly nun associated with the doorway. A nun fell in love with one of the soldiers who guarded her priory and they eloped together. Both for her broken vows and for his going absent without leave, a group of soldiers was sent to capture them and they were brought back to the priory. The soldier was executed for desertion and the nun walled up to die of starvation or asphyxiation. The nun is occasionally seen to enter or leave through the bricked-up doorway. The wall in which the doorway is positioned is currently the perimeter wall of the Friends Meeting House. The current caretaker of the Meeting House took us around to see the old photographs of the Meeting House as it was over the past decades, but was himself sad he had no drawings of the old monastery. He was aware of the nun reports and had heard several contemporary accounts right up to 1997, but he was cautious. 'Most of the sightings are at night, in the dark. And there are a lot of wine bars and pubs around here,' he said, with a laugh.

SEE ALSO:

- Brighton Pavilion.

WHILE YOU'RE THERE:

- Visit the ruins of Bramber Castle near Steyning, which are host to phantom children, seen in December. They are believed to be the children of William de Braose. William de Braose had angered King John, who, in retribution, imprisoned William, his wife and his four children at Windsor, where they starved to death. It is at Bramber that their pitiful cries are heard, however. William de Braose annoyed King John by being one of the barons who united against him, resulting in a meeting at Runnymede on 15 June 1215 where John was forced to put the Royal Seal upon the Great Charter of Liberties – the Magna Carta.

Leith Hill
(near Dorking, Surrey)

A few miles south of Dorking is a National Trust area favoured by walkers, picnickers and locals exercising their dogs, known as Leith Hill. At 967 feet above sea level, it is the highest ground in south-east England. Atop the area is the sixty-four foot tall Leith Hill Tower, built by Richard Hull in 1766.

In 1997 we received an account from Anthony Long of a strange occurrence he had experienced there. Anthony is a very down-to-earth man, currently working as a ski-instructor. He had been walking his dog, but the dog had disappeared and was missing for two hours; this was very unusual, as the dog usually stayed near him. When Anthony found him – in the same place where he had last seen him – he was frightened, nervous and eager to be away. The following day the dog displayed unusual nervousness at the same site. Although Anthony himself could not detect any reason for the problem, a friend later described seeing a ghost in the same area of the woods, a shadowy gliding figure that had disappeared. Had Anthony's dog seen the same thing?

WHILE YOU'RE THERE:
- Take a trip to Leatherhead a few miles north and visit the parish church of St Mary and St Nicholas; it is said to be haunted by a hermit-like monk who once lived there.

Lochbuie
(Isle of Mull, Scotland)

One headless horseman is believed to be a portent of death for members of the MacLaine clan from Lochbuie. The ghost is that of Ewen of the Little Head, once the son and heir of the clan. He was apparently impatient with his father's unwillingness to die and allow him to inherit, and the two got into many feuds and fights. They fought a duel, accompanied by their two respective supporters. During the battle the son was beheaded, but his ghost has continued to ride apparently even to the modern day.

Perhaps Ewen appears as a portent of doom not only because of his anger or desire for revenge but also because he himself suffered just the same experience on the night before his death. According to local legend, on the night before he died he saw the fairy washerwoman, one of the many fairy folk who appeared to those about to die, and similar to the Welsh 'dribbler' and the Irish banshee. The washerwoman washes the blood from the clothing of those about to die. Ewen was apparently by the side of a stream when he saw an old woman washing a pile of blood-stained shirts. When he asked her if his own was among them, she confirmed that it was. According to the legend she told him that he would avoid his death if the next morning his wife – unprompted – served him butter with his breakfast. (Curious the sort of details on which the outcomes of battles are said to hang!) The next morning Ewen munched his dry bread probably somewhat disconsolately and then rode off to his death.

Maghull
(Merseyside)

Just a few miles north-west of Liverpool is the small town of Maghull which is allegedly haunted by the sounds of ancient battle. It is not certain which battle people believe they are hearing; certainly the two most famous in the area are from the Second English Civil War, the battle of 17–19 August 1648; and the Jacobite battle of 1715.

The manifestations heard have included sounds of horses and the battle clash of swords. There have also been occasional reports of apparitional horsemen.

SEE ALSO:
- Golborne.

WHILE YOU'RE THERE:
- 1974 and 1975 were times of considerable numbers of sightings of UFOs around Liverpool. In May 1975 an object was reported to have landed at Norris Green and witnesses claimed they could see the occupants looking out at them.

Markyate Cell
(Markyate, Hertfordshire)

In Hertfordshire there is probably no more famous a character from history than the Wicked Lady of Markyate, Katherine Ferrers. The Tudor mansion known as Markyate Cell, north of the village of Markyate, was originally part of a nunnery. By the seventeenth century Markyate Cell was the family seat of the Ferrers family. By about 1635 the elderly Sir George Ferrers and one son, Sir Knighton Ferrers, lived there. Sir Knighton married an heiress, the Lady Katherine, but died within a year, before the birth of his only child, a daughter named Katherine. Lady Katherine then married Sir Simon Fanshawe, a Royalist who fought with King Charles's army. At the legal age for marriage, twelve, Katherine Ferrers was married off to Sir Simon's own blood-son, Thomas, in order to secure the family fortunes. But she was neglected by her husband and went to live alone at Markyate Cell.

There she met farmer and highwayman Ralph Chaplin, who no doubt introduced her to the art and craft of highway robbery. Chaplin was caught and shot on Finchley Common, leaving Katherine Ferrers alone again. But she embarked on her now famous crusade as a highway-woman, though it appears less for the sake of robbery than either bravado or perhaps revenge on a society that had let her down. Her exploits included arson, cattle slaughter and murder, often without obvious gain. For a long time she was able to keep her identity a secret, living the life of a lady during the day and that of a highway robber during the night. It is said that in Markyate Cell she had a secret staircase starting on the ground floor and leading up to a chamber where she stored her highway robber's equipment and disguise. Lady Katherine's last adventure is, however, well known, taking place near St Albans. A wagoner was taking wood from St Albans to an inn at Gustard Wood and gave a lift to two men who lay down out of sight in the back of the wagon. As the wagon crossed Nomansland Common near Wheathamp-stead, Lady Katherine appeared and shot the driver. However, she was obviously unprepared for the people in the back of the wagon, one of whom managed to shoot her; she raced away over the common. It is said that she reached Markyate Cell and died there but it is not known where she is buried. She is certainly not buried at Markyate and it is believed that her body might have been taken to the Church of St Mary at Ware, though it appears also not to be buried in the Fanshawe vault there. (One telling of the story has it that her body was found at the entrance to her secret room still dressed in the highway robber's outfit.) A fire destroyed much of Markyate Cell in 1841. Lady Katherine's ghost has been seen at Markyate Cell and she is believed to be the phantom highway robber seen in several other Hertfordshire locations.

One apparent sighting of Lady Katherine was reported by Augustus Hare in his journal of 19 November 1894. 'Lord Brownlow . . . talked of a neighbouring house where a Lady Ferrers, a freebooter, used to steal out at night and rob the pilgrims coming from St Albans . . . She constantly haunts the place. Mr Ady who lives there now, meets her on the stairs and wishes her goodnight. Once, seeing her with her arms stretched out in the doorway, he called out to his wife who was outside, 'Now we have caught her!', and then they rushed upon her from both sides, but caught nothing.'

Lady Katherine is commemorated by the pub 'The Wicked Lady' on Nomansland Common near Wheathampstead.

SEE ALSO:
- Markyate in Bedfordshire: A5.
- Woburn Abbey.

WHILE YOU'RE THERE:
- Visit the Devil's Dyke in Wheathampstead. This dyke, together with one known as the Slad to the east, once formed one huge earthwork of around 100 acres. Devil's Dyke is around forty feet deep and ninety feet wide. It is thought to be the site of Julius Caesar's attack on the headquarters of the tribal leader Cassivellaunus in 54 BC.

Mildenhall
(near Marlborough, Wiltshire)

On 12 May 1879 a tragedy took the life of fourteen-year old Alfred Henry Watts in a small cutting on the B4567 near Mildenhall in Wiltshire. A team of three horses pulling a heavy coal wagon suddenly got out of control and despite the attempts of the carter and the boy with him, Watts, galloped down the hill. Watts fell under the wheels of the wagon and as the local paper reported: 'There was no hope for the poor lad, every rib and bone in his body being fractured, and the interior parts crushed, and he expired the same evening, two hours after the occurrence'. As the local paper also reported: 'The team of three horses, none of which had ever been know to run away, suddenly started from an unknown cause . . .'

Watts' demise was commemorated by a stone cross set up on the side of the road next to where he died. In October 1956 Frederick Moss and three friends were driving home from Marlborough in the late evening when suddenly the car headlights picked out in the road ahead of them a tall, lean man standing in the road at the point where the memorial stone stood on the verge. The man wore a long brown coat. He was standing in the road with his back to the stone cross, staring intently, perhaps glumly. It seems he was standing either on or looking down directly at the point where Watts had died nearly a century earlier. Despite the onrush of headlights the man made no attempt to move, indeed Moss blew his horn but was forced to stop the car. He opened the car door to inquire what was happening and in the moment in which he took his eye off the figure it disappeared. The passengers with him had been looking at the figure and they were quite certain that it 'blinked out'. There one minute, gone the next.

The group tried to rationalize the situation; they all got out of the car and searched around the area for the man, unable to account for his disappearance. They even remained silently in the car for some ten minutes, hoping to catch sight of him again, but they never did. Eventually they drove home. Mr Moss described the incident to his wife, who was able to tie up the sighting with the earlier death of the boy. She had been born in the village and from her childhood knew well Alfred Watts's father, Henry Watts, a tall lean man who habitually dressed in a long brown coat. He had died just after the turn of the century. Although it was very common in Edwardian England for men to sport whiskers, Henry Watts had not; his clean-shavenness was noted by the witnesses to the apparition.

It appears that Moss and his friends had come across the apparition, perhaps the recording, of the boy's father standing over the spot where his son had died and mourning his loss.

SEE ALSO:
- Littlecote House, near Ramsbury.

Northwich
(Cheshire)

Ghostly horse-riders are said to haunt the area around the River Weaver at Northwich in Cheshire.

For example, one couple living in the area described seeing, several times, a ghostly horseman riding in the direction of Winnington Bridge. Following publicity in the local press, several locals were prompted to respond. One related the time when together with a friend they had heard horses approaching them; they both stepped aside to let the horses pass but when they did so were shocked to discover that both the figures were dressed in Royalist uniforms. This is said to be consistent with the escape route of the Royalist army following the last battle of the English Civil War.

SEE ALSO:
- Tarporley, Cheshire.

WHILE YOU'RE THERE:
- Nearby Knutsford sports a ghost seen on Higher Tower Common. A tavern-keeper murdered a rent collector and stole his money but spent his life being haunted by his victim's ghost. He confessed to the crime on his deathbed.

Oldbury
(near Avebury, Wiltshire)

Yet another detachment of Roman soldiers was reported marching along the road near Oldbury camp in Wiltshire. They were seen by a shepherd, who described them as 'men with beards, wearing skirts and big helmets with hair on the top. And a girt [*sic*] bird on a pole a'front on 'em'. This could easily be a description of Roman unit carrying its eagle standard.

SEE ALSO:
- Calne, near Chippenham.
- Mildenhall.

WHILE YOU'RE THERE:
- Watch out for crop-circles; you are in the heart of crop-circle land where some very elaborate patterns have formed – for example at Barbury Castle to the north-east.

Reston House
(near Ings, Cumbria)

Reston House is situated between Windermere and Kendal and is thought to have been built for Robert Bateman, a marble merchant, in the mid 1700s. He set out from Italy, where he was conducting business, to come to his new home but died at sea. Rumour has it he either died naturally or was murdered by the captain and thrown overboard. His ghost has often been seen around the property, watching from the gates but never entering the house. It is also said that Bateman was a misogynist and that no woman has been able to live in Reston House for a long period either as owner or tenant.

SEE ALSO:

- Tebay.
- Cark Hall / Holker Hall, near Cartmel.
- Gaythorne Hall, Tebay.
- Rydal Mount.

WHILE YOU'RE THERE:

- Visit Kendal church, where you will find a helmet on the north wall. It is supposed to be the helmet of the Royalist Sir Robert Philipson – known as Robin the Devil. He was attacked by Colonel Briggs, Roundhead magistrate of Kendal, and rode into Kendal the following Sunday seeking revenge. He did not encounter Briggs, but during the ensuing confusion he lost his helmet and sword. Sir Walter Scott immortalized the incident in the poem *Rokeby*.

Salcey Forest (Northamptonshire)

Visitors to this area have been alarmed at the sight of a spectral intruder. Indeed, there are many such dark figures reported from the area. The figure is said to be a tall man dressed in a dark cloak and hood. It is seen floating above the ground, and was particularly noticed gliding across a field of corn.

SEE ALSO:

- Grosvenor Centre, Northampton.

WHILE YOU'RE THERE:

- A cross-country trip to north of Bedford will bring you to a tiny road that runs between the villages of Wilden and Ravensden. There is another 'outdoor' ghost here – a phantom hitch-hiker of sorts – a witch-like woman in black seen usually in daylight. Her expression is said to be one of evil.

Sedgemoor
(Somerset)

The battle of Sedgemoor took place in 1685 following James II's succession to the throne. On 11 June 1685 the Duke of Monmouth, together with eighty-one largely untrained members of his 'Peasant Army', sailed into Lyme Regis harbour. His rebellion looked as if it could be successful. Within a few days up to 6,000 West Countrymen sided with his cause against his uncle, James II. This period of loyalty to the Duke of Monmouth became known in English history as the Duking Days. However, the lack of training and equipment meant that the 'Peasant Army', for the large part armed with rusty implements and pitchforks, and the lack of money – Monmouth was broke – meant that the Duke was largely under-supported in battle where it was to matter most. For up to a month the Duke ruled Somerset and indeed Monmouth was proclaimed king in the Taunton market place. James II's troops, present at the time, did nothing to stop him, though clearly they reported these events. On the night of 5 July James II fought back and routed the Duke's troops in the Battle of Sedgemoor. Monmouth himself was captured, taken to London, and despite pleading for his life and promising to turn Catholic, he was beheaded on 15 July on Tower Hill. James's response to the people of Somerset was to send the infamous Judge Jeffreys to Taunton to deal out his justice for him. At the Bloody Assizes, 200 or more people were hanged and 800 transported to the West Indies. Judge Jeffreys himself and his victims play a large part in the hauntings of the area, as indicated by other entries in this book.

There have been many reports of ghostly horsemen and troops seen but not heard in the fields and lanes around the battle site near the River Carey. The sounds of battle have also been heard and there are many reports of balls of light and anomalous light phenomena in the area, often on 5 July, the anniversary of the battle. Other witnesses have reported groups of sad, dishevelled, tired soldiers clutching pikes and shouting, 'Come on over'.

One local farmer reported that on a foggy night he heard coming across the moor what he took to be the shouting of a drunk, 'Come over and fight,' but was told later that this was the last cry of Monmouth men as they were slaughtered by a cannon firing across the River Carey.

Fugitives from the battle also are alleged to be responsible for other local ghost sightings. For example, John Plumley, lord of Locking Manor, was chased to his home but was found hiding when the barking of his dog gave away his concealment. It is then said that his wife grabbed the dog and together they plunged to their deaths in the Locking well. Her ghost, still carrying the dog, is said to haunt to this day.

A legendary association with the site concerns the betrayal of one of the Duke of Monmouth's men. Having been captured, the story has it that he was offered the chance to save his life if he could win a running race against a horse. In fact he won the race but was none the less killed. It is said the sound of a galloping horse and a man's strenuous and exhausted breath have been heard and also that the ghost of the man's lover has been seen, she having drowned herself after his death. These sounds of the horse and runner are supposed to be heard at Weston Zoyland, near the battle site.

An event which was reported in 1951 may have some connection for the Battle of Sedgemoor. Around twenty miles away to the west lies Dunster. In 1951 Joyce Nicholls and Frances Robinson were holidaying there. During one day they came across Conygar Hill, a steep tor on the peak of which is a small tower, a folly built in 1760. Although private property, they decided to enter the grounds and climb to the tower. They climbed a ramp inside the tower and reached the top. Although they were tired from the steep climb and having to push their way through tight branches and shrubs, they had enjoyed the bright warm summer's day. However, when they stood in the tower they became aware of a change of atmosphere. The sun was still as strong but the wind was so cold it was as if winter had onset. They also felt a darkening, as if a cloud was passing in front of the sun, although there were no clouds in the sky. Then they received their shock. They could hear, coming from the north, a sound they were certain was of a huge group of people marching towards them. They realized from the steepness of the tor and the thickness of the undergrowth that no one could be marching so rhythmically up that hill, but furthermore, they were certain that the marching was coming towards them at a horizontal level despite the fact that they were raised very high above the natural ground level. They were certain that a ghostly army was marching towards them. They felt the wind increase, the darkness deepen, and as they were certain that the troops had become close to them, they ran. Their flight was so panic-stricken that they were badly cut by thorns and branches as they scrambled down the hill. When they arrived at the roadway below they could feel the warm sun and the still air. They could hear that the trees were motionless and there was no sound of the spectral army. It is by no means certain that even if they heard an army it was one relating to the Monmouth rebellion, but there are no other major battles known in the area. The local Dunster Castle was alternately occupied by both sides during the English Civil War and it is possible that what they heard related to the one or two engagements there. Perhaps they related to a time further back when Dunster Castle was an active fortress, and local legend even relates activity in the area to the times of King Arthur.

SEE ALSO:
- Heddon Oak, near Stogumber.

WHILE YOU'RE THERE:
- You are close to what has been referred to as the 'mystical centre of the world' – Glastonbury. Glastonbury Tor, with the tower of St Michael dominating the skyline, has inspired a great deal of history and mysticism. It is believed to be the place where the first Christian church in Britain was built, a place where Christ visited as a boy, but also a holy site of significance 1,000 years before Christianity reached England. It is supposed to be the burial place of King Arthur, who was carried, mortally wounded, to the Isle of Avalon. There is good evidence that Glastonbury was indeed Avalon; Glastonbury was once an island in the marshes that existed in the area.

The Siege House
(Colchester, Essex)

This story starts not in Colchester but many miles away, on the M6 motorway. When twenty-two-year old Geoffrey Wright, in January 1974, used the toilet in the Keele Service Station on the M6 at 11 a.m. in the morning it must have been a time and place when he would have least likely expected to see a ghost. But standing against the urinals was a man 'like one of those pictures you see of Puritans'. He apparently wore a wide-brimmed hat, a wide white collar and buff-coloured clothing. Geoffrey, and his friend Francis, noticed that no one else seemed to be paying any attention to this otherwise eccentric dress. At the time they assumed that the person was someone dressed up, perhaps to do with a film or advertising stunt. On leaving the toilets, however, they could see no trace of him and friends outside had not seen anyone dressed like that leaving. The matter was dismissed but, as it turned out, only for a time.

Some months later Geoffrey was at his parents-in-laws' house, which faces the Siege House in Colchester. The Siege House is a famous local building, the last retreat of the loyalist forces before they were defeated by the Parliamentarians during the English Civil War. Suddenly Geoffrey saw the same figure he had previously seen in the toilets walking along the pavement. No one else seemed to be noticing him or at least paying any attention to him. Geoffrey called his wife and mother-in-law and together they all looked out of the window. However, only Geoffrey could see the figure. Eventually it walked out of the range of view and Geoffrey could see it no more. However, it was now clear to him that he alone was seeing the figure, and that with the exception of Francis, perhaps that had also been true at the Keele Service Station.

Geoffrey reported one other sighting of the figure in fields near Colchester but admitted that by now his thoughts on the previous sightings may have made him imagine it in some way. He made one point, however: 'If I had been going to imagine someone from the past I would have found a person much more interesting than this one,' he said, having no interest in history generally, nor the English Civil War in particular.

If we assume Geoffrey's sightings to be genuine then it is very difficult to categorize them. They do not seem to fit into the 'recordings and replays' category as these tend to be seen by any witnesses present at the time. More importantly, from the point of view of challenging the 'recordings' theory it hardly seems probable that the Puritans of centuries ago would have somehow stopped to urinate against a tree or in a field at the exact position where the urinals were positioned in a modern motorway service station. On the other hand the ghosts seen by Geoffrey were not interactive with Geoffrey. His accounts of sightings offer more questions than answers and perhaps even demand some rethink of the broadly accepted categories of ghost sightings.

SEE ALSO:
- Berechurch, Colchester.
- Mersea Island.
- Langenhoe Church (site).

WHILE YOU'RE IN THE COLCHESTER AREA:
- Travel twenty miles or so to Finchingfield and visit St John the Baptist Church. Carved on the window sill is the 'board' of the game 'Nine Men's Morris'. Similar ancient carvings of the game have been found on the steps of the Acropolis in Athens, on the deck of a Viking ship in Norway, and on a Roman tile excavated at Silchester. It is a game

that has a history throughout the world and was known in the Amazon, India and China. It was also immortalized in Shakespeare's *A Midsummer Night's Dream*.

Stalybridge
(Greater Manchester)

In *Ghosts of North-West England* Peter Underwood relates the tale of a Mrs Vera Bottomley in the mid 1930s, reported some forty years later. Vera, then nineteen, was, one summer, staying in a house at the foot of the Pennines near Stalybridge with her cousin, Jessie, who was a couple of years younger. They set out for a walk passing by nearby reservoirs. Suddenly they heard music and were instantly aware of two men in Highland dress; kilt, sporran and both playing bagpipes. They were unaware of how the two men could have got so close to them. They could see the stretch of road for a quarter of a mile ahead yet they had to step aside quickly as the Highlanders disappeared round the bend in the road from which they had just come. They also noted that neither of the Highlanders so much as glanced at them, as if from their perspective the girls were not standing there. Later investigation by Mrs Bottomley discovered that 'Bonnie' Prince Charlie had stayed in the area prior to his excursions north.

SEE ALSO:
• Hyde.

Stondon Massey
(Essex)

Stondon Massey is a small village just a few miles to the north of Brentwood in Essex. The story was related first-hand to ghost researcher Joan Forman, and included in her collection *Haunted East Anglia*.

In 1935, a Mrs M. C. Jones lived in Stondon Massey in a bungalow which was part of a building development on an old estate. One summer's night Mrs Jones was awoken by what seemed to be the sound of someone opening her bedroom door. She assumed it was one of her young twin sons, then aged five. But she saw the door was still closed and became aware of the shadowy outline of what appeared to be a woman standing at the foot of the bed. She appeared dressed in Edwardian style, wearing a lace scarf and a large picture hat. Her hands gripped the railing at the end of the bed, making her knuckles white. Mrs Jones asked, 'Who are you? What do you want?' She got no reply and gradually the apparition faded away.

It was some time later when Mrs Jones was with the Village Hall Committee that she overheard talk of a ghost in the area. A Miss Edith confirmed that there was a ghost, saying that her sister had seen it. Her sister had seen the ghost appear at the back of the rectory, walk along the Canons Walk and then disappear into the woods. Based on her own sighting, Mrs Jones indicated, 'I know where she goes when she leaves the wood,' though whether or not her analysis of tying up the two sightings was correct is uncertain.

It is believed that the ghost is that of a young woman who courted Miss Edith's brother and who, in her youth, had lived in the locality. Miss Edith remembered that the couple used to meet at the edge of the wood and the young lady's route to meet her suitor matched the alleged walk of the ghost.

WHILE YOU'RE THERE:

- Travel through a few small by-roads to come to the Stock-to-Ingatestone road off the A12. This road is haunted by the ghost of a cavalier.

Verulamium
(St Albans, Hertfordshire)

St Albans in Hertfordshire, famous for the Roman city ruins of Verulamium, is named after the first English Christian martyr, St Alban. Quite who Alban was is unclear. One story suggests that he was a man who protected a priest, became converted to Christianity and was martyred at Verulamium. Another suggests that Alban was a Roman soldier who was converted to Christianity in Rome, who then came to England, and who died on the spot now commemorated by St Albans Abbey.

St Albans is rich in ghost stories, not least of the shades of Romans and Roman legions. But one sighting often repeated is that of a vision of St Alban. For example, Miss Toulmin, who as a young girl was living in Redbourn Road, St Albans, saw the vision at the remains of a monk's rest near the abbey. 'It was a figure in white with light streaming from its head and shoulders,' she describes. 'It was quite motionless and perfectly lovely. It stayed absolutely still for about three minutes and then as I turned, it vanished.' Throughout the time Miss Toulmin watched it she described it as the vision of a man with a golden radiance about his head and as she watched the radiance gradually encompassed the whole figure. There have been several such sightings of 'the saint', for example in the previous century by a Mr Bolton, the butler and later mace bearer to the Mayor of St Albans. One theory is that the vision marks the place where Alban's body was hidden to prevent attacks on his tomb.

SEE ALSO:

- St Albans.
- St Albans Abbey.
- Salisbury Hall, St Albans.

Wenlock Edge
(Shropshire)

A story of astonishing escape and survival comes from the wild country around Wenlock Edge in Shropshire, and dates back to English Civil War. Wilderthorpe Manor, now in the care of the National Trust, belonged in 1645 to Major Smallman. Smallman was a Royalist and he became a target for the Parliamentarians. At one point it is reported that Parliamentarian horsemen surrounded Wilderthorpe Manor and that Smallman escaped on horseback and was chased along Wenlock Edge. Reaching what is now known as Blakeway Coppice, he leapt over the edge of the scarp slope which dropped almost 100 feet. The Parliamentarians called off their chase, convinced that Smallman must be dead. In fact his horse was killed but Smallman survived by crashing into a crab-apple tree some way down the drop. Whether Smallman was a brilliant strategist or just plain lucky is unclear. Also, it is not certain exactly where this event took place as records are vague, though the event is commemorated by the area known as 'Major's Leap'.

At Easter 1965, Eva and Alick Knight were driving in the area at around 3.30 in the afternoon when they were surprised to see a rider on horseback standing on a single track ahead of them. Both rider and horse were seen in shades of greys and black; no colour was evident. The rider wore a wide-brimmed plumed hat, cloak and breeches. Suddenly the horse and rider leapt into the field to the left of track, galloping parallel to the road right past the car. Despite the close proximity the Knights heard nothing. They did not believe that the horse and rider had moved as a response to their own proximity but believed that they had not been noticed. Eventually the horse and rider disappeared from sight. Mr Knight believed that they had gone over the brow of a hill; Mrs Knight believed that the horse and rider had vanished when they should have still been visible.

The Knights tried to discover whether or not it was likely that this was a local rider, perhaps taking part in a pageant, but they could find no trace of this and considered the possibility that they had seen ghosts. Even if they did it is by no means certain they saw the ghost of Major Smallman. However, some analysts believe this is possible. Although his apparition was seen some nine miles from where it was believed he had effected his disappearance, the location is uncertain. They believe also that the generally accepted view that Major Smallman originally escaped to the north-east is unlikely to be correct, as that would have taken him into territory held by the Parliamentarians; they believe that a north-west escape – the route taken by the rider that the Knights had seen – is more likely.

SEE ALSO:

• Castle Lodge, Ludlow.

WHILE YOU'RE THERE:

• It is a short distance to travel to Chirbury, near the Welsh border. Just nearby you will find Mitchells Fold Stone Circle dating from the Bronze Age. Fifteen stones remain out of probably twice that number originally. The stones were taken from nearby Stapley Hill. Legend has it that a giant cow lived on the moors and provided milk for visitors, but was made to disappear by a witch who was in turn captured and contained within the stone circle. The legend is told in stone carvings at Holy Trinity Church in Middleton-in-Chirbury.

CHAPTER 8

~

ROADS OF THE PHANTOM HITCH-HIKERS

The A435 at Arrow
(Warwickshire)

Known as the phantom hitch-hiker of Ragley Hall, this spectral figure may have been identified. Several people, including care worker Anne Cooke and her husband, have encountered the figure of an old lady that stands outside the gates of Ragley Hall, apparently seeking a lift. Drivers have told how they have picked her up, taken her to Dunnington Cross and then sought to drop her off only to find that she has disappeared.

Anne's husband, John, first encountered the figure on Valentine's Day. Incredibly his car headlights picked out the figure up in a tree. As he approached closer the figure jumped off a branch and was dangling by the neck. He stopped, expecting to have to cut down a suicide, but the figure was gone. The following year he saw a figure by the side of the road in the same location and the following night Anne herself saw the figure gesturing as if for a lift. Alerted, and afraid, Anne drove past. 'Nothing will convince me that what I saw wasn't a ghost', she said.

But perhaps the figure is identifiable. An examination of the location unearthed the skeleton of an elderly woman who had been buried at the roadside.

Bebington
(near Birkenhead, Cheshire)

It is said that Poulton Road is haunted by the ghost of a nun who died at Poulton Hall while returning to her nunnery. She was seen by several witnesses both in cars and on foot in the 1970s. For example one driver travelling along Poulton Road from Higher Bebington saw a figure. He slowed down alongside and saw that the figure was of a young girl, perhaps with long hair, wearing a long dark coat and standing at the roadside. Concerned that the girl should be out so late, he stopped and asked if he could assist or offer a lift. He leant across the car and opened the passenger window and as he did so he watched the figure slowly dematerialize. Of this particular aspect he was quite certain. The girl did not move away or run into the darkness but while standing absolutely motionless she gradually faded away. On reflection he realized that he had never actually seen her face but he was certain she was female. He was one of many people who had reported the same experience and the same dematerialization.

In the summer of 1970 there were two other incidents of people seeing the figure; one a woman walking from Clackerbridge Hospital and another a motorist.

WHILE YOU'RE THERE:

- Nearby Leasowe Castle has had a chequered history. The castle dates from 1593. Once the summer home of the Earl of Derby, it has been a hostel for sailors, a hotel, a convalescent home, a nurses' home and is presently a hotel again. At one point, dilapidated, it was known as Mockbeggar Hall. There are many ghost reports from the castle, in particular of a man and a young boy whose origin is unknown. One local story has it that the father killed his own son and then committed suicide.

Blackwall Tunnel
(London)

In October 1972 a motor-cyclist just south of the Blackwall Tunnel (under the River Thames, in London) gave a lift to a male hitch-hiker. The hitch-hiker, riding pillion, gave his address to the driver in a shouted conversation. Coming out of the tunnel the driver turned to shout again to his passenger but found that the hitch-hiker was no longer on the motorbike. Fearing that he might have fallen off, the motor-cyclist went back and retraced his journey through the tunnel but found no trace of the missing man.

The story continues the next day, when the motor-cyclist visited the address of the hitch-hiker to be told that a person of that description had died years before. This is not an uncommon ending to hitch-hiker reports, though they must be considered as similar to urban legend in nature. We have found that similar reports of motor-cycle hitch-hikers in later years include the description of the passenger wearing a helmet, as the law now insists.

SEE ALSO:
• London's various locations; mainly palaces and theatres.

Blue Bell Hill
(Chatham, Kent)

One of the most famous, at least the most persistent, of phantom hitch-hikers is the young woman who haunts Blue Bell Hill. For the drivers she encounters she is also the most disturbing. Mr Sharpe reported in November 1992 how he had been driving on Blue Bell Hill when suddenly a girl appeared and ran towards him. She looked straight at him just as they collided, and then fell under the car. Mr Sharpe, terrified, sure the girl had been killed and was lying under his car, knelt down to see her. There was no body under the car, nor could he locate her in the vicinity. After trying to attract the attention of other drivers, Mr Sharpe drove to the police station and told the police that he had run over a woman but could not find the body.

The police went back to the roadside and, when they found no body, tried to assure Mr Sharpe that he had experienced a ghost. Mr Sharpe reported: 'It was the most scary experience of my life . . . I know I wasn't seeing things, I definitely saw a girl and she looked human, not like a ghost with pale skin.'

Eighteen years previously a Mr Goodenough had had a similar experience on the same stretch of road. At around midnight on 13 July 1974, driving on Blue Bell Hill, he saw a young girl apparently about ten years old who appeared from nowhere in front of his car. He tried to stop, failed, and hit the girl. Finding her lying on the road, bleeding, he carried her body to the roadside and covered it with a blanket. Then he drove to Rochester police station to report the incident and get assistance for the victim. Returning with the police they found the blanket, but no body, no blood-stains, and no tracks. There were no subsequent reports of anyone who claimed to have been injured, or whose child had been injured, at that location at that time.

Calne
(near Chippenham, Wiltshire)

In the *Bristol Evening Post* of 29 October 1965 there was a report of a classic phantom hitch-hiker. Garage proprietor Ray Viner believed he had run over a man in Calne and heard 'two distinct bumps as though both sets of my car wheels had passed over him'. Viner stopped his car and ran back immediately. He saw the man disappearing into some nearby trees, followed him but could not trace him. The man was never located.

SEE ALSO:

• Oldbury, near Avebury.

WHILE YOU'RE THERE:

• A woman driving near Corsham in September 1968 passed what she described as an American-style car driving with headlights full on. As it overtook her again she saw that it had no driver.

Carlisle
(Cumbria)

Phantom hitch-hiker stories seem to be prone to legend. Particularly noticeable is the way in which such stories have naturally well-tied-up endings. Such a story arises from Carlisle as related in *Lakeland Ghosts* by Gerald Findler. A driver in pre-motorway days gave a lift to a man thumbing cars at Shap. As they talked they shared their common interest in playing chess. The old man who had been picked up promised the driver that he would give him an interesting chess conundrum that he had been working on if the driver would call at his home; and he handed him his address. He also told the driver that if he wasn't there he would leave the conundrum written down for him in a tobacco jar positioned on the mantelpiece.

In due course the driver called at the address and, talking to the woman who answered the door, discovered that the old gentleman had died three days prior to the time when he had thumbed the lift on the road. Remembering the further promise, the driver asked if there was a tobacco jar on the mantelpiece. On being told there was, he asked if the woman would look inside it. Inside was a piece of paper with the problem written on it.

SEE ALSO:

• Corby Castle

WHILE YOU'RE THERE:
- To the south-east lies the village of Croglin, location of one of Britain's relatively rare vampire stories. The story would seem to pre-date Bram Stoker's *Dracula* by 200 years, and certainly appears in print prior to the publication of Stoker's work. The story probably relates to Croglin Low Hall, once known as the Grange. A woman sleeping in the Grange saw two lights coming from the direction of the churchyard and as they got closer realized that they represented a 'ghastly something'. They turned into a creature that broke into her room and bit her throat. The story concludes that at a time of a later attack the creature was shot and chased to a burial vault where it was destroyed by fire.

Golborne
(Merseyside)
The streets of Golborne are said to be haunted by a floating White Lady who drifts out in front of passing traffic, causing crashes and injuries. In 1970, for example, a motor-cyclist crashed avoiding such a figure, but when he reported it at the local police station he was told that it was the same figure that had caused several other incidents and that the police had no explanation.

Tradition has it that the White Lady is seeking revenge on passing traffic because at some time in the past her lover was killed on that stretch of road. An alternative explanation is that she herself was a victim of a crash.

Since the M6 motorway was built through Golborne the volume of sightings of the White Lady seem to have diminished, though there are reports that she has been seen on the motorway itself, unusual since phantom hitch-hikers seem rarely to appear on these modern, busy, fast, arterial routes.

SEE ALSO:
- Rivington Castle, near Horwich.
- Samlesbury Hall.
- Burtonwood, near Warrington.

M4 Motorway
(near Heathrow, Greater London)

In the early hours of the morning, around one or two o'clock, one September or October night in 1993, Becky was travelling home from Reading. She was driving towards London along the M4, between junctions 4 and 3. She was driving fast, the motorway was empty, and the stretch of road was lit up brightly by orange motorway lighting. Suddenly, ahead of her in the distance, Becky could see a figure walking down the outside lane of the motorway towards her.

She told us: 'My first thought was that someone had broken down. And I considered that where you break down and there aren't any footpaths you're supposed to walk towards the traffic, but that hardly seemed to apply on a fast motorway. She could have at least walked down the central reservation if she didn't want to get over to the hard shoulder, but she was just walking down the traffic lane.

'I particularly noticed that there was no traffic on the motorway, it was very empty. There were no cars in front of me and there were no cars coming from the London direction either. I quickly looked for a broken down car, but I couldn't see one. I looked then on the other side of the road to see if her car was on the hard shoulder there, perhaps she had crossed the motorway to get to a nearer breakdown phone and there was no car over there either. In any case, I later realized that she had already passed a breakdown phone so she obviously hadn't decided to stop at that.

'Of course I was getting nearer to her all the time. I must have been doing over 80 miles an hour. Obviously I started to slow down, but I didn't brake. I just slightly lifted my foot off the accelerator and I moved into the middle lane. I was straddling the outside lane and the middle lane when I actually flew past her. And the freaky thing was that she never flinched, she never seemed to jump or even notice. She was just staring straight ahead.

'It was a woman. She was dressed in black, and it crossed my mind that you don't want to be walking on the road in dark colours. She was carrying two bags; she had a bag in each arm and she was just walking down the motorway and staring straight ahead. She was all in black and she looked like she had a rain mac on, it was like a heavy sou'-wester rain mac rather than a lightish one and she looked wet but it wasn't raining. She had a hat on, an unstylish rainhat, and she was carrying these two bags; one looked like an old leather shopping bag. She wore sturdy walking shoes, black lace-up, and dark tights. I thought she looked like she was from a 'Catherine Cookson' era.

'Even to this day I can tell you what her face looked like. When I shot past I took it all in. She had a very pinched, very drawn face and she had chin length, straight, bobbed hair. It was very dark with a fringe, almost like black hair. It was a very severe cut, there was no style to it. She was an older woman, perhaps around sixty. Very harsh and bitter-looking in a sense, very sharp, beaky almost. She looked like she was out for a walk, and prepared for all weathers.

'As I pulled over and was passing her, a car came up the inside lane, and overtook me on the inside. I hadn't noticed it before. I think I must therefore have been slowing down quite a lot as I got near to her, and he just shot past me. I saw him swerve, but I really don't know if that was because he saw what I saw, or because I swerved and he had to avoid me.

'I thought should I stop and phone the police on one of the breakdown phones, but I thought it better not to stop on the motorway, you don't know what could happen. I came off at Junction 3 and I got to the roundabout, the first roundabout with the White Hart pub on it, and I stopped there at the phone box and phoned 999. They took the details and said they would get a car out on the motorway. While I was talking to them a car literally screeched to a halt with two guys in; one just flew out and he was really pale and I wondered if he had been on the motorway and had seen the same thing. But I didn't feel it was sensible at that time to strike up a conversation with them.

'I thought about it for ages and ages afterwards. What was concerning me was, if it was a woman, should I have stopped and helped her? Secondly, did she get hit by a car? It was all these guilt feelings that I was feeling, like I should have done something more constructive than just phone the police. And then I felt, if it was a ghost, wouldn't the police have more reports and wouldn't they have said something to me at the time on the phone?'

Becky's encounter was not a one-off. She saw the same figure again at around six o'clock one evening in the same place. It was about a month later, and this time she was with her partner, Conrad. But although Becky saw the woman, Conrad did not, as he also confirmed to us. Becky was so surprised at this that she thought Conrad was 'winding her up', pretending he couldn't see the figure.

'In a way I felt like I was replaying it in my mind to try and describe it to him and I was almost seeing it like a recording on the telly and he wasn't seeing the same picture and it was really irritating me. But he couldn't see it.'

This time they took a roundabout turn-off and came back on to the motorway travelling back the way they had come, to see if they could spot the figure. But they did not.

SEE ALSO:
• Windsor Castle.

Markyate
(A5 Bedfordshire)

There have been several reports of a figure around 6 feet tall and dressed all in white seen on the busy A5 road between Dunstable and Markyate near the Pack Horse Inn. On a Sunday morning in 1970 a taxi driver suddenly saw the figure step out in front of his car and, unable to stop, the driver 'went straight through him'. Agitated and alarmed, the driver parked the car and ran back to see what injuries had been caused but could find no one there. The car itself was undamaged and showed no signs of collision. The local press discovered that there were several stories of people who had seen what they thought was a cricketer standing on the side of the road who, they assumed, was a hitch-hiker leaving the Pack Horse.

The cricketer connection seems to be the favoured explanation for this phantom hitch-hiker, arising from an incident in 1958. In that year a cricket team belonging to the Kenwood Manufacturing Co. Ltd., were returning from a match and at that spot on the A5 were involved in an accident, which killed two members of the team, Sidney Moulder and Jerry Rycham; three others were injured.

SEE ALSO:
• Markyate Cell.
• Woburn Abbey.

WHILE YOU'RE THERE:
• At nearby Studham, in January 1967, a group of children around the age of ten reported seeing what became known as the 'Little Man of Studham Common'. They described the figure as 'a little blue man with a tall hat and a beard'. He was short, wearing a very tall hat and carrying a small black box. As they stood watching the figure would disappear in a puff of smoke, then reappear elsewhere; this

happened several times. They heard the figure talking in what they described as 'foreign sounding babble'. They told their teacher, who separated them and asked them to write out their accounts. These were then collected together as a report on the entity, and retained by the school.

Mersea Island
(Essex)

Mersea Island, at the estuary of the River Blackwater, is a small island linked to the mainland by a causeway known as Strood, part of the road to Colchester. The whole area was one of the major Roman outposts during the Roman occupation. There are several stories of Roman ghosts in the area. It none the less also has some of the characteristics of the phantom hitch-hiker. The first is a centurion who has been seen marching from East Mersea across the causeway and along the road towards the little village of Peldon by many drivers and pedestrians. As related in *Essex Ghosts and Hauntings* No. 3, one motorist driving along that road on a foggy night nearly ran into the figure and two naval ratings actually did so. However, they were even more stunned to pass through the figure rather than to hit it. They then spent time outside the car looking around, unable to find the injured man.

One witness leaving a pub in West Mersea claimed on a radio phone-in that he had been in a taxi when he encountered several Roman soldiers in the middle of the road. The taxi driver had apparently driven straight through the apparitions, which had disappeared when he looked back.

On the island itself there have been many reports of the sounds of battle though no visual sightings; these include the sounds of sword clashing, shouting, cries of pain and so on. Around Barrow Hill there have been many reports of the sound of wheeled carts and horses tramping along.

West Mersea Hall, built on the site of a Roman villa, is haunted by the laughter of an unseen female. She is thought to have been a guest of the Emperor Claudius staying at the villa who drowned during a midnight swim, her laughter being the echo of happier times.

SEE ALSO:
- Berechurch, Colchester.
- Langenhoe Church (site).

- Visit nearby Layer Marney. Lord Marney died in 1523 before he had completed the building of the tower there; and his ghost is still said to haunt the structure.

Mitchell, also Hayle
(both in Cornwall)

Elizabeth Bain was driving through the village of Mitchell in the late summer of 1965. It was a warm day, the middle of the afternoon. Driving slowly through holiday traffic, Ms Bain saw a girl, aged about nine, skipping out of one of the quaint shops in the town. Her dress was Victorian in style: navy blue and white, pleated pinafore, boots and dark stockings.

Terrifyingly, Elizabeth Bain saw the girl dance out into the traffic straight into the path of a lorry in front of Ms Bain's car. Anticipating the inevitable accident, Ms Bain braked but the lorry did not even adjust its accelerating speed. As the road cleared Ms Bain could see that there was no child lying in the road or standing on either side of the street.

But what made this case more extraordinary was that some thirty miles on, at Hayle on the north coast of Cornwall, Ms Bain narrowly missed an accident. A van in front of her turned left and a lorry pulled out into the road; Ms Bain avoided the collision but almost immediately saw again the apparition of the same little girl. This time the head and shoulders were directly in front of her on the windscreen as if reflected from the back seat of the car. The girl was smiling at Ms Bain but clearly identifiable as the same apparition.

It was Ms Bain's general feeling that somehow the girl was a warning to her and may have in some way prevented a collision at Hayle in which Ms Bain could have been injured or killed. This phantom hitch-hiker, if Mrs Bain's feelings are right, seems to have fulfilled one of the basic requirements of this genre of ghost; a protective ghost.

Saltwood
(Kent)

A stretch of road running to Sandling Station is not only haunted but has quite a variety of manifestations associated with it. One claimed manifestation is a ball of fire from which a man appears carrying a lantern. He is thought to be William Tournay, who died at the end of the Edwardian period and was buried on an island in a nearby lake.

One report from four teenagers walking from Saltwood to Sandling Station was of watching the ball of light dip down below a hill and then seeing a figure appearing on the road ahead 'like a man in a red cloak carrying a lantern'. It apparently reached the railway bridge and disappeared, implying perhaps the days when railway workers carried lanterns while working at night around the tracks. Despite the fact that the air was generally very cold, the temperature immediately outside the station – where the figure had vanished – was very warm, implying the exact opposite of most ghost sightings where a temperature drop is noted. On another occasion a courting couple saw a glowing light in a field at Brockhill School and then saw a dark figure standing in the field. As they approached the light it suddenly disappeared, causing the girl to faint.

Other local apparitions include a Roman soldier, a Victorian farmer, and several reports of a Grey Lady on the roads of the area, and on one occasion boarding a bus.

In his privately published manuscript *Ghosts of Shepway*, Paul Harris, a local researcher, relates the story of an ex-Scout leader who ran over a figure looking like a 'black robed monk' outside Brockhill School, stopped his car, got out but found no-one there.

SEE ALSO:
• Dover Castle.

Sheriff Hutton
(North Yorkshire)

A protective ghost is thought to haunt the A64 north of York in the area around Sheriff Hutton. The story reaches back into the coaching era, when a couple called Nance and Tom lived in the village. Tom was a coachman working the long-distance runs to the north of England. While he was away Nance fell in love with a man from London and disappeared with him. In a scene of great melodrama Tom later encountered her sitting on the side of the road while he was driving his coach towards York. She, together with a baby, had been dumped by her lover and was dying from exposure. Both Nance and the child died and Tom was left in despair. However, Nance apparently sought to make amends for her wrongdoing and her ghost was held to guide him safely when he was driving his coach. She is believed still to haunt that stretch of the A64, guiding present-day drivers.

SEE ALSO:

- Treasurer's House, York.
- National Railway Museum, York.
- Theatre Royal, York.

South Cerney
(Gloucestershire)

On 13 January 1968 the *Bristol Evening Post* reported that Arthur Gibbs, driving along the Cirencester to Cricklade road, thought he had struck a person near South Cerney. Gibbs stopped and searched the area but could find no one. He then called the police, who confirmed that he had definitely struck something because there was a dent in the top of the offside door and the wing mirror was twisted. No one could be located who had been struck by the car.

Stockbridge Bypass
(near Sheffield, South Yorkshire)

According to newspaper reports, the Stockbridge bypass near Sheffield is haunted by a ghost that jumps into cars. He is blamed for the fifty-seven crashes that have taken place at that spot, resulting in eight dead and eighteen seriously injured in the six years up to April 1994. A report of a strange figure 'hovering overhead' caused P.C. Dick Ellis to investigate. He told the newspapers: 'I saw it next to my Panda and then something banged on the back.'

Tarporley
(Cheshire)

The A51 from Crewe to Chester runs between Tarporley and Tiverton, two small villages just south of the Delamere Forest. A small lane between the two villages is said to be haunted by the spectres of a man and his dog.

In September 1971 a Mr A. Pressick, driving alone, became disorientated and found himself on the small country lane. He saw a man with a dog ahead, and slowed down to get directions. The man appeared to be wearing a khaki smock, khaki trousers tied below the knees and a floppy rain-proof hat. Mr Pressick noticed that although it was a calm windless night both the man and the dog were acting as if they were walking into a strong wind; the man's body seemed to be tensed against an oncoming force and Mr Pressick noticed that even the dog's saliva was blowing backwards. Nevertheless he drew up alongside the man and asked for directions. He received no reply; the man and dog kept on walking. Mr Pressick drew up beside them again and shouted his query, thinking the man might be deaf. This time he got a reaction. The man looked towards him (did he finally hear him through the rush of whatever wind he was perceiving?). However, the interaction was far from pleasant. The man's eyes were glaring and still he ignored the question. This time Mr Pressick became aware of the sound of wind and, thinking there was something odd, he drove off quickly. When he looked back in his mirror he could see neither man nor dog and he could see no way in which they could have left the road, which was bordered by unbroken hedges.

It was some years later that a farmer told Mr Pressick that a man walking his dog had been knocked down and killed in the lane during a night of fierce storms.

SEE ALSO:
- Northwich.
- Lyceum, Crewe.

Warminster
(Wiltshire)

On 16 December 1965, Reginald Roberts was alarmed when a grey-clad figure with streaming fair hair jumped in front of his car while he was driving near Colloway Clump, Warminster. Roberts stopped and ran back but could find no one there.

Just five days later what seems to have been the same figure was seen again at nearby Shearwater. A couple ran over a figure that rushed out from a hedge, apparently throwing itself under the wheels of the car. The car was stopped and the woman was sick by the roadside. However, her husband, searching, could find no body or bloodstains. This figure was also described as wearing grey and having long hair.

SUDELEY CASTLE

The figure of a Victorian housekeeper has been seen guarding the staircase, still apparently intent on keeping the sexes apart as was her duty in former days

THE BATTLEMENTS OF ROCHESTER CASTLE
Said to be haunted every 4 April by the ghost of a 'white lady'; thought to be
Lady Blanche de Warren who was killed in an accident there

BRAMBER CASTLE
The children of William de Braose, whose family were imprisoned
here, have reportedly been seen and heard amidst the castle
ruins and in the streets of the town

BORLEY CHURCH
Teams of investigators have reported many strange
happenings in this most famous of haunted sites

Credit: Paranormal Picture Library

THE TOWER OF LONDON
Said to be the most haunted buildings in the world, reports have
included almost every type of ghostly phenomena

Credit: Paranormal Picture Library

THE THEATRE ROYAL, YORK
This theatre sports one of the most famous 'grey lady' ghosts in theatreland

Credit: Paranormal Picture Library

REDWORTH HALL
The hotel is thought to be haunted by Lady Catherine

Credit: Redworth Hall

CHARLTON HOUSE, GREENWICH
During experimental research in this south London mansion the
authors had a ghost sighting shared with several others

Credit: Paranormal Picture Library

KATHERINE'S CROSS
The white apparition of a man on horseback has been seen
riding from Katherine's Cross to a nearby stream

Credit: Paranormal Picture Library

LINCOLNSHIRE AVIATION HERITAGE CENTRE
The authors interviewed a witness to a haunting here that left him so
disturbed he would not enter the building again for years

Credit: Paranormal Picture Library

IVY DENE COUNTRY HOUSE
Haunted by a 'politically incorrect' ghost who makes his
presence known by the smell of his smoking pipe

Credit: Ivy Dene Country House

THE BELL, TODDINGTON
The authors interviewed several witnesses to ghostly happenings in this pub

SEE ALSO:
- Longleat House.
- Frome.
- Farleigh Hungerford.

WHILE YOU'RE THERE:
- The town of Warminster was the site of the most famous upsurge of UFO sightings in England during the mid 1960s into the early 1970s. Known locally as 'The Thing', these sightings gave birth to many books about the subject, mainly by local writer Arthur Shuttlewood, and put England firmly on the world UFO map.

Whaley Bridge
(Derbyshire)

A most extraordinary account of a haunting was given in the *Stockport Express* in December 1974. The story was told by Brian Mohan, who on 30 November was driving a black taxi along the A6 through Great Moor after having dropped a passenger at Whaley Bridge. While driving along, knowing his cab was empty, he looked in the rear view mirror and saw, sitting on the back seat, an old woman. His first thought was to rationalize the sighting and assume that there was some odd reflection, so he kept driving, but when he checked, the woman was still sitting there. She was upright, still and expressionless. She appeared to be between fifty and sixty with long hair, wearing a black overcoat, pointed collar, white blouse and black bow. Brian himself made the point that he was not tired, hungry or drunk and there was no reason for him to see something that was not there. In Stockport he pulled the cab over, opened the glass partition between the passenger segment and his driving cab, and turned to ask the lady for an explanation but immediately saw that the seats were empty. Still trying to rationalize the sighting, he got out of the cab, walked around it, looked up and down the street but could see no sign of the figure he had been watching in the back of his cab. As reported in the newspaper, Mohan said: 'I saw her both when we were in darkness, at the Convent, and when it was light. So it can't have been an image. No one could have jumped into the cab because of the noise of the door and the interior light. We have spent hours trying to work out what it could be but we haven't come up with any answer. I know it wasn't just me seeing things because I looked three times to make sure and she was there each time'. The owner of the cab company, Ray Normansell, confirmed that Brian Mohan was very frightened when he returned to his base that night and was not the kind of person to make up ghost stories.

All the drivers in Normansell's company refused to use the cab after that experience.

SEE ALSO:

- Lyme Park, near Disley.
- Bosley, Macclesfield.
- Northern Moors, Peak District.

WHILE YOU'RE THERE:

- Travel east to Chesterfield, south of Sheffield, and visit Hardwick Hall. Built in the sixteenth century, this imposing building sports a spectral monk with no hands or feet, but a luminous white face. In 1976 a couple driving through Hardwick Park saw it in their headlights; two police officers have also reported the phenomena.

~

CHAPTER 9

THE RIDES OF THE PHANTOM COACHES

Brockley Combe
(near Congresbury, Somerset)

There are several ghosts associated with the bright open picnic area of Brockley Combe, but of particular interest is a phantom coach and horses said to ride at night along the winding lanes of the Combe. The roads bordered by tall overhanging trees, can become very gloomy at night, adding to the haunting atmosphere.

There is an account of a haunting by a phantom coach and horseman given in *Ghost Stories of the South-West* by Tony Wells and Melanie Warren, which, if it has been related to them accurately, may give us some very important clues as to the nature of hauntings. The story involves a Ben Brown, who knew of the stories of 'a phantom coach drawn by four black horses and driven by a headless horseman' which was alleged to drive along that lane. Brown was a sceptic and walked the lane quite unmoved by such stories, but one night at midnight he became somewhat apprehensive, the atmosphere of the lane perhaps 'getting to him'. He armed himself with a few stones – presumably to ward off more earthly attackers – when suddenly he heard the sound of coach wheels rumbling behind him. Presumably thinking of the legends of the lane, and perhaps acting slightly irrationally, he hurled stones at the driver of the coach. Unfortunately it was not the phantom carriage at all but a coach carrying a football team whose driver did not appreciate Brown's gesture. Brown ran off down the lane with the football team pursuing him and it looked as if they were likely to catch him, when suddenly 'a hearse-like coach pulled by four black horses' appeared in front of them. The whole parade of people scattered.

Before considering this, let us also look at a few other such reports. The same phantom coach with its headless driver was apparently seen by a cyclist in the lane who was unable to get out of the way due to the rocks and trees which form a border down sections of the lane; the coach went right through him. All he felt was 'an icy chill'. He was of course somewhat shaken by the experience.

A cyclist appears to have encountered a very classical ghost; without warning or without apparent cause the apparition appears and acts as if it is some form of recording, i.e. completely oblivious to the surroundings, it carries on doing whatever it is doing and the witnesses simply have to watch it, in this case at alarmingly close quarters!

But the Ben Brown story is different. As experienced ghost researchers will testify, a great deal of time can be spent in haunted castles, old ruins and open roads and areas of land waiting for ghosts which never appear. It is speculated that a certain frame of mind is required to perceive ghosts and probably not the analytical mind of a ghost-researcher looking for clues. That Ben Brown should have been sufficiently thinking of a ghostly carriage just moments before one appears is almost too good to be true but at least it fits the logic that perhaps his state of mind, not rational but instinctive, was just the state of mind needed to perceive the carriage; perhaps in the right state of mind the carriage is always in the lane driving up and down and it just takes a certain attitude to see it. Interestingly, we note that Brown only saw the coach after he had stopped looking for it, not while he was looking for it. But this does not explain why the football team would also be in such a frame of mind. Indeed it appears that their own attitude was a very different one. If, therefore, this story is related accurately, the possibility would seem to be that Brown did not perceive the carriage so much as manifest it in a way in which others in any state of mind were then able to see it.

There are one or two instances of an individual being able to create hallucinations which others can see, in particular 'Ruth' studied by Dr Morton Schatzman. But these are rare instances and the hallucinations were particular to the individual. In this case the phantom coach and horses may have been manifested by Brown sufficiently for others to see but it also exists as the phenomenon in that lane witnessed by others. Therefore we have the possibility that Brown has been able temporarily to manifest this phantom, and in a way in which others can perceive it.

Whatever we think about the case, it adds questions to the mystery and questions that will need to be answered before the mystery of ghosts can become even close to being solved.

SEE ALSO:

- Theatre Royal, Bath.
- Theatre Royal, Bristol.

Bungay
(Suffolk)

A stretch of road between Bungay and Ditchingham is said to be haunted by a coach and horses. In the early 1970s a driver was driving along in the late evening when he came to a point where the new road joined what was the old road, the latter having been relegated to the role of lay-by. He sudden realized that there was a vehicle on the road ahead of him heading straight towards him. Even more shocked, he realized that it was a coach pulled by four horses, that two people were seated on the top and a carriage lamp hung either side of the coach. He tried to swing round the coach but then realized that it had moved aside, in fact 'floated away' was his description, into the lay-by.

Many local people regard the place as evil, though with no specific reason and nothing particularly associated with the apparition seen by the driver.

WHILE YOU'RE THERE:

- Visit the church. Bungay was also host to a famous black dog encounter. On the morning of Sunday, 4 August 1577 a spectral black dog appeared to the congregation of a church. It ran down the aisle and struck dead two worshippers. It 'shrivelled' a third person (who none the less remained alive), broke the church clock and scratched the doorway. The scratches on the door can still be seen today.

Cammeringham
(Lincolnshire)

Cammeringham is a small village on the B-road between Lincoln and Ingham which runs parallel to the Roman Ermine Street. There is a phenomenon there which locals believe may be the apparition of one of the most famous women of Britain.

One witness in the earlier part of the century was walking to work at dawn when he saw among the various patches of mist one particular large block of mist apparently coming towards him. As he watched, a chariot drove out of the mist pulled by one black and one white horse. Aboard the chariot was a woman in a long flowing dress draped in fine gold jewellery, whipping the horses along. The witness noticed that throughout the whole visual experience no sound was heard whatsoever.

He was only one of many people to have seen the apparition known as the Cammeringham Light, and it is the local belief, and the belief of this witness, that it is the apparition of Queen Boudicca.

Boudicca was an incredible woman, queen of the Iceni tribe, who inhabited the area now constituted by Norfolk and Suffolk. During the Roman occupation this territory was seized on the death of Boudicca's husband, King Prasutagus. Boudicca herself was tortured, her daughters raped and the Iceni enslaved. Boudicca gathered together an army and attacked and defeated the Roman armies at Colchester, Londinium and Verulamium, killing, according to the Roman historian Tacitus, 70,000 Romans. She was eventually defeated by an onslaught of the Romans under the leadership of the Roman Governor of Britain, Suetonius Paulinus, and she took her own life by poison, but not before she had become famous for her image of riding at the head of her troops in a horse-drawn chariot with knives attached to the wheels.

Boudicca is not known to have been particulary active in that part of Lincoln, nor was it the site of her final defeat, which almost certainly took place somewhere between London and Chester, but she was active against the Romans for almost the last twenty years of her life and no doubt covered a great deal of territory.

Hyde
(Greater Manchester)

A stretch of the A57 road between Hyde and Mottram-in-Longdendale is said to be haunted not by a phantom person but by a phantom lorry. The story arose when a twenty-nine-year-old bus driver, Charles Ridgway, from Hyde, was killed in a road accident on that stretch of road. He had been riding pillion on his cousin's motorbike and in the early hours of the morning both men were discovered seriously injured. His cousin, Albert Collinson, had a fractured skull yet survived his injuries, but Ridgway soon died. Collinson reported that as he approached a crossroads near which there was a small opening next to a tavern, a lorry had backed down into the road in front of him. Despite his certainty this story did not seem credible, as investigation by police found that there was no such opening nor were there any tracks of a lorry. The coroner, Stuart Rodger, was concerned enough to ask the jury to accompany him to the scene at midnight to try to find some explanation for Collinson's report. It was Rodger who coined the phrase 'phantom lorry' in February 1930 during the inquest. In fact Rodger was unable to come to a satisfactory conclusion, but a more extraordinary analysis was yet to follow: it was discovered that during the previous twenty-two months sixteen accidents had taken place involving all kinds of motorized transport and pedestrians. These had resulted in three people dead and twenty-five injured, and eighteen vehicles badly damaged. In every case no satisfactory explanation had been discovered. It did not seem to be a factor of the road itself; the surface was good, the road straight.

Whether connected to the phantom lorry or not, that precise area also appears to have been the haunt of an 'invisible walker'. Several people, including the licensee of the inn near the crossroads, then a Mr William Gratton, claimed that they had heard footsteps but could see no one. One local person said that she often heard what sounded like a heavy man walking on the roadway just prior to accidents and crashes.

As sometimes happens where no explanation is forthcoming, the interest gradually died away. However, just a year after Ridgway's death there was another series of accidents: a large lorry ran into a lamp post, a motor-cyclist was tossed over a hedge and two cars crashed on a wide part of the road. Even more interestingly, a pedestrian was run down by a lorry that appeared suddenly and silently in front of him and then disappeared, implying that for a time the lorry had substance.

One local driver crashed despite being very familiar with the area. He claimed that his vehicle went out of control despite his efforts to right it. Examination of the car showed that there was nothing mechanically wrong with it. A cyclist was found lying by his bicycle just 200 yards from where the phantom lorry had previously been seen. He never regained consciousness and was therefore never able to tell his story.

Since the 1930s there has not been a high intensity of incidents in the area but there are still ghostly reports and a lingering long local memory. The area has been changed by the introduction of the M67, which runs more or less parallel to the A57 and has obviously taken a good deal of traffic from the A-road. In any case significant structural changes to locations are thought to affect frequency and ghost sightings and perhaps this has had its effect.

SEE ALSO:

- Stalybridge, Greater Manchester.

WHILE YOU'RE THERE:

- Nearby Smithills Hall in Bolton sports a footprint impressed into the stone stairs. It is said to have been made by the Protestant martyr George Marsh, who was interrogated there prior to being burnt in 1555. The footprint is said to represent a divine criticism of George Marsh's treatment.

Kensington
(London)

Foreign tourists to London list among our most famous and notable features the double-decker red buses which travel the Greater London area. Perhaps they should not be overly surprised, then, to find that one has appeared in spectral form in the Kensington area of London. The precise spot of the manifestation is the junction of St Mark's Road and Cambridge Gardens; it is a blind bend and has been the cause of many accidents. Several accidents were alleged to have been caused by the sudden appearance of a speeding No. 7 bus tearing down St Mark's Road in the early hours of the morning, well after the night bus service has ceased. One report was as follows: 'I was turning the corner and saw a bus tearing towards me. The lights of the top and bottom decks and the headlights were full on, but I could see no sign of crew or passengers. I yanked my steering wheel hard over, and mounted the pavement, scraping the roadside wall. The bus just vanished'.

During one accident a driver was killed when his car hit a wall. At the inquest one eyewitness said that he had seen a bus hurtling towards the car just before the driver spun off the road. The coroner raised questions on this but many residents confirmed directly to him and to the local media that they had had sightings of the 'ghost bus'. Perhaps the most extraordinary such report was from a transport official, who claimed that the bus had actually drawn into the bus depot, stood with its engine running and then disappeared.

As a result not of the ghost bus but of the many accidents on that corner, the local authority undertook to redesign the bend, eliminating the blind spot and reducing the risk of accidents. Since that time the bus has not been seen.

SEE ALSO:
- London's various locations; mainly palaces and theatres.

Modbury
(Devonshire)

In 1967 a driver on the road from Modbury to Garabridge saw a black 1920 Daimler Landaulette coming towards him at 7.30 in the evening. As he reached the bend where the two cars should pass each other, he could see no sign of the vehicle nor anywhere that it could have turned off. Just a week later at the same place he saw the same car, but again before the two got together the vehicle had vanished. The same witness experienced this on three occasions and also found two other local people who had seen the same apparition. They were able to add that they had seen the driver who was wearing a peaked chauffeur's cap and dark jacket.

Certainly the description seems to relate to the type of vehicle which in the 1920s and 30s would have driven the roads of Devon, a favourite place for the wealthy to take excursions and picnics in their chauffeur-driven cars.

SEE ALSO:
- Berry Pomeroy Castle.

WHILE YOU'RE THERE:
- Totnes, to the north-east, was the starting point of a trail that zig-zagged about 100 miles through fields, gardens and gates, and over haystacks, walls and roofs, finally ending at Littleham near Bideford. It was a trail known as the devil's footprints – a single line of hoof-prints in the February snows of a particularly harsh winter in 1855. The prints were about eight inches apart and seemed to indicate a biped rather than quadruped creature.

Moretonhampstead
(near Exeter, Devon)

Electrical effects and car stops are a familiar characteristic of that most modern of paranormal encounters – the UFO experience. However, there are one or two accounts of similar effects that seem to be related to ghost sightings. On 4 April 1969 a Mr and Mrs Hunter reported such an experience at four o'clock in the morning on the B3212 near Moretonhampstead, a few miles south-west of Exeter. About half a mile from Moretonhampstead Mrs Hunter pointed out that there was a car coming along the road towards them; they could see the headlights approaching from some couple of hundred yards away. Mr Hunter, concerned at the speed the car seemed to be moving, swung the wheel over and ditched their car on the side of the road – but no car passed them. On trying to restart the car Mr Hunter found the battery was flat although it had performed faultlessly prior to that. A garage mechanic at Moretonhampstead was puzzled by the problem and commented: 'Every bit of energy has been drained out'. He himself had also been on that road and was sure that no car had gone in the direction the Hunters had indicated for at least two hours. The Hunters also learned that theirs was not an isolated report but that several other people had seen the same thing on misty mornings in the same area; an AA patrolman recalled that a vehicle had crashed on that bend about five years ago and the driver had been killed.

This electrical effect implicitly connected to the proximity of the ghost sighting was one also reported in November 1960 by a Mrs Dorothy Strong, who was in a taxi at Otterburn in Northumberland and saw a phantom army that had been reported by others. As she described it: 'Suddenly the engine died, the fare meter went haywire and the taxi was as if it was being forced against an invisible wall. The soldiers seemed to close in on us and then fade into thin air.'

Many ghost-researchers have indicated that manifestations must require some form of energy, and point particularly to the temperature drops associated with many apparition sightings. In this instance perhaps we are seeing a different 'sucking up' of energy – of electrical rather than heat energy.

SEE ALSO:
• Cheriton Cross.

Penhill Beacon
(Wensleydale, North Yorkshire)

Philip Atkins, of the National Railway Museum in York, reported to us a ghostly story that had happened to a close friend of his. Driving in the tiny green lanes around Penhill Beacon, near Wensleydale, his friend saw what seemed to be two headlights approaching. What he could see was two beams coming up from over the other side of the hill further down the road, one beam slightly stronger than the other. But they disappeared and no car was seen. His friend saw the lights several times and even took his girlfriend to see them. (Philip Atkins later went with him but unfortunately saw nothing on his visit.)

SEE ALSO:

• Richmond Castle, Richmond.

Uplyme
(near Lyme Regis, Dorset)

In 1970, when he was nine years old, a boy was out cycling with friends at Uplyme in Dorset. He got some way ahead of his friends and was out of their sight when he saw what he described as a stage-coach 'like you see in pictures'. Red and black with gold trimmings, it was pulled by four horses. The driver wore an eye mask and had a red feather in his cap; there were two other men riding outside the coach. The boy saw the coach turn out of a white gate and come straight towards him. He momentarily looked away and when he looked back it had vanished.

Some of the details seem to tie in with the history of the road. It was in fact the old coaching road at Whitty Hill, and at the point where the boy saw the coach there used to be white gates, probably unknown to him at that time.

SEE ALSO:

• Parish Church of St Mary, Beaminster, Dorset.

Wool
(Dorset)

One of the most famous phantom coaches must be that which Thomas Hardy fictionalized in 1891 in his novel *Tess of the D'Urbervilles*: 'There momentarily flashed through his mind that the family tradition of the coach and murder might have arisen because the D'Urbervilles had been known to do these things'.

The real story arises at Woolbridge Manor, once the home of the Turbervilles. The ghostly carriage rides from Woolbridge Manor to the old Turberville Pile at Bere Regis. It is said that it can only be seen by those of the Turberville blood. One local bus driver saw the coach and stopped his own coach to allow it to pass, much to the amazement of the passengers, who could see nothing.

SEE ALSO:

- Corfe Castle.
- Clouds Hill.
- Priory Church, Christchurch.
- Town Museum, Poole.

WHILE YOU'RE THERE:

- You are very close to Owermoigne and Moigne Downs, where Angus Brooks had a significant UFO sighting while walking his dog in October 1967. At a time when there were many reports from the south of England of cross-shaped lights at night, Angus reported one of the few star-shaped, indeed shape-shifting, UFOs during a daylight sighting of some duration.

CHAPTER 10

~

GHOSTS OF THE RAILWAYS

Great Northern Line

During the last century an engine driver of the great steam locomotives that ploughed the Great Northern Line told the story of a protective ghost he encountered one night. He was driving the 8.30 train from Kings Cross north and for the first time in his life felt nervous about the ride. He stated: 'I don't know nothing about ghosts of spirits, or apparitions – call 'em what you like – but I am ready to swear before any judge today that I saw something of the kind that night, and no amount of argument will change my belief. It was just when we were passing through Hatfield when, I would take my oath for all I am worth that a man stepped from the platform to the foot-plate, just as easily as though we weren't travelling about fifty-five miles an hour. I can see his face and dress to this day. It was the saddest face I ever came across. The eyes seemed to look you through and through; and when on top of that I saw that he was all in black, I never was so afraid in my life.' The driver pointed out that the fireman saw nothing and continued acting as if there was nothing amiss. The driver continued: 'I soon noticed that the strange-comer never went to any other part of the foot-plate except to the spot whereon I stood, and he even hedged up so close to me that I went cold all over, and my feet were like lumps of ice. I think I must have acted mechanically, for I watched the man put his hand upon the regulator, and I put mine on with him. The touch of it was like the touch of snow, but I couldn't loose it, and before I knew what I'd done, the steam was cut off and the train was slowing.' The fireman apparently thought the driver had gone mad and came down to see what was going on as the train slowed down. Up the line, the signal indicated that the way ahead was clear. However, 'there were two trucks across the main line, and although the signals were off, the way was blocked, so that me and the passengers behind me, wouldn't be living to tell the story if I hadn't been compelled to pull up as I did.'

Mayfield Station
(Greater Manchester)

In the 1950s Mayfield Station, a parcels depot, had a reputation for being haunted by those who worked there. Even then it was run down, dilapidated and in desperate need of repair, no doubt adding to the eerie atmosphere. One night, after the station had been closed for some hours, one man was on duty in the foreman's office. He heard the clear sound of footsteps approaching from another office, pass the office he was in, pause at the window and then continue towards a baggage hoist. The footsteps then stopped. Two others, Ted Dyson and Charlie Movey, also heard the footsteps. On the second occasion Movey heard them he turned on the lights all over the station and was able to see that no one was present, though he could still hear the footsteps coming towards him. He heard them pass close to him and then they ceased. The foreman, Fred Jinks, heard the footsteps three times but never saw anyone. However, he did know the history of the baggage hoist: one night a workman had fallen to his death into the fifty-foot deep shaft.

In addition to the accident at the baggage hoist there had been two suicides in the station, which may have had some bearing on the hauntings. Both involved hanging, one in the indicator box and the other in the men's toilets.

Mayfield is no longer in use as a parcels depot, the lines having been removed. As you approach Piccadilly Station you can still see where the old spur used to be, running away to the left from the main line. The site is now often used for television and film locations: for example, the reader may have seen the area in the television series *Cracker*.

SEE ALSO:
• Belmont Road, Bolton, Greater Manchester.
• Stalybridge, Greater Manchester.
• Hyde, Greater Manchester.

National Railway Museum
(York, North Yorkshire)

In 1997 Mr Philip Atkins, librarian of the National Railway Museum in York, assisted us with several questions relating to ghosts of the railways, and also related to us stories of alleged hauntings in the Museum itself.

The main centre of the reports would seem to have been around the photographic studio. There, a revolving door often turns 'purposefully' and leads people to expect someone to walk out, but there is no one there. In the dark-room several people have felt a 'blowing' or 'breathing' on their necks, though again there is no one present.

In the second exhibition hall one journalist interviewing there – during the day, in broad daylight – felt her necklace being tugged. No one was present at the time.

Perhaps most dramatically, there is a belief that a sleeping car in the museum that was used on night ferries is haunted – it was believed that during the war the Germans used it as a brothel. Perhaps some of the emotions that it saw then have come to the present time!

SEE ALSO:

- Theatre Royal, York.
- Treasurer's House, York.
- Sheriff Hutton (A64).

WHILE YOU'RE THERE:

- Visit the churchyard of St Denys and St George. It contains the tomb of Dick Turpin, probably the most famous highwayman in England, who was hanged at York in 1739. His ghost has been reported in various parts of the country. The leg irons that held him while awaiting execution are displayed in York Castle Museum.

Southend-on-Sea
(to Shenfield, Essex)

The Southend to Shenfield railway runs past Southend Airport through Rochford, loops around Hockley and goes inland through Wickford and Billericay to Shenfield. An event on the line was reported in *Ghosts and Hauntings* No. 7. In 1919 a Shenfield man had been to the Southend Hippodrome with his girlfriend, had walked her home but had lingered too long and was in danger of missing the last train to Shenfield. He was running through the station as he heard the guard's whistle allowing the train to leave, did not stop to get a ticket and threw himself into the moving carriage at the last moment. The carriage was empty.

At Rochford a ticket inspector entered the carriage. The man explained why he did not have a ticket and the inspector made out a docket, handed it to him, wished him goodnight and left the carriage. Later in the journey, near Billericay, another ticket inspector awoke the man, who had fallen into a doze. The man again explained his circumstances but told this inspector that he had already paid the previous inspector. The inspector now standing in front of him was adamant that he was the only one on the train. The man pulled out the docket he had been given and handed it to the inspector now standing in front of him, who asked for a description of the first inspector.

The description was given: 'About forty, clean shaven, reddish hair, I'm certain about that because he took his hat off, and he had a large scar on his forehead.' The inspector was shaken. The description he had just heard was of Ginger Rhodes. He had died while saving a child who had fallen on the rails at Rayleigh, part of the same line. On looking at the docket they realized that it was not dated 1919 but 24 December 1913, which the inspector confirmed was 'the night Ginger was killed'.

This is a fascinating story, but one that experienced ghosthunters recognize as just 'a little too good'. We might speculate that perhaps the true story is that some form of ghostly apparition was seen and that the story became embroidered over the years. We have introduced this story as a caution both to 'believers' and 'sceptics' alike; stories are embroidered over time usually in a way which 'ties up the loose ends' in a way that the confusing spontaneity of actual ghost interaction rarely allows for. But by the same token the case should not be totally dismissed, as the story may well be an embroidery but based on a real event.

If we assume that the case is genuine but we had to attribute what probably reality we thought applied to it, then we might bear in mind that at least on part of the journey the man was dozing because he was woken up by the second, 'real', inspector. Perhaps his interaction with Ginger was while he was dozing, i.e. in a lightly altered state. Perhaps he picked up psychic traces of Ginger, perhaps Ginger's ghost was able to interact with him because of his state of mind; all of that may well be plausible and possible.

SEE ALSO:

• Rochford Hall (cyclical ghosts).

Tebay
(Cumbria)

The *Westmoreland Gazette* of 1983 reports that railway enthusiast David Johnson accidentally photographed what appears to be a ghost at Tebay in the Lake District. Seeing an old steam train, a Britannia Class locomotive, on an isolated section of the main line, he photographed it. On developing the film, he could see standing on the embankment the cloaked figure of a woman he was certain had not been there when he took the photograph.

Johnson, knowledgeable in local legend, convinced himself that it was one Mary Baines. Baines, sometimes known as the Witch of Tebay, died in 1811 at the age of ninety and was locally notorious for her powers of prophecy. One of her prophecies was that 'carriages without horses shall run over Loups Fell'. Mr Johnson believes that perhaps the figure he photographed was Mary Baines, proudly checking on her prophecy.

Although it would be speculation at best, it is an interesting exercise to 'play the game' and consider another possibility still. How did Mary Baines know that one day 'carriages without horses' would run in the area? Perhaps somehow she projected herself into the future and saw them and, if so, was her projection the ghost that Johnson photographed not checking up on her prophecy but actually in the process of discovering something she would later prophesy?

SEE ALSO:
- Rydal Mount.
- Cark Hall/Holker Hall, near Cartmel.
- Gaythorne Hall, Tebay.
- Reston House, near Ings.

GHOSTS WITH A PURPOSE

As this book shows, the word 'ghost' is a term that covers a wide range of phenomena, from phantasms of the living (there are two reports in Chapter 17 of people seen in bilocation – two places at once), to 'recordings' of the dead. Perhaps 'ghost' also contains a reference to remnants of the deceased which have survived after death, but this is by no means as certain as popular belief would make out. However, if there is a claim for such, then ghosts with a purpose would seem to be evidence for it.

The ghosts in these accounts seem to have had some mission to accomplish after death, and appeared as ghosts to the living. John Thurlow Reade's ghost, for example, an apparition seen by his mother in a time of distress, does not seem to have brought her much comfort, but it did suggest his imminent death which turned out to have been correct. The rock-climber on Scafell has a mindful friend to thank for his attentions. The staff at Sudeley Castle and Althorp House continuing to do their jobs seems strange – most people look forward to retirement however much they enjoy their jobs, but perhaps they were exceptions. The young subaltern seen at the Coliseum, St Martin's Lane, seems not to have much mission to undertake, perhaps just to see the show again, but who knows what is important to an individual? Grimshaw's sense of injustice is easier to understand; though his manner of imparting the information of his innocence certainly veers towards the dramatic.

But there are other possibilities which relate to the purpose being that of the living rather than the dead. To Reade's mother, was the apparition her way of picturing her fears about his death, already inspired by his unusual break in his habit of writing? Or perhaps even a telepathic sensing of his distress or death? Was the image of the friend to the rock-climber actually a complex construction by the latter to access his subconscious memory for knowledge of a way out of the difficulty in which he found himself? It is said that everything we sense is recorded in our memories; it is the accessing of the memories that is sometimes hard – perhaps constructing a ghost to 'lead the way' is a theatrical way of allowing the subconscious to lead. In any case, in modern America such a figure would probably not be regarded as a ghost but as a guardian angel; there is a rich body of material about modern angels which is similar to British ghost stories.

The pleas of the lady of the Hungerford family, passed through a psychic, that she is unhappy about being 'on show' could so easily be a projection of the respectful concern of the native American. Perhaps a certain amount of more 'frantic' purpose is shown by the desire of skulls to remain in their homes and designated locations. But why skulls?

Although it is true that hauntings have been associated with all sorts of parts of the body – religious relics include skulls, hearts, hands, etc. – skulls predominate in these non-religious reports. Hauntings have also been associated with non-human objects, as we have catalogued in our other books on the subject, objects such as the Hexham heads, a haunted model cottage and a number of paintings endowed with ghostly qualities.

But skulls are the most common such objects. The entries here are only a small list of the total around the country. Many are in private homes and not appropriate to this book, and a few are in homes which have traditionally allowed visitors but where an endless parade of ghosthunters – asking the same old questions, one man told us – have made the owners retire from publicly discussing their relics, at least for the time being.

But why skulls? We are emotive about skulls presumably because the skull surrounds and protects the mind, which is thought to be the seat of where the person 'really' lives in his or her body. It is the place where the consciousness is deemed to be – though even that is a matter for philosophical debate.

Whatever the truth or logic of the argument, we must remember that the preservation of the skulls sometimes starts with the living, not just with mythology. Catherine Griffith, for example, asked for her skull to remain in the house. For others, such as Dorothy Cook's victim of the Philipson family, the skull represented the haunting itself. We might consider that the skull also has more emotive imagery than other parts of the bodies. The 'grinning' teeth, the empty eye-sockets, are a powerful image. The skull and crossbones was the flag of fear of pirates, using the same image.

As with all ghost reports, when we study ghosts that seem to have purpose we stand a chance of learning something about ghosts, perhaps something about death, and certainly something about the living and the human mind.

CHAPTER 11

~

GHOSTS WITH A MISSION

Althorp Park
(Northamptonshire)

Althorp Park is the family home of the Spencer family, including the late and much-loved Lady Diana Spencer, Princess of Wales.

One of its well-known ghosts, though sighted only once in the early 1800s, is that of a groom to George John, 2nd Earl Spencer. The story was recorded in *Haunted Houses and Family Traditions of Great Britain* by J. Ingram, published in 1900. A guest at the house, a clergyman named Drury, retired late to bed after a game of billiards with Earl Spencer's son-in-law Lord Littleton, but was awoken during the night by a bright light shining in his eyes. He saw a male figure in a striped shirt and flat cap standing by his bed. The figure was holding a bright lantern. He enquired as to the reason for the intrusion and was probably somewhat annoyed by the total silence which he got in response. Indeed, it is reported that after being continually ignored he lost his temper and shouted that he would report the intrusion to the Earl in the morning. In response, if response be the word, the figure by his bed silently lowered the lantern, turned away and walked towards the dressing-room. Drury turned aside and fell asleep. The following morning he reported the incident to Lady Littleton, suggesting that perhaps the man had been drunk, though admitting there was no other reason for supposing that other than the insolence of the intrusion. Lady Littleton explained the position. Drury had probably seen her father's favourite groom, who had been especially charged with going round the house to ensure that all lights had been extinguished, particularly to ensure that guests had not fallen asleep leaving lights burning. Her father had a considerable fear of fire, something which Drury had been informed of at the end of his billiard game the night before. Lady Littleton explained to Drury, however, that the groom in question had died a fortnight earlier. Whether some conscious part of the groom's spirit was still carrying out his instructions or whether he represented that category of ghosts known as recordings is uncertain. The fact that the apparition was non-interactive, completely ignoring Drury, suggests the latter.

Another ghost seen around the turn of the twentieth century was a young child seen in the picture gallery. One of the young Spencer girls often saw the child coming through a doorway. The apparition's clothes were at least half a century out of date. It is believed that the child was an ancestor of the family; records indicate that there were a number of Spencers in the eighteenth century who died in childhood.

Again, whether the apparition was interactive or not is uncertain. The apparition did not speak to the young girl who saw her, though it appears she did smile at her. Much more recently the ghost of Albert Edward John Spencer, 7th Earl, grandfather of the Diana, Princess of Wales, has been seen. He died in 1975, but was seen by several young relatives at a party for his son and new wife several months later, apparently mingling and smiling with the guests. The wife of the butler at Althorp twice saw the 7th Earl's ghost, the first time even addressing him: 'How nice to see you, my Lord,' before realizing precisely what she was doing! The 7th Earl apparently smiled by way of response. Shortly afterwards a workman in Althorp also saw the same ghost. The 7th Earl apparently loved Althorp Park; many believe that that is why he has not yet left it.

When we spoke to those at Althorp in 1997 they confirmed the sighting by the housekeeper but were unaware of any recent hauntings.

SEE ALSO:
- Grosvenor Centre, Northampton.

WHILE YOU'RE THERE:
- About five miles to the south of Althorpe is the A5 near Weedon. It was on this road in November 1978 that Mrs Elsie Oakensen, head of Daventry Teacher's Centre, saw a UFO, suffered a 'missing time' episode and believes that she was contacted by non-human beings and given a spiritual 'scanning'.

Belmont Road
(Bolton, Greater Manchester)

One of the more dramatic, almost classical, ghost sightings associated with phantom hitch-hikers is that of Belmont Road in Bolton, apparently haunted by the ghost of an executed highwayman. The ghost appears with ropes still hanging round his neck, eyes bulging and desperately trying to speak but able to make no sound.

The story is that a highwayman by the name of Horrocks who operated in the area left some stolen booty in a place where he could recover it later. However, it was discovered by a man called Grimshaw, who took the opportunity to keep it and try to sell it rather than report the find. Grimshaw was eventually charged with the highway robbery in which the jewellery had been stolen, and the court did not accept his plea of having found the goods. Consequently Grimshaw was hanged at Preston in 1780 and it is his ghost that is seen, perhaps still trying to mouth his protest at his sentence or plead his innocence.

SEE ALSO:
- Mayfield Station.
- Rivington Castle, near Horwich.

Coliseum
(St Martin's Lane, London)

A young subaltern died during one of the last battles of the First World War on 3 October 1918. His last hours in England had been spent at the Coliseum, for which perhaps he had an affinity; those hours were at the very least his last peace-time memory. At the precise moment of his death, friends of his who were in the Coliseum saw him walk down the gangway of the circle and take a seat in the second row. They did not learn of his death until a few days later.

Although there were reports of the subaltern's ghost appearing several times subsequently, they shortly ceased altogether and have not been reported since.

SEE ALSO:
- London's various locations; mainly palaces and theatres.

Farleigh Hungerford
(near Trowbridge, Somerset)

Farleigh Hungerford Castle dates from the fourteenth century. It was built by Sir Thomas Hungerford on the site of an even older castle and today consists of castle ruins and a chapel.

Ghost-researchers Tony Wells and Melanie Warren interviewed Maggie, who worked in the ticket office, who told an interesting story. A native American who was in England on his first visit apparently received 'impressions' and a message from one of the Hungerford ancestors while he was visiting the crypt. The crypt holds the coffins of six adults and two children of the Hungerford family from sixteenth and seventeenth centuries. He told Maggie, 'Excuse me, but she is very unhappy; you've got her on show and she doesn't like people staring at her'. The visitor told Maggie that 'the Hungerford ancestor' had asked to be covered over with green velvet. If Maggie was feeling dismissive of the message for one reason or another, she was startled when the man specifically asked if she was Maggie, by name. He then told her that the 'woman' in the crypt had given him a message for her. The message was: 'You are not to worry about your night in the crypt, as she will look after you'. Now Maggie had to sit up and think. She had mentioned to her husband spending the night in the crypt in a sponsored fund-raising night for charity. The event had not yet even been organized and she was certain there was no way the tourist could know of her intentions.

However, the one ghost that is seen is a lady in the chapel next to the crypt, usually seen around eleven o'clock on Saturday mornings. The one thing often mentioned is that she wears a green dress.

SEE ALSO:

* Theatre Royal, Bath.
* Frome.
* Warminster.

WHILE YOU'RE THERE:

* Drive along the Frome–Nunney Road, but beware of who you pick up hitch-hiking there. In 1977 a witness offered a hitch-hiker a lift; he got into the back seat and the driver secured the doors. They talked very little, the hitch-hiker commenting that he was cold. When the driver asked his guest a question he got no response, and when he looked round there was no one in the car. Police were not unused to these reports, commenting: 'We have had people coming here in a state of virtual hysteria'.

Ipsden Church
(Ipsden, Oxfordshire)

In the country lanes around Ipsden is a memorial of white stone topped by a pyramid on which can be read:

John Thurlow Reade
Esquire
Sehaarunpore
November 15 A.D. 1827
'Alas my brother'

The stone, and an organ loft screen in Ipsden Church, were erected by John Reade's brother Edward in 1860. The memorial must be one of very few in the country erected on the site of, and in response to, a ghost sighting.

John Reade left England for India in 1817 to work for the East India Company. He was a devoted member of the family, regularly corresponding with his mother, for whom he had great affection. After an unexpected length of time, during which she received no letter, she had an intuition that she should walk down the road to obtain news of her son. While walking down the road she saw the apparition of her son, obviously distressed. She became convinced that he was dead but also that he had been buried without a proper Christian service, and she was able to persuade the local vicar to hold the burial service which would bring her son peace. The above monument is erected on the site of the apparition.

Her intuition proved to be correct. She was later informed of her son's death and that his servants had buried him on the spot where he had died.

Louth
(Lincolnshire)

Louth's most famous and popular ghost story has inspired a song called 'The Spanish Lady'.

Thorpe Hall is a Tudor mansion on the Elkington Road, just outside Louth. During the Elizabethan wars with the Spanish the owner of Thorpe Hall, Sir John Bolle, fell captive to the Spaniards and was imprisoned. He was regularly visited in his cell by a Spanish noblewoman and over time they fell in love. It is said that she bribed his gaolers with jewels. They allowed him to escape and she paid his way back to England with her remaining jewels. She, of course, hopelessly in love with Sir John, wished to accompany him, but he was married and could not allow her to return to England with him. Her passion would not subside, however, and she followed him to England, arriving at Thorpe Hall dressed in a beautiful billowing dress of green. But she arrived only to see Sir John with his family and, despairing, took her own life by stabbing herself in the garden, under an oak tree.

Her ghost, always seen clad in green and known as the Green Lady, has been seen many times. She once walked out in front of a cyclist, who fell off his bike trying to avoid hitting her. He got up ready to remonstrate with her but found she was nowhere to be seen. In the 1930s the vicar of Elkington, driving home during heavy rain, saw the woman dressed in green walking in the middle of the road. He wound down the window to offer help but noticed that her dress, far from bedraggled and wet, was perfectly dry and blowing as if in a summer breeze. Almost immediately when he looked for the figure again the road was empty.

It is said that in more recent years there have been fewer sightings. If she is a 'recordings' ghost, then the replay is perhaps becoming weaker. If she is interactive, then perhaps she is finally moving on to a more peaceful existence.

SEE ALSO:

• Cawthorpe.

Scafell Crag
(Cumbria)

A.H. Griffin in *In Mountain Lakeland* recalls a crisis apparition which appeared to a rock climber on Scafell Crag. The climber was a friend of a rock climber of considerable reputation who was away fighting in France during the First World War. During a climb one summer's afternoon this friend, who he had thought was in France, joined him. The climber was pleasantly surprised, as he had not realized his friend was home on leave. Together they walked the fells but later the soldier parted company, promising to see the other later. Some days later he received a letter from France telling him that his friend had been killed in action on the very afternoon that he had walked with him on the fells.

Sudeley Castle
(near Winchcombe, Gloucestershire)

The original castle is now largely in ruins but there was substantial restoration in Victorian times. It is from this era that the following known haunting dates.

The figure seen was described as a Victorian housekeeper, dressed in a long grey dress, striped apron and cap. She is believed to be 'Janet', who took it upon herself to make sure that when the owners were away for the season in London she would keep the men and women servants apart. She apparently sat on the staircase to ensure that no 'hanky-panky' took place by preventing contact between the men servants who were quartered 'below stairs' and the female servants whose bedrooms were upstairs. In the 1980s a school party visiting Sudeley Castle included a girl of twelve who was walking up the stairs when she saw the apparition standing in her way. 'Janet' apparently brushed a feather duster into the girl's face, frightening her considerably. An elderly housekeeper at Sudeley confirmed that the girl's description sounded very much like Janet, whom he remembered from his youth at the castle. There have been several other reports of the figure.

SEE ALSO:

- Deerhurst Priory, near Tewkesbury.

WHILE YOU'RE THERE:

- Winchcombe itself sports a 'recordings-style' figure, possibly a monk, suggestive of changes in the ground level. He is seen walking from the direction of the railway station two feet above the present ground level.

CHAPTER 12

~

SCREAMING SKULLS

Brigham
(near Cockermouth, Cumbria)

It is alleged that Brigham used to have a churchyard which was haunted by the Carlisle hangman, Joseph Wilson, after his suicide by drowning at Cockermouth in 1757. Apparently the sexton of the graveyard, concerned about the constant hauntings, dug up Wilson's skull and gave it to the occupants of the cottage where Wilson had lived. The skull remained in the cottage and the haunting ceased.

WHILE YOU'RE THERE:

- Red Tarn is a small mountain lake between Wrynose and Langdale, situated to the south-east of Brigham, and used to be the hiding place of a smuggler called Lanty Slee. Jessica Lofthouse, in *North Country Folklore*, wrote in 1976 of an incident which her friends experienced – of following footprints in the snow from Wrynose Bottoms to the Tarn where they ended, with no sign of anyone, nor any hole in the ice.

Burton Agnes Manor House
(Burton Agnes, East Riding of Yorkshire)

An Elizabethan mansion, Burton Agnes Manor House contains bricked up in its walls the skull of Catherine (Anne) Griffith. Burton Agnes Hall Preservation Trust Ltd., were kind enough to send us information relating to the Hall and to Catherine's ghost.

Catherine, the youngest of three daughters of the Hall's builder, Sir Henry Griffith, died in 1620 while the manor house was being built. She loved the Hall and spoke of little else, but on a trip to nearby Hapham she was waylaid and robbed. She died of her injuries a few days later at Burton Agnes. She told her sisters, perhaps in delirium, that she would never rest unless her head was allowed to stay in the Hall. The sisters humoured her, but she was buried, intact, in the churchyard.

Her ghost was seen restlessly walking, particularly in the Queen's State Bedroom. The sisters, remembering her wishes, were able to get the local vicar to agree to exhume the body, remove the skull, and have it brought into the house. While it remained there, there was peace. But each time it was removed horrible screaming was heard until such time as it was returned, and often the ghost was seen to walk.

The skull is now said to be bricked into the structure of the Hall, but no one knows for sure where. Some say it is behind the panelling of the Great Hall. Since it was made permanently 'resident' the ghost has been quiet and not seen or heard.

SEE ALSO:
- Scarborough Castle.

Calgarth Hall
(Lake Windermere, Cumbria)

Calgarth Hall stands on Lake Windermere, near Troutbeck Bridge. It belonged many years ago to the Philipson family, one of whom was known as Robin the Devil. It was said that Robin murdered two people and that their skulls could not be taken from that place.

What is thought to be a more reliable version of the story is that Myles Philipson framed two neighbours, Kraster and Dorothy Cook, when they refused to sell him a parcel of land. He accused them of stealing a silver cup which he planted on the land, and the Cooks were hanged. Dorothy cursed the land, and the house which Philipson built there was troubled by ghostly skulls which could never be removed. Even when taken away and destroyed they would be found back in the house again. Eventually the house was exorcized by Bishop Watson of Llandaff who bought the estate.

A lot of these stories were rumours put around by Cromwellians or Royalists during the Civil War to discredit the opponents. By the same token the rumours were often based on some core of true story.

SEE ALSO:
- Rydal Mount.

WHILE YOU'RE THERE:
- At nearby Langdale, the Langdale Outdoor Education Centre occupied a site where, in an early part of the twentieth century, a gunpowder

factory was located. In September 1916 there was an explosion at the factory which killed four men. A ghost frequently seen at the centre is believed to be one of them, John Foxcroft. Described as bearded, with a pock-marked face and wearing an old-fashioned collarless shirt and flat leather cap, he was seen in several parts of the centre looking through windows, walking in passageways and dormitories, etc. According to the *Westmoreland Gazette* he was seen last in September 1979. Several schoolchildren reported seeing him and sketched what they saw, and these pictures and descriptions closely match the features of John Foxcroft.

Threlkeld Place
(Threlkeld, Cumbria)

When a farmer took over a property from a tenant farmer he found that one room had been unused. In it he discovered a skull occupying a hole in a wall. This he removed and buried out of respect, but shortly afterwards discovered it back in its place. Determined to be rid of it, now that it had frightened him, he threw it out to sea but found it had returned again. Ultimately he bricked up the skull in the place where it seemed to want to be and the matter seems to have been left there. This legend is similar to many around the country.

GHOSTLY EXTRAS

There are experiences that fit into the category that we loosely call 'hauntings' but which are arguably not ghosts – a word that encompasses so much that it has almost become meaningless. In this section we look at cases of two types of commonly reported such phenomena: timeslips and poltergeists.

A timeslip is the perception of seeing into another time, usually the past, though occasionally the future. There are a great many accounts of 'time-slips' from around the world, generally exhibiting the characteristics of the cases included here. Assuming that we eliminate pure imagination, then we are looking at several possible 'mechanisms' to explain these visions.

Perhaps the sighter is seeing a huge 'recordings' ghost, not just of a person but of a whole scene. This is not too unlikely, given the reports of whole battles replayed and so on. But there is something in the quality of the experience, according to the witnesses involved, that seems to make this a less likely explanation. One woman we spoke to who had experienced walking into a room that used to be an old theatre, seeing it active in its full glory of centuries ago, certainly seemed to feel that she was 'really there' rather than just viewing.

That leaves us looking for alternatives. One of these is that the person is viewing through a sort of 'doorway', a bridge, between times. Another is that the person is somehow, presumably psychically, 'time-travelling' and becomes a part of the time they perceive. Another is that they see through the eyes of a person living in that previous time. There are cases that suggest all possibilities, and indeed perhaps there is more than one answer to these types of cases. Perhaps Mrs Rawlings at St Albans saw through the eyes of someone who once really watched the Roman procession she witnessed. The people seen in Dallington Church were 'transparent'; perhaps it was the effect of viewing through time. Perhaps Air Marshal Sir Victor Goddard actually travelled in time and flew over Drem years later. We know of one case where passengers on a modern electric train saw what seemed to be a Victorian station-master waving a lantern at them, and he looked as shocked as they did – who was the ghost there? Who was doing the timeslipping?

As quantum physics opens up possibilities for new understanding of the nature of the universe, so probably it will change our view of the nature of time. And who knows what the possibilities are?

Poltergeists are the original 'things that go bump in the night', and for many people represent the most well-known form of haunting. Yet there are many possible explanations offered to account for poltergeists, not all of them ghostly in the strict sense.

There are four front-runner theories to account for a poltergeist:

- The spirit of a dead human.
- A mischievous entity from 'another plane'.
- A living focus in a certain state of mind to allow the manifestation of the actions of one or other of the above.
- A living focus creating, subconsciously, RSPK – recurrent spontaneous psycho-kinesis.

There is certainly a body of evidence, as we have set out in our book *The Poltergeist Phenomenon*, that at least some poltergeist activity is internally generated by the 'witnesses' themselves as a response to their personal circumstances. We believe that stress, and particularly extreme and unrelievable frustration, may be the driving energy that 'exteriorizes' and creates the sounds and movements which are the typical poltergeist manifestation. One case we know related to a woman who had undergone a mastectomy; one of several pairs of ornaments were found broken. As her cancer worsened, her other breast was removed and the breakages became more 'random'. As she came to terms with her condition, the poltergeistery stopped. It seems highly unlikely that a deceased person, or even a mischievous spirit, would cause such specific damage, and more likely that it represents the woman's own frustrations.

That said, there are other cases, the Enfield case of the 1970s for example, that suggest more than just RSPK. There were stories of hauntings in that location, and information coming through the focus that related to a death in the house. If we believe that there are such things as ghosts, and haunted sites, then we must consider that sometimes the most spectacular cases of all – rarely, perhaps thankfully – are the combination of a person able to generate RSPK in a site that is already haunted. Langenhoe in Chapter 14 might represent such a site.

The personal nature of poltergeists is also suggested by our entry on the Great Bed of Ware (page 227). Of all poltergeist phenomena there is probably no more consistent area of a house that is 'affected' than the bedroom, and specifically the bed itself, and the bedcovers. Covers have been reported thrown off, moving on their own, and so on. We consider that it is possible that the bed is also the most personal of locations, and that this should be so affected suggests that the poltergeist is not only personal, but relates to the intimate side of our psyche. On the other hand, perhaps the bed was simply haunted: it would not be the first inanimate object to carry ghosts around with it. We have known of many such objects, including haunted paintings, haunted cars, and more.

CHAPTER 13

~

TIMESLIPS AND TIME PORTALS

Dallington Church
(Northampton, Northamptonshire)

In 1907 two young girls visited Dallington Church and were somewhat surprised to find the place full of visitors kneeling at prayer. They became more alarmed when they realized that the figures were 'transparent' – a rarer claim for ghosts than many imagine, incidentally. Apart from this mass gathering, which seems to suggest something of a timeslip, there are also reports from the church of the ghost of a grey-haired lady seen from time to time.

SEE ALSO:

• Grosvenor Centre.

WHILE YOU'RE THERE:

• Visit Becket's Well. It contains a medieval style of well housing. The waters are reputed to ease blindness.

Drem Airfield
(East Lothian, Scotland)

In 1934 Air Marshal Sir Victor Goddard was flying over Scotland on a misty and rainy day. As he flew lower, looking for a landmark, he saw bathed in sunlight the disused airfield at Drem. He was able quite clearly to see yellow aircraft on the runway with technicians dressed in blue overalls. Air Marshal Goddard flew on and thought no more about this until 1938, when the airfield was back in action as a flight training station. The aircraft were, for the very first time, painted yellow and the ground crew were issued with a new-style blue uniform. It seems Air Marshal Goddard had a view in 1934 of how the airfield would look later when it reopened.

SEE ALSO:

• Holyrood House, Edinburgh.

WHILE YOU'RE THERE:

• On the road back towards Edinburgh you will find Tranent and nearby Penkaet Castle to the south-east. A murder took place here; the castle is haunted by the sounds of knockings and of dragging across the floor. Charles I's ghost is also said to haunt here.

Farnham Parish Church
(Farnham, Surrey)

A classic 'little old lady' ghost appears to be the most common apparition associated with the parish church in Farnham. Several people have seen her walking into the church and have even occasionally followed her, only to discover on entering the church that she is not there and has disappeared. A curate, the Reverend Allan Wheeler, has seen the ghost several times and commented, 'I thought she was absolutely real and so did a colleague who was with me on one occasion'. In addition there would appear to be a ghostly priest, whom even the church warden spoke to only to discover the priest was not real.

There are reports of the sounds of horses, heard as if behind the church; sounds suggesting horses tethered and standing, perhaps 'champing at the bit' and occasionally scratching their hooves on the ground. Though there are no horses there at present, it is known that the church was used as stables during the English Civil War. Other sounds emanating from within the church include Latin chanting, reported during the Second World War.

The church also has a report from the 1960s of what would appear to be a classic timeslip, suggesting again that there is something particular about this church or its location which 'captures' elements of the past. A visitor to the church, sitting alone, suddenly saw the building full of people and watched all the ornamental finery of a Catholic High Mass being observed. She could even smell the incense. The vision was experienced in silence; the usual music and singing of the Mass was absent. She turned as the door of the church opened and saw the Rector entering; when she looked back towards the altar the church was once again deserted and 'normal'.

SEE ALSO:

• Farnham Castle.

WHILE YOU'RE THERE:

• Farnham, like Pluckley in Kent, is a town heralded by some as 'the most haunted town in England', so the keen ghostwatcher will not be short of possibilities. Take a walk down Castle Street: there are reports of a phantom coach which deposits a drunken dandy on to the streets. East Street sports the ghost of a woman seen in old-fashioned dress, and West Street has received many reports of a ghostly black dog. At Bourne Mill there are reports of a spectral woman dressed in crinoline.

Hastings Castle
(Hastings, East Sussex)

This castle, on the East Sussex coast, may have been built on the site of a very ancient church. There are church ruins in the grounds and it is thought that the church held an important position; Archbishop Anselm is thought to have preached to King Stephen there and Thomas à Becket probably preached there too.

The castle reports an anonymous ghost which walks on the cliff edge. The curtain wall of the castle ends where the cliff has eroded, and clairvoyants have reported to the custodians that they have felt a 'presence' there.

The castle also appears to be prone to 'time-slipping' if the reports of local fishermen are correct. Some say that on sunny, misty mornings they have seen the castle in its former glory, with pennants flying from the turrets.

SEE ALSO:

• Brede Place.

WHILE YOU'RE THERE:

• The abbey at Battle, to the north, marks the actual site of the Battle of Hastings. There is a belief that the ground seeps blood during rain – the Normans called the site Senlac, the Lake of Blood – though if there is any origin to the belief it is probably that iron in the soil sometimes adds a red tinge to the puddles that form.

Letham
(near Forfar, Angus, Scotland)

On 2 January 1950 Miss E.F. Smith was returning home from a party. She was driving in appalling weather, on treacherous roads, and eight miles from her house in Letham she skidded off the road and ditched the car. She was left with no alternative but to walk home, taking, and for the most part carrying, her dog with her. At around two in the morning she was approaching Letham when she saw figures moving around in a field carrying torches. They were walking a circular path and apparently searching the ground as if looking for something. As she got closer she could see that the men were dressed in the outfits of a former time, rough tights and tunics and carrying swords. Miss Smith's dog became agitated and she hurried home, hoping that the barking of the animal would not wake her fellow villagers.

Investigators for the SPR (Society for Psychical Research) concluded that it was possible she had seen a ghostly shadow of the aftermath of the Battle of Nechtansmere, which had taken place there. In AD 685 the Picts and Northumbrians had battled around the shores of a lake now long gone, the culmination of which was the death of Ecgfrith, King of Northumbria. What she may have seen was the post-battle search for the dead.

SEE ALSO:

• Glamis Castle.

WHILE YOU'RE THERE:

• Just a mile or so to the north is a splendid example of Pictish incised stones. Three stand on a grass verge next to the B9134 outside Aberlemno. There are images carved into the stones of a serpent, a double disc and Z rod, a mirror and comb shape and cup markings. The code to translate these symbols has still to be broken.

St Albans
(Hertfordshire)

St Albans stands on the site of the Roman Verulamium. Certain moments of history seem to produce a large number of recordings-type ghosts, timeslips, and so on, in particular the English Civil War and the Roman occupation. One such imprint arose at the Verulamium arena when a Mrs Rawlings, from Barnet, North London, saw a procession of Romans entering. They were marching in rank and file in full uniform, and the standard-bearers carried what were presumably the unit insignias and in particular the eagles so associated with Roman history. They were preceding an individual dressed in white and wearing a laurel crown, presumed to be a high-ranking official, even perhaps one of the emperors who visited the area. This individual moved to a chair in the centre of a platform area and two standard-bearers positioned themselves on either side. The image then disappeared and Mrs Rawlings was again looking at the Verulamium ruins as they are in modern times.

SEE ALSO:

- St Albans Abbey.
- Verulamium.
- Salisbury Hall.

WHILE YOU'RE THERE:

- Nearby Tyttenhanger House, just south of Colney Heath, is said to be haunted by its builder, Sir Henry Blount, who lived there in the 1600s.

CHAPTER 14

~

POLTERGEISTS

Cecil Higgins Art Gallery
(Bedford, Bedfordshire)

There are a number of haunting and poltergeist-like stories here, described by Jennie Clarke, a secretary at the Gallery.

Poltergeist reports include: in the Back Lobby, when a previous telephone system was in use, dialling could be heard by loud clicking noises audible at the back entrance. Several times an attendant, and also the acting curator, called in during the night would hear the sounds of dialling even though the building was empty and the offices were locked. (In a famous poltergeist case at a workplace in Rosenheim in Germany, use of the telephone was a major aspect.)

On one occasion a member of staff heard the lift door open and the lift move, even though the building was empty. In the general office it is reported that a typewriter started typing on its own. On another occasion a member of staff could clearly hear the chair in front of the typewriter creaking as if occupied, though it – and the room – were empty. In another office a photocopier lid opened and closed spontaneously, and a drawer came out for no reason. This happened twice.

A clock in the Burges Room was inspected and believed to be in desperate need of overhaul, due to the cog teeth being completely worn down. Suddenly, the clock restarted and was working, and chiming, perfectly.

'Hauntings' phenomena: a member of staff looked out of an office window and saw a man leaving the building; he was dressed in an old-fashioned black suit and bowler hat. She questioned the attendants on duty at that door, who stated that nobody had come in or out in the previous half hour.

In the loft area some workmen apparently had an experience they did not feel they wanted to discuss. They left, stating only that they would never again return there. There are reports from upstairs rooms of 'presences'. One member of staff reported hearing mutterings and feeling warm air (like breath) on her back. When she turned round nobody was there. The room was empty.

SEE ALSO:

• Bedford.

• Chicksands Priory.

WHILE YOU'RE THERE:

• Pay a visit to Ampthill Park and Woodlands. Ampthill Park contains Katherine's Cross, carved with melancholic verses and representing the site of the old Ampthill Castle, where Henry VIII imprisoned Katherine of Aragon before and around the time of their divorce. It is a beautiful park, open to the public and containing many ramblers' walks. The white apparition of a man riding a horse has been seen cantering from Katherine's Cross to a nearby stream. Some, perhaps romantically, have described the apparition as a knight in armour. No one has offered a specific identity for the figure.

Epworth Rectory
(Doncaster, South Yorkshire)

The Old Rectory in Epworth was the home of John and Charles Wesley. John was the founder of Methodism and Charles (the poet of the Methodist) composed nearly 7,000 hymns.

The house was built in 1709 by their father, the Reverend Samuel Wesley, for his large family, and remained a rectory until 1954. From December 1716 to January 1717 the family were disturbed by poltergeist phenomena, centred, it seems, around one of the girls, nineteen-year old Mehetabel, known as Hetty. The main events reported were knocking noises, which were often responsive. For example, when Samuel Wesley tapped his stick against the floor the poltergeist would reply in knocking form. On a few occasions he also felt himself being pushed by 'an invisible power'. The family also reported the sounds of breaking glass, groaning and cackling sounds, all apparently without explanation, and they saw objects moving or 'dancing' mysteriously. The family did not find the poltergeist frightening; in fact they nicknamed it 'Old Jeffrey'.

Many of the reports were recorded in correspondence written by Mrs Wesley to her son. For example: 'One night it made such a noise in the room over our head as if several people were walking; then . . . running up and down stairs, and was so outrageous that we thought the children would be frightened so your father and I rose and went down in the dark to light a candle. Just as we came to the bedroom at the bottom of the broad stairs, having hold of each other, on my side there seemed as if somebody had emptied a bag of money at my feet, and on his as if all the bottles under the stairs (which were many) had been dashed in a thousand pieces.'

Today the rectory is laid out as a museum and also contains the Gwyron Aston Library of Methodist History. The rectory is open between March and October for visitors; it is also possible to spend the night in the bedrooms. A must for the enthusiastic ghost-hunter.

We spoke to the warden, Mr Colin Barton, who explained that visitors have reported a strange feeling of 'unwellness' when on the top floor. Three people working at the rectory have reported hearing footsteps when they were sure no one else was there. Mr Barton himself has heard noises that were inexplicable, and remembers being told that one of the rectors left the rectory for a while because he was being so disturbed by strange happenings. However, not everyone is so affected; we spoke to a guide who had slept in the 'haunted room' but he had not felt anything untoward.

The Great Bed of Ware
(Victoria and Albert Museum, London)

The Great Bed of Ware, displayed in the Victoria and Albert Museum, inspired the poem in 1596 by Prince Ludwig of Anhalt-Köhten:

> At Ware was a bed of dimension so wide
> for couples might cosily lie side by side
> and thus without touch each other abide.

At one time it was believed that the Great Bed of Ware was the largest bed in England, but its origins are uncertain. It appears in *The Holly Tree* by Charles Dickens as a comparison to a sofa in an inn. It also appears in Shakespeare's *Twelfth Night* when Toby Belch comments: 'Although the sheet were big enough for the Bed of Ware in England'. Ben Johnson used it in *The Alchemist* and John Taylor wrote of it in *Honourable and Memorable Foundations*.

It is a huge four-poster measuring eleven feet square and was well known even in the reign of Queen Elizabeth I. It has been claimed that it was commissioned for Henry VIII, but others believe that it may be older and that it was made for the Earl of Warwick, who lived between 1428 and 1471. At one time it was the property of Thomas Fanshawe, the Lord of Ware Manor, whose family is associated with the Wicked Lady, Lady Katherine Ferrers. It seems to have been sold perhaps when the Fanshawe family moved to their new mansion at Ware Park, and after that appears to have become something of a tourist attraction at various inns in the area.

The theories of its haunting start with those who believe that it was the work of a carpenter known as Jonas Fosbrooke, dating from 1463. It is said that Fosbrooke haunts the bed and when he disapproves of guests prevents their sleeping by scratching and pinching them. A further legend has it that the Master of the Horse to Henry VIII, Harrison Saxby, fell in love with the daughter of a rich miller living near Ware and offered to do anything to win her hand in matrimony. The King ordered the girl and all those who wished to be her suitors to appear before him and offered her hand in marriage to anyone who would spend the night in the Great Bed of Ware. Saxby was the only one who took up the challenge and endured all that Fosbrooke's ghost could do, succeeding in gaining the hand of the lady.

A number of other writers have included the Great Bed in their accounts, including Sir Henry Chauncy of Ardeley in his *Historical Antiquities of Hertfordshire* and Ned Ward in *The Writings of the Author of the London Spy*. The Great Bed's last romantic interlude is in Byron's poem *Don Juan*.

Langenhoe Church (site)
(Langenhoe, Essex)

Between the mid 1930s and 1960 Langenhoe Church and the neighbouring manor house were the focus of a variety of ghostly and psychic phenomena. The Reverend Ernest Merryweather took over as rector in 1937 and within weeks began to experience a series of phenomena which lasted until his retirement twenty-two years later. Many of the manifestations were witnessed by him alone, but researcher Peter Underwood, who knew him for many years, has stated that 'Mr Merryweather impressed me as a good witness'. Many of the manifestations were also shared by others, including whole congregations. In fact prior to the Reverend Merryweather's appointment it seems the church already had a local reputation for being haunted; for example a lady from nearby West Mersea remembered a 'lady in black' haunting from around 1910.

Poltergeistery seems to have been the first phenomena triggered during Merryweather's time, and started, like most poltergeists, with small movements and sounds. The church door slammed inexplicably, flowers placed in the church would be found replaced elsewhere or completely gone, there were noises that couldn't be explained, such as the ringing of bells in the church when no one was there, and so on. Merryweather, and indeed several locals, heard the coughing of what seemed to be an old man coming from a bricked-up doorway. The doorway had been an exclusive entrance for the family that lived in a neighbouring manor. In 1947 Merryweather was looking over the manor with its then owner, who explained to him that she never used one bedroom because it felt strange. While in the room Merryweather had the extraordinary sensation of being embraced by a naked woman. It was an entirely tactile experience, no vision, sound or smell, but the clear sensation of being touched by naked arms, breasts and torso.

The following year Merryweather felt the need to bring an ornamental dagger he owned into the church for protection, as there had been several bursts of hooliganism. The dagger was pulled from him while he was standing near the altar and a woman's voice shouted, 'You are a cruel man'.

The following year the phenomena stepped up a notch. While holding Communion, Merryweather looked up and saw a woman, apparently about thirty years old and dressed in a long white dress, walk across the chancel and disappear through the wall. Old photographs from the 1800s show that at the point where she disappeared there had once been a doorway.

Smells became the next form of ghostly phenomena, when in September 1950 the church was filled with the pungent smell of violets from no obvious source. A few days later music was heard coming from the church and the vicar heard the sound of a young girl singing; no one was present at the time who could have caused the sounds and they ended with the sound of heavy footsteps. A week later workmen outside the locked building heard the same singing and were astonished at the rector's suggestion that the church was empty. He proved it when together they searched the church thoroughly and found no one inside. The year 1950 ended with the sighting of a vague apparition of a man in modern dress.

During the next two years there were several outbreaks of poltergeistery and sightings of the apparition of a young woman described as having a 'strange sad look'. Once when a candle blew out, although there were no draughts or people sitting close enough to have blown it out – one of many times this had happened – several members of the congregation were absolutely certain they had heard a deliberate human blowing sound.

In 1958 a medium, Mrs Lampart, attempted to contact any spirits in the church and succeeded in contacting a man, Sir Robert Att Ford, and a girl, Mary. The story is that Sir Robert – a lord of the manor in the time of James I – quarrelled with Mary, one of his servants, and stabbed her to death in the church.

The church may well have been the focus of this paranormal activity, but several researchers have pointed out that the whole area seems prone. There are tales of hauntings in the Manor House nearby, and in private houses all around the area. In one cottage a man shot and killed his fiancée in 1948, swearing that his finger was never on the trigger. In fact the area has suffered more than its fair share of violence: in the fourteenth century several murders at the hands of a lord of the manor, Lionel de Bradenham, and in the sixteenth century tragedy within the Waldegrave family, who also at one time owned the village of Borley (see Borley Church, page 44). Nine children of the owner of the Manor House died in the nineteenth century, followed soon after by their mother. Several owners of the Manor House committed suicide, including the famous Belgian financier Alfred Loewenstein.

It has been pointed out that the majority of the hauntings have displayed a basic femininity. The figures seen were women, the tactile impression was of an embrace by a woman and the voices heard were definitely female.

The church was demolished in the early 1960s and is today represented by a wild and unkempt graveyard. The area none the less merits a visit. It is atmospheric, very much a place filled with English history, and the main road through leads to the 'island' of Mersea which has several unusual hauntings of its own (see Chapters 8 and 13).

SEE ALSO:
- Mersea Island.
- Berechurch, Colchester.

Sandringham House
(Sandringham, Norfolk)

Sandringham House is the Queen's private residence, but open to the public. Just after renovation work on the kitchens in the 1980s, during a house party, one overnight guest awoke at approximately two o'clock in the morning and found the room seemingly illuminated. Her bedroom door opened and a young boy entered, apparently carrying a long candle-snuffing pole, and walked around the room reaching up the walls, snuffing candles not there in the present but presumably there in the past. The scene vanished and the illumination died away.

Helen Cathcart, in her book *Sandringham*, reports, though somewhat sceptically, that Prince Christopher of Greece saw a ghost while staying there. He caught sight of a young beautiful woman in his dressing-table mirror, her expression pleading and melancholy. When visiting Houghton Hall the following day the Prince recognized the figure he had seen in one of the portraits of the Cholmondeley family.

There are also reports of poltergeist phenomena occurring, most commonly around Christmas, and of an oppressive presence described as 'a pulsating paper bag'. Christmas cards are often thrown around the floor and it is reported by some servants and guests that unoccupied beds are ruffled. Peter Underwood reports that maids refuse to enter the footman's corridor on the second floor alone and insist on working in small groups. This is where the 'presence' has been reported, together with heavy footsteps and doors opening and closing spontaneously.

SEE ALSO:
* Castle Rising Castle.
* Castle Acre Priory.

WHILE YOU'RE THERE:
* At nearby King's Lynn there is a heart shape apparent in a brick on a house wall in the north-west corner of Tuesday Market. Margaret Read was burnt at the stake as a witch in 1590, a rarer form of execution in England than generally supposed. It is said that as she died her heart burst from her chest and imprinted itself in the wall.

Selside Hall
(Kendal, Cumbria)

North of Kendal, Selside Hall, just off the A6, had a very active ghost which would rush about the house putting out lights in pre-electricity days. No one knows where or how the ghost originates, but the local legend is that it is the revenge of a hanged sheep stealer. A yew tree in the grounds of Selside Hall was used for hangings in earlier centuries.

SEE ALSO:

- Tebay.
- Cark Hall/Holker Hall, near Cartmel.
- Gaythorne Hall, Tebay.
- Reston House, near Ings.

GHOSTS
WITH A
TIMETABLE

If ghosts were so predictable that their arrival or manifestation could be predetermined accurately, they would have been filmed, photographed or witnessed by thousands long ago. The fact is that ghosts are notorious for standing up their dates! But we should not be too cynical and reject real observations along with the healthy chunk of salt it is worth taking with stories of such compliant regularity.

There is little doubt that legend overlays many tales of ghost sightings, and perhaps more so these historical stories. Stories mutate over time; the actual sighting dates may be forgotten, but they may become associated with anniversaries – and given the strong belief that ghosts represent the dead, many anniversaries are said to be of the deaths of those seen. But the core of the stories is probably that something was seen at some time, and in such a way as to impress on the witnesses a sense of surprise, or fear, or some other emotion. This might be the reality that we should avoid rejecting too easily. So even if the precision of 'anniversary ghosts' is a myth, the basic reality of their existence might still be true.

In support of the theory of recordings ghosts – and these seem to be the commonest type of ghost reported at anniversaries – has been the suggestion that any one spot contains hundreds of ghosts who have lived there or passed that way, but that part of the replay mechanism is a living agent focusing on individuals. If we are at Hampton Court we are likely to be thinking of King Henry and his wives – perhaps that makes their manifestation more likely than another such ghost.

But if the ghosts are actually not that reliable perhaps we should consider how the idea of regular visitations got started. Perhaps such ghosts appear 'around' certain times of the year and the significant date is imposed; if so, why? Perhaps the climate and other natural conditions of humidity and temperature play a part in the 'playback' of the 'recording'. If so, then it is possible that a specific ghost – 'recorded' at a certain time when, say, it is foggy – might only appear when it is similarly foggy. If so, then it is more likely for that ghost to appear in, say, November than August.

We would be dishonest to suggest that merely by being in the right places on the dates given you are going to see a ghost. However, it is possible that you will increase the odds of success, particularly if you 'stake out' a place for a period of time around the anniversary.

CHAPTER 15

~

ANNIVERSARY
GHOSTS

There are many reports of ghosts that appear with frequency on the anniversary of certain events. This section is subdivided into months, offering the reader a selection of ghostly sites to visit each month around areas of Britain.

January

19 At the Biggin Hill airfield, Greater London, an unseen Spitfire is sometimes heard making an approach to landing. However, it was during the summer that one witness, Patrick Muirhead, a radio presenter, was flying a light aircraft over Biggin Hill and saw the Spitfire. He was later assured by his instructor that no Spitfires were in the air at that time and it is assumed that he saw a ghost aircraft.

19 The sound of horses' hooves can be heard at Braddock Down in Cornwall; the site of the defeat of Cromwell's army in 1643.

31 At Huddington, Worcestershire, the headless ghost of a woman walks around the moat and along an avenue of oaks on the anniversary of the death of her husband, Thomas Winter, who was executed on that date in 1606 for his part in Guy Fawkes's notorious gunpowder plot to blow up Parliament.

February

12 In the Bloody Tower, in the Tower of London, a vague white shape is seen. This is the anniversary of the death of Lady Jane Grey, who was executed on that day in 1554.

15 Hickling Broad in Norfolk is host to the apparition of a 'drummer boy'. The Broad is also the location of the ghost of the 'skating soldier' and the 'punting woman'.

25 At the Old Court House, in Hampton Court, the ghost of the famous architect Christopher Wren is said to appear on the anniversary of his death. King William III engaged Wren to undertake major changes in the designs of Hampton Court. Wren spent the last five years of his life there; he died in 1723.

March

1 St David is said to have been born near the now ruined chapel in St David's, Pembrokeshire, which was dedicated to his mother, St Non. During the nights before and after St David's Day, 1 March, ghostly singing is said to be heard from the ruined chapel which overlooks St Bride's Bay.

17 At the Ferry Boat Inn in Holywell, Cambridgeshire, there is the reputed appearance of the ghost of Juliet Tewsley, who hanged herself there centuries ago. (This story is covered in detail in Chapter 17.)

April

4 At Rochester Castle, Kent, the apparition of Lady Blanche de Warren is said to walk the battlements. She was accidentally killed in 1264 by an arrow fired by her lover, Ralph de Capo, during a siege of the castle.

7 At Acle in Norfolk there is a bridge which was the scene of a gruesome death, possibly two. Josiah Burge is said to have killed his wife, and her brother then slit Burge's throat in revenge on the bridge. A further elaboration of the story is that the brother had his own throat cut a year later by a spectral skeleton, again on the bridge. On 7 April a ghost, and fresh blood, is said to appear on the bridge.

9 At Orme House, Newport, on the Isle of Wight, in the early hours 9 April, the ghost of an elderly lady thought to be from the eighteenth century has been seen as recently as 1992. She wears a long skirt, shawl and boots.

26 At Penfound Manor, now no longer open to the public, Kate Penfound's ghost is said to walk. (The story is related in Chapter 3.)

May

1 A silent, phantom army is said to appear at dawn on the shores of Loch Ashie near Inverness in Scotland. This is the site of an ancient battle between the local forces and an invading force from Norway led by King Ashie.

1 It is said that if you should see the first rays of the sun through the Godstow nunnery chapel at Wolvercote, in Oxfordshire, you will also be privileged to hear the ghostly chanting of medieval psalms. The nunnery is also the site of a Grey Lady, the ghost of Rosamund Clifford, mistress of Henry II, who died there in 1177. She was murdered by Henry's wife, Queen Eleanor.

12 (or the third Tuesday in the month) At Salthouse in Norfolk a ghostly midnight Mass has been heard and sometimes seen on the shore of Salthouse Pool.

19 A phantom coach is said to drive towards Blickling Hall in Norfolk, built on the site of the house once occupied by Anne Boleyn. The coach fades away as it gets near. The 19th is the anniversary of the death of Anne Boleyn in 1536, and some reports of the carriage hold that it contains the ghost of Anne, sitting with her head in her lap.

31 At Potter Heigham in Norfolk a phantom coach is said to crash into a bridge over the River Thurne at midnight, perhaps re-enacting a tragedy of years past. In 1741 Sir Godfrey Haslitt and his new bride, Lady Carew, were fleeing from a fire that was ravaging their home; they crashed into the bridge and died in the waters of the river. Other local stories claim that Lady Carew had sold her soul to the devil who was claiming his own.

June

2 At Soham railway station in Cambridgeshire there are reports of a phantom train running along the tracks. On 2 June 1944 an ammunition train, fifty-one wagons long and carrying hundreds of 500-pounder bombs, caught fire and exploded. Twenty-two-year-old fireman James Knightall and signalman Frank Bridges were killed instantly in the explosion; the driver Ben Gimbert survived, though badly injured. The driver who had worked with James Knightall the day before the event remembered Knightall saying that he did not think he had much longer to live.

14 Goodrich Castle on the banks of the river Wye, in Herefordshire, was besieged by Roundheads during the Civil War in 1646. The leader of the Roundhead forces was Colonel John Birch, and trapped within the castle was his niece, Alice, who had taken up with a Royalist lover, Charles Clifford. The couple attempted to escape but were drowned together in the River Wye. It is said that on or near 14 June – particularly if it is a stormy night – their cries can be heard. There have also been sightings of the pair on horseback, diving to their deaths in the waters.

15 At Hitchin Priory, in Hertfordshire, a spectral cavalier is said to appear.

20 Between North and South Barrow, near Castle Cary in Somerset, is the site of an ancient causeway. It is said that on 20 June, Midsummer's Eve, King Arthur and his knights, with teams of footsoldiers, are seen riding. They are supposed to be heading from the nearby Cadbury Castle to Glastonbury.

21 The longest day of the year, Midsummer's Day. At the West Kennet burial mound in Wiltshire, a neolithic tomb, a spectral black dog is said to appear. Black Dogs are a particular feature of English ghost-lore; they were once guardians of graveyards and this claim could be the sighting of the 'recordings' ghost of just such a guardian. There are also claims of a white-dressed priest entering the tomb at sunrise on Midsummer's Day, accompanied by a white dog with red ears.

27 At St Mary's Church, Beaminster, Dorset, it is said that the ghost of murdered John Daniel, who died there in 1728, appears. The story is recounted in detail in Chapter 2.

July

1 At Smithfield in London stands the church of St Bartholomew the Great. The ghost of Rahere, the founder of the original monastery and hospital on the site, built in 1123, is said to walk in the church at around seven o'clock in the morning on each 1 July.

3 At Burgh Castle, on the Norfolk/Suffolk border, a seemingly tragic re-enactment takes place. What appears to be a body shrouded in a white blanket or flag is flung from the ruins on to the foreshore below. The real-life origin of this presumed death is not known.

5 Strange sights and sounds are reported over the site of the Battle of Sedgemoor, in Somerset, which took place in 1685.

27 In the sky above the Pass of Killecrankie, in Perth in Kinross, a red glow marks the scene of the bloody battle fought there in 1689.

28 On the site of the now-destroyed Borley Rectory at Borley in Essex, on this day the famous ghost nun is said to walk. She has been seen by many people; Borley Rectory and Church have been heralded as the most haunted buildings in the world. Certainly they have attracted a great deal of attention (not always welcomed by local people, however, so be diplomatic if visiting). The hauntings of Borley Church are described in detail in Chapter 2.

August

11 (and 22) At Beeleigh Abbey, near Maldon in Essex, on 11 August 1553, Sir John Gate was awaiting execution; he was beheaded at Tower Hill in London on the 22 August. The sounds of his crying and wailing in despair have been reported on the anniversaries of both the 11th and 22nd of the month.

15 At Rock in Northumberland a grey lady is said to have been seen walking from South Charlton to Rock (now crossing the A1) each 15 August, which is locally believed to be the anniversary of her husband's death. She is thought to be a former occupant of nearby Rock Hall.

17 The ghost of the nun Berta Rosata is said to appear at Chicksands Priory in Bedfordshire. (The story is related in Chapter 2.)

September

13 At Newark Castle, near Selkirk, Borders (Scottish), the sounds of the slaughter of men, women and children are heard on the anniversary date of a slaughter in 1645. (See Chapter 1.)

28 At Sherborne Old Castle in Dorset the former owner, Sir Walter Ralegh, is said to return. He is also reported at midnight on the 29th, sitting in Ralegh's Seat. (The hauntings at Sherborne are described in Chapter 1, and other manifestations of Ralegh are described in Chapter 4.)

October

23 The sights and sounds of the 1642 battle of Edge Hill are re-enacted at Edge Hill in Warwickshire.

29 At Rye in Sussex the Mermaid public house is the scene of a ghastly and ghostly re-enactment. A swordfight duel takes place, with the victor killing the other and then dragging the body to a corner of the room and lowering it through a trapdoor.

30 At Lydiard Millicent, near Swindon in Wiltshire, Lady Blunt's ghost is said to appear in the garden of the manor house each 30th October, the anniversary of the date she witnessed the murder of her betrothed 200 years ago.

31 Perhaps unsurprisingly, Halloween is a popular time for anniversary ghosts:

- At Cliviger Gorge near Burnley, Lancashire, a spectral huntsman and his hound are seen.
- At Armboth Fell in the Lake District, there are reports of both a phantom dog and the ghostly pealing of bells.
- At Minsden chapel, now ruins in a field in Hertfordshire, a ghostly monk is said to walk; he is presumed to be the same one that was photographed in 1907. Some witnesses have reported the pealing of bells just beforehand.
- At Netley Abbey, on Southampton Water, the ghost of a Cistercian monk known as Blind Peter is seen apparently guarding the treasures of the Abbey. Rumour has it that an attempt to locate the treasure left one man, Mr Slown, frightened literally to death.

November

1 The ghost of Sir John Jocelyn is said to ride on horseback down the drive of Hyde Hall, Sawbridgeworth, Hertfordshire. He and his favourite horse are buried there.

3 At Bruce Castle in Lordship Lane, Tottenham, North London, the ghost of a suicide at what was once known as Tottenham Manor House, Lady Coleraine, appears, screaming and running through certain rooms in the museum, as it is now. She is also heard to jump from the balcony. The curator, Penny Wheatcroft, has had no experiences herself, but believes that the ghost's screaming was heard by people in the nearby park in 1996.

Bruce Castle is thought to date from the early sixteenth century. Henry, 2nd Lord Coleraine, took over the house after his father's death and later named the house Bruce Castle. Henry married his first wife, Constantia, possibly in an attempt to restore family fortunes lost during the Civil War. But it is possible that even then he was in love with Sarah, the daughter of Sir Edward Alston, with whom he had had and was perhaps continuing an affair. (He later married Sarah.) Whatever the reason, it seems that Henry turned against his wife, first confining her to certain upper rooms in the house and lastly enclosing her in the small rooms of the clock tower. On 3 November 1680 Constantia – with her infant son in her arms – forced her way on to the balcony and flung herself to her death below. It is said that this event is somehow replayed each year on the anniversary; her form is seen and a despairing cry heard. A printed reference to the Ghostly Lady of Bruce Castle comes from 1858, in the March edition of the *Tottenham and Edmonton Advertiser*. Bruce Castle was later home to Sir Rowland Hill and as well as containing records of local history and an archives collection its exhibits include displays of the early postal services.

13 At the Royal National Orthopaedic Hospital in Stanmore, Greater London, the ghost of a Grey Lady is said to walk.

December

22, or thereabouts. At Studland, in Dorset, a phantom white donkey stands on the heath. The local legend is that its owner was killed and robbed, and that the animal returns each year hoping to find him.

24 Christmas Eve is a popular time for ghost sightings:

- At Hever Castle, near Edenbridge in Kent, Anne Boleyn's ghost has been seen.
- At Strata Florida, Ceredigion, to the north-east of Tregaron, there is the reported ghost of a monk wandering through the ruins of the old abbey.
- Roos Hall in Beccles, Suffolk, is visited by a ghostly coach and four, driven by a headless groom. Perhaps he is connected to the oak tree in the nearby park, which once supported a gibbet; the ghosts of those hanged there are supposed to re-visit occasionally. Inside Roos Hall it is said that the Devil's footmarks are visible in a wardrobe – and local legend says that the Devil can be conjured up by walking round the oak tree six times.
- In the graveyard near Rochester Castle the ghost of Charles Dickens has been seen walking between the gravestones. It was a place he loved throughout much of his life. He wanted to be buried in the graveyard, though he is in fact buried in Westminster Abbey. His ghost has also been seen at midnight on Christmas Eve outside the Corn Exchange, setting the hands of his watch.

- From Bomere Pool, near Shrewsbury, Shropshire, a supposedly sunken bell is said to be heard ringing. Ringing bells have a particular fascination in ghost-lore and even more so at Christmas periods: at Combermere Abbey, at Nantwich in Cheshire, it is said that the monks removed the bells when the original abbey was dissolved and that one fell into the water from the boat on which it was being transported – that bell is sometimes said to be heard ringing from the depths of the lake, often accompanied by sightings of a ghostly monk.

- At the Tudor mansion of Madingley Hall, Cambridgeshire the ghost of Lady Ursula Hynde, wife of the Hall's builder, Sir John Hynde, has been reported. She was apparently distressed at her son's destruction of the local church of St Ethelreda in Histon to provide building materials for the Hall and forever walks the Hall wringing her hands in despair. It is said that each Christmas Eve she walks between the Hall and the church.

- At Sandringham House, Norfolk, the servants' quarters are subject to poltergeist activity on Christmas Eve and around the Christmas period, and there are reports of a 'pulsating' presence being reported. (Sandringham's ghosts are recounted in Chapter 14.)

27 Thomas à Becket is said to ride through the village of Lapford in Devon, two days prior to the anniversary of his death. Several authors have pointed out that there is some confusion over the logic of this ghostly ride. He appears to be heading for Nymet Rowland, but possibly should be heading for Nymet Tracey. Sir William de Tracy was one of the four men who murdered Becket in 1170; he built a church in that village as part of his penance for the crime.

29 One of the killers of Thomas à Becket, who died on this day in 1170, is said to be the origin of the ghost in armour that visits the church at Kemsing, near Sevenoaks in Kent. The knight rides in on horseback, ties up the horse and enters the church, kneeling at the altar. During this prayer, the figure disappears.

31 New Year's Eve, again not surprisingly, is one of the most popular times for 'anniversary' ghosts:

- Peel Road, Bootle, Merseyside, is the reported scene of a phantom horse and rider.

- Bramhall Hall, in Greater Manchester, is the scene of the 'Red Rider'. He was originally a traveller who rode into the Hall's courtyard one 31 December in the 1630s, dressed in red cape and hood. He was given hospitality for the night but by the following morning had disappeared and the owner of the hall, William Davenport, was found dead.

- At Purse Caundle Manor, near Sherborne in Dorset, a pack of the King's hounds is said to appear on the Bowling Green. When John Aleyn lived there in the thirteenth century it is said that he had the job of 'keeping and lodging the King's (John) sick and injured hounds'.

- A phantom carriage pulled by headless horses is said to cross the frozen waters of the Loch of Skene, near Aberdeen in Scotland. It is thought to be 'occupied' by the ghost of Alexander Skene, who died in 1724. He was a warlock said to raid the local graveyards for the bodies of unbaptized children which were fed to his familiars – a jackdaw, a hawk, a crow and a magpie – which travelled in the coach with him.

- At Andover in Hampshire a ghostly pig is said to put in an appearance.

- At Ranworth Old Hall, east of Norwich, in Norfolk, there are reports of a black horse galloping out of the drive.

- At Knighton Gorges, on the Isle of Wight, the Manor House was demolished long ago, but it is said that at dusk on New Year's Eve its apparition briefly reappears.

- At St Bartholomew's in Arborfield, Berkshire, at midnight, it is said that the ghost of a young bride appears next to the yew tree near the church. She was apparently murdered by a jealous would-be lover on the eve of her marriage.

- At East Wellow in Hampshire a spectral coach and horses is seen driving to the church from Embley Park at midnight. The area has several ghosts in its repertoire; Florence Nightingale is buried in St Margaret's and it is thought that she is the ghost seen in the church where in life she frequently attended, and the ghost of Colonel William Morton – who signed Charles I's death warrant – is said to walk from the old manor to the churchyard.

CHAPTER 16

~

CYCLICAL GHOSTS

At the Bradfield Hall estate at Kentisbeare in Devon it is said that the ghost of a farmworker rides on a horse-drawn roller every night at midnight.

And at Bridgnorth in Shropshire there is a report that a lady in black appears, crossing the high street, every night at midnight.

If only it was that easy to spot ghosts . . .

On Thursdays at the Coliseum Theatre in Oldham, Greater Manchester, the main event is the appearance of the ghost of the actor Harold Norman. He was killed on a Thursday in a stage fight during a performance of *Macbeth* in 1947.

Clear nights of the full moon in June. At Tidmarsh, Berkshire, on such nights, it is said that you can see the ghost of a drowned boy rising from the river in which he died, near the rectory.

Any July day. A ghost nun is said to appear during July in the cloisters at Exeter Cathedral, Devon, usually at around seven o'clock in the evening. She is said to materialize through the south wall of the nave and disappear through the south wall of the Church House. There is also a report of a ghostly monk in the cathedral close.

Third week in August. At Burgh Island in Bigbury Bay, Devon, the ghost of the hanged pirate Tom Crocker, executed in 1395, is seen. He used the island as his base of operations until his death.

Any day in September. This is the month in which it is believed a soldier was brutally murdered at the Grenadier public house in Wilton Row,

Knightsbridge, London. His shade is said to haunt the pub during this month. (See Chapter 17.)

Just before Christmas a ghostly coach drawn by headless horses is said to appear at Penryn, in Cornwall. Local legend has it that unless witnesses avert their eyes the coachman can spirit them away.

The twelve nights following Christmas. On these nights Rochford Hall, at Rochford in Essex, is said to be visited by the headless ghost of Anne Boleyn.

On 13 February 1748 the schooner *Lady Luvibond* sank with all lives lost on the Goodwin Sands, off the Kent coast. (The story told is that a jealous fight over the captain's new wife had taken place on board and the ship was deliberately grounded and sunk by the first mate. But if lost with all hands, how is this known?) It is said that every fifty years the ship re-enacts the journey and the tragic ending. In 1798 it was seen by the master of the ship *Edenbridge* and by the crew of another vessel nearby. In 1848 the ship was seen by longshoremen of Deal, who were so convinced the sight was real that they launched a rescue, but found no ship present. In 1898 and 1948 there were reported sightings on the anniversary date. (By the time this book is published the ship either will, or will not, have made its 1998 appearance; we intend to be there to see whether or not it appears and to report on it.)

GHOSTS . . . ON THE MENU?

Ghosts and hauntings seem to arise in all kinds of buildings and other locations. It is not surprising therefore that there are many accounts of such events in pubs and hotels around the country. We know of a few people that are reluctant to 'go public' about the hauntings associated with their premises but for the most part many regard it as a fortunate extra. These ghosts and hauntings do not usually inspire fear, but rather a great deal of interest.

We have therefore contacted a number of such locations so that the more active ghost-watcher can, while touring around visiting scenes of reported hauntings, stop off for refreshment or an overnight rest at locations which themselves provide stories of interest. In most cases the proprietors have expressed their interest in receiving first hand stories, and many will probably be interested to speak to experienced ghost-watchers to share stories from around the country.

To add a little tongue-in-cheek humour to the listing we have graded, not the premises themselves, but the hauntings, with 'ghost ratings', e.g:

The ratings are (very subjectively) given on the basis of the nature, frequency, and range of phenomena reported. We should be pleased to hear of recommendations for changes to those ratings, or of new premises to be included in later editions of this book, or in future written work.

CHAPTER 17

~

HAUNTED HOTELS AND PUBS

Albright Hussey Hotel and Restaurant
(Ellesmere Road, Shrewsbury, Shropshire)

Situated in the heart of historical England, just a few minutes' drive from Shrewsbury and within easy reach of such sites as Ironbridge Gorge, the Severn Valley Railway and haunted Ludlow Castle (south on the A49), this hotel has a reputation for the noisiest – and perhaps boldest – of ghosts, one not completely camera-shy.

A wedding was held at the hotel. The happy couple were booked in for three nights. During the night the bride woke up and saw a tall, dark-cloaked person standing at the foot of the bed. Photographs taken in the room all show the impression of a shadow-like figure. A professional photographer could not explain the effects.

On another occasion the proprietor, Franco Subbiani, was snow-bound in the hotel one night; he was the only person there. Twice he was awoken by a knocking at the door of his room, but there was never anyone there when he opened it, and no footprints in the snow.

Those who are prepared to brave the anonymous caller at the door, and wedding parties willing to accept uninvited guests, will also find the hotel suitable for more conventional historical encounters. The Albright Hussey Hotel dates back to an entry in the Domesday Book itself. It is situated near the site of the Battle of Shrewsbury, where, in 1403, Henry IV defeated Hotspur. During the Civil War Charles I garrisoned his troops there. The wood panelling, beamed ceilings and large open fireplaces all lend an atmosphere steeped in history.

The Angel Posting House and Livery
(Guildford, Surrey)

According to the *Surrey Advertiser* of 27 February 1970, the Angel Posting House and Livery, a hotel in High Street, Guildford, has a ghost. Mr G. Dell of London saw the ghost in a wardrobe mirror at three in the morning. He and his wife had been staying at the hotel over the weekend of 30 and 31 January. The ghost, dressed in military uniform, was a middle-aged man with a moustache, a very compelling expression in his eyes, and visible from the waist up only. The uniform was thought to be foreign, probably from the Continent and dating from the late nineteenth or early twentieth century. Mr Dell later made a sketch of the apparition.

Mr and Mrs Dell were staying in Room 1, known as the Prince Imperial of France Room, and the newspaper noted that a previous guest who had stayed in the same room had been so petrified by the supernatural that she had requested a transfer to a different room. She had only been aware of a presence, and the assistant manager of the hotel, Mr Colin Anderson, believes that Mr Dell was the first to actually see the ghost.

As the paper reported, tradition has it that the Angel has foundations of monastic origin and was once linked by tunnel 'from the Angel to the castle'. It is the oldest inn in Guildford. Perhaps associated with the military ghost is the mystery of a bullet found in one of the old beams by W.T. Madden of the Surrey Trust.

The Bell
(Toddington, Bedfordshire)

In 1996 we visited the Bell public house in Toddington, where in September 1995 the landlord had left saying he was tired of being woken every night by a mysterious presence, thought to be the ghost of a young girl who had some time in the past been imprisoned in the room that was now his bedroom.

The landlord of the pub at the time of our visit was Mr Howard, who had then been there for some weeks. In that short time he had noticed a few abnormalities, for example three glasses falling from the shelves spontaneously, confirmed by the barmaid, Rose. She further admitted that this had been a problem in the pub for quite a while. Rose went on to tell us how one area of the bar had been active when a particular member of staff was around.

Mr Howard also told us how some strange things had been noticed by him from the bedroom, and that some guests who stayed the night were decidedly unhappy. Mr Howard had on a couple of occasions seen an apparitional shape but pointed out that this could be misperception. He has an open mind but is interested in the events. He thinks some of the problems may come from vibrations; the pub, being fairly close to the road is passed by some heavy traffic. This may well explain some of the reports, but in our view could not explain them all. Mr Howard also said that he had been told by his regulars of strange problems noticed in the past.

Later we spoke to Alan, a member of a music group setting up to play in the pub, as they regularly do. He described unexpected power failures – equipment would not work, yet the socket was not faulty and the equipment would always work when removed from the pub.

The Bridgnorth Croft Hotel (Bridgnorth, Shropshire)

Jill Wilding reported to us several instances of hauntings in the hotel. Two ladies staying in Room 12 apparently complained of hearing bells ringing all through the night, they also felt a tugging at their feet and stated that they did not wish to stay in that room any longer. Apparently there used to be stables in the garden, now converted to cottages, and it is believed that the horses that pulled the fire-truck were stabled there. Whenever there was fire the bells would be rung, and the horses brought out for action.

A guest staying in Room 2 apparently woke to find 'a friendly companion' standing at the foot of the bed. This guest stays regularly in the room, regarding the ghost as a 'companion'.

Two business people reported a lady dressed in black walking through the dining-room. Apparently the ghost walked from the bar cupboard at the top of the cellar access, past the inglenook fireplace, along the hallway and to a cupboard that now houses the boiler but might once have been a room.

The Buckingham Arms
(Old Road, Linslade, Bedfordshire)

The *Leighton Buzzard Observer* and *Linslade Gazette* of 13 February 1996 reported some hauntings in the Buckingham Arms in Old Road, Linslade. According to the newspaper report, the landlord, Roy Gates, discovered that the front gate opened and closed with a clang at 5 a.m. in the morning every day though it was not evident why – and the milkman was ruled out. One barmaid became trapped in the pub – she had been upstairs after the pub had been locked up and heard 'this almighty racket' in the cellar. It sounded as if someone was kicking barrels around. She was so terrified she refused to come down from upstairs and had to stay all night in the pub. However, in the morning there was no evidence of any damage or intrusion.

Roy Gates himself sought to investigate the ghost and stayed in the pub one night. He didn't see any apparitions but felt the icy cold which often accompanies ghost reports. 'It was as if someone had opened the door and there was a gale blowing. It was very weird.' Doors and windows were in fact firmly locked.

The Castle Hotel
(High Street, Conwy, Conwyn, Wales)

Heather Knight of the Castle Hotel told us: 'Some time before the hotel was bought by Trust Houses in 1927, the hotel was owned by the Dutton family. At this time tourism was just beginning to take off and staff were hired locally and from further afield. A young girl from Anglesey looking for the excitement of the bright lights of bustling Conwy came to work as a waitress. One day she approached Miss Dutton, who was a very formidable lady by all accounts, saying she wished to return to her home in Anglesey as she was going to die! Miss Dutton severely admonished her for such foolish notions and told her to pull herself together and get on with her work. Some weeks later at the height of the holiday season the young girl died. She was hurriedly buried in St Mary's churchyard nearby.

'After that, very strange things started happening in the hotel. The head waiter, entering the restaurant with a laden tray, tripped over nothing at all and sent the dishes flying across the room. A housemaid looking away from her bucket for a moment found it had disappeared, never to be seen again. The oil lamps refused to light. Jugs used for hot water broke into a thousand pieces.

'Miss Dutton was at her wits' end, as these disturbances were causing uneasiness among the guests and staff, so she decided to approach the local vicar for his advice. She related the story of the young waitress, as she believed there was a connection with her and the strange happenings in the hotel. The vicar said there would be no peace in the hotel until the deceased's wishes were carried out. So arrangements were made for the coffin to be removed from Conwy to a resting place on the Menai Straits, where the girl's heart had always been. After that, tranquillity reigned once more at the Castle Hotel.

'This is a true story which was recounted to me some years ago by the local plumber. As a young lad in the 1920s he was contracted to attend to the hotel plumbing so was privy to the internal affairs of the hotel.'

The hotel is much quieter these days, though unexplained incidents do occur. For instance, a male presence has been felt by guests and staff but these events are now very infrequent.

The Cauld Lad Public House (Sunderland, Tyne and Wear)

The Cauld Lad pub is positioned close to Hylton Castle near Sunderland in Tyne and Wear, and is named after the legendary victim of a murder from the early 1600s. The pub was built in the 1960s on the grounds of the castle, which itself is dated from 1072. The pub is subject to typical poltergeistery: in particular keys go missing, things are moved, strange smells are detected and members of staff feel the presence of someone behind them when no one is there. All pretty typical of pub poltergeistery. As one of the staff said, 'After a while, you just get used to it'. Mrs Armstrong, wife of the proprietor, in particular felt the cellar was haunted; others in the pub have felt the same. One customer in the pub apparently saw a figure in a grey suit, there one moment and gone the next. And a cleaner in the pub has seen footsteps on a mopped floor, seemingly a child's naked footprints. These have been attributed to the Cauld Lad himself, original visions of the murdered child being seen stark naked and hence given the name.

The Copper Kettle
(Kendal, Cumbria)

The Copper Kettle is a café in Widmanstreet, Kendal. In 1981 the *Westmoreland Gazette* reported that poltergeistery of some sort was under way in the property. On one occasion one of the women running the café was pushed down the stairs by unseen hands, the lights having gone out just prior to that. She claimed she could feel the imprint of the hands for two hours after the incident.

The Crown Hotel
(Market St Poole, Dorset)

Trudy Clarke told us that twins born in the late seventeenth century were kept chained in an upstairs room in what is now the Crown Hotel. This was because they suffered from deformities – they were probably hunchbacks. It is also rumoured that when they died they were buried under the floor in what is now the larder area. The sound of children playing in the courtyard has been heard at times when there is nobody there. Adam, the son of a previous landlord, saw the ghost of a young girl in a nightdress leaning on the banister at 2.15 a.m., one November night when he went to the bathroom.

We spoke to Trudy in 1997 and she told us of events that had occurred more recently. During January, a tax inspector walked into the bathroom and spoke to a man he saw there, but he became frightened when the man disappeared. In fact the inspector was so frightened that the hotel staff had to give him a double brandy to calm him down!

Trudy explained that they have suffered problems with electrical items failing for no apparent reason. One evening she told her stories to Richard Forsyth, for *Encounters* magazine. After she had spoken for over an hour it was found that the tape recorder had failed so the exercise had to be repeated. The second time it recorded the interview but on replaying Trudy's voice another voice was heard in a distorted manner, threatening death to those listening.

The hauntings continue at the Crown Hotel. It is not certain that they directly relate to the legend of the seventeenth-century twins but it may be that an atmosphere of evil – and chaining up children is surely evil – can in some way hold psychic imprints, or manifest the ghosts at the location.

Visitors to the hotel should speak to Trudy, who will point out the areas of interest and would be interested to hear of any further sightings in her hotel.

Donington Manor Hotel
(Castle Donington, Leicestershire)

This hotel recently celebrated its 200th anniversary, having been built as a coaching inn in 1794. The hoteliers were advised that there was a ghost when purchasing the property in 1967, but gave no particular weight to the claim as there were no specific incidents mentioned.

Mr Grist told us, however: 'While renovating what was a derelict building, I had a very unnerving experience in one of the bedrooms. About seven years later, a guest in that same bedroom checked out in the middle of the night describing a similar experience and refused to stay any longer. In both cases, a very unpleasant woman was apparently present in the room.'

Since then there have been incidents in other rooms when members of staff have been utterly convinced that there has been an unnatural presence.

Eastwell Manor Hotel
(Eastwell Park, Ashford, Kent)

Although the present building is relatively recent, following a fire in the early 1900s, the foundations date back to 1086; there is, as we were told, a lot of history in the hotel.

The hotel has alleged hauntings going back a number of years. When we spoke to Alan Standing, a porter and night porter on the staff, he told us of a night when he was on duty with Ben Prout. They were playing snooker when they heard a loud 'donk' coming from within the walls and the floor of the room; it seemed to be moving around the room. They could not explain the noise so Alan left the room to look around, thinking he would trace the source. But Ben, left alone, heard a really loud 'donk' and at the same time felt something like an electric shock – a tingling sensation. He left, very scared. Alan pointed out that he's a big chap – over six foot – and not usually scared easily. Neither of them could find any reason for the noise, which stopped when they started working. They admitted they were at the time 'skiving': was it a ghostly remonstration from an ex-member of staff that they should keep on working, they wondered?

Ben Prout, in the cellar the next night, was beside a door which scared him when it started banging, as if being kicked. He no longer likes to go into the cellar alone.

In the 'steel room' one of the barmen was sitting six feet away from a strong, sturdy, steel shelf when a cafetière fell off the shelf and smashed; he could see no reason for this. The chef was also present and was shocked by what he saw.

Other porters have reported the ghost of a White Lady; one saw her enter the bar but when he went to serve her there was no one there. Another saw her float past reflected in a mirror.

A rather grisly tale came from a housekeeper: she entered a function room to clean and saw the vision of a man with a noose round his neck hanging from the ceiling. She left the hotel, and refused ever to work there again.

These hauntings seem to appear to affect the staff rather than visitors, who enjoy peaceful nights at the hotel. But the determined ghosthunter might get lucky! Those wanting to know more about the hauntings should talk to Alan or Ben, who will be happy to discuss these accounts, and more.

Elderton Lodge Hotel
(Thorpe Market, North Walsham, Norfolk)

Elderton Lodge Hotel was once the sporting lodge to the neighbouring Gunton Hall Estate and Deer Park, home to the Earls of Suffield since the Middle Ages. Built in 1780, it retains much of its Georgian elegance and was much frequented by Edward, Prince of Wales (later to become Edward VII). It was here that he often met with Lily Langtry in the latter part of the last century. One room has her initials etched into a glass windowpane.

It was about this time, when the lodge was being used for hunting parties, that one of the chambermaids, having been severely rebuked by the head housekeeper, hanged herself from the servants' staircase. To this day it is not uncommon for those sensitive to the paranormal to feel a distinct chill when treading the eighth and ninth step of the old staircase. Many also report a feeling of falling backwards at this point on the staircase.

The chambermaid has appeared in the adjoining bedroom on several occasions standing at the foot of the bed. Recently footsteps have been heard in the lobby at the top of the staircase by two hotel guests but, as far as we are aware, she has never been seen 'above stairs'. Mr Worby told us that he has not experienced the ghost himself, but he has been told of sightings and guests have occasionally felt their bedcovers tugged at during the night.

The Elephant and Castle Public House (Amwell, Hertfordshire)

In a letter to the *Daily Mail* (8 May 1996) a Ms Kathleen Dempster of Cornwall described a ghostly encounter in the Elephant and Castle Public House at Amwell. She was staying there with her mother, sharing a bed in a room above the taproom. One morning she awoke feeling the sensation of a presence leaning over her. 'I felt terrified and reached out for my mother and tried to call her but my voice came only in a whisper.' On other occasions Ms Dempster had seen the apparition of a woman in a black dress with golden hair and pearls, standing on the landing. The figure had its hands out 'as though pleading'.

According to Ms Dempster, a former licensee had committed suicide in the room in which she had stayed, after murdering his wife.

The Falcon Hotel (Castle Ashby, Northamptonshire)

At the time of the English Civil War, Arthur was the village blacksmith in Castle Ashby. As a servant of the Marquis of Northampton, he was a staunch and loyal royalist. On the night before the battle of Naseby, outlying forces of Cromwell's men passed through the village and commandeered the farm that now forms part of the hotel. Their horses needed re-shoeing and they enlisted Arthur, but mindful of his master's loyalties, he refused and on the morning of the battle was hanged from the walnut tree in his garden. Arthur's forge is now part of the Falcon Hotel and there is still a walnut tree in the garden.

Two of the hotel bedrooms are said to be haunted. Visitors should ask for a glass of 'Arthur's Walnut Wine' in the cocktail bar and while there might like to watch the bottles. It is said that Arthur also likes a 'wee dram'.

Arthur is remembered on the anniversary of his death, 14 June. Mr Watson told us that Arthur had been quiet since the two hundred and fiftieth anniversary in 1995, but he expects to hear from him again soon.

The Ferryboat Inn
(Holwell, Cambridgeshire)

Arguably the most famous haunted pub in England, not just for the ghost but for its alleged cyclical nature, the Ferryboat Inn stands on the Great Ouse at Holywell near St Ives, Cambridgeshire. It derives its name from a ferryboat which used to operate on the site crossing the river. Constructed in Anglo-Saxon times, the Ferryboat Inn regards itself as England's oldest inn and records that liquor was on sale as early as 560 AD; foundations of the inn may go back 100 years further.

In the floor of the inn is a slab that marks the grave of a seventeen-year-old girl named Juliette Tewsley, who was buried there at 1050 AD. It is said that Juliette committed suicide as a result of unrequited love for the woodcutter Thomas Roul. The Ferryboat Inn's own literature states: 'He was tall, handsome, arrogant and well aware of the effect he had on most women. Juliette fell completely and hopelessly, and fatally in love. Day and night she brooded and dreamed of him only. There was no other meaning to life, nothing left in the world if she could not have Tom. At last, desperate with love she could neither hide nor control, she took to roaming the woodland paths. At last her dream came true! He was walking towards her! Shyly, diffidently, her heart overflowing with innocent love, she stepped into his path mutely offering the flowers she had just gathered. Thomas sneered at such girlish foolishness and rejected her brusquely, cruelly and went into the tavern laughing. Heartbroken, crushed, the devastated girl ran home ashen faced and shocked. All night [she] lay sobbing and as dawn broke she took a length of hempen rope from her father's barn and hanged herself from a willow tree in clear view of the nearby inn. The suicide was adjudged guilty of self-murder and denied burial in consecrated ground. Juliette sleeps – but does not rest – under her tombstone inside the Ferryboat Inn, and on each anniversary of her death, 17 March, walks again to seek her lost love inside the ancient walls of the Ferryboat Inn . . .'

It is said that on the anniversary of her death the inn bustles with those seeking to catch a glimpse of the ghost of Juliette, which is said to walk around the inn and then point to the flagstone which is her alleged burial site. There is one claim that she made herself known a little earlier than usual: on one 16 March the innkeeper told a group of people who had come specifically to see Juliet that 'she'll not make herself known tonight', at which point an unseen force apparently tore a tankard from its hook and flung it to the floor.

Garden House Hotel
(St Martin's, Stamford, Lincolnshire)

The hotel was built in 1796 as a place of residence for wealthy families of the area and now has twenty en-suite rooms. Ghosthunters should ask for one of the rooms on the top floor, which would have been servant quarters in days gone by but are now rooms 18 to 21. Housekeeping staff regularly check the rooms; sometimes they have found the curtains in Room 18 closed when they should have been open. On another occasion a regular guest here at the hotel woke to find a figure looking in the window – this room is on the second floor! He has since refused to stay in that room.

The hotel also houses a Psychic Fair twice a year. Visiting psychics have told the management of a number of spirits in the hotel, mainly female, and in particular one who watches them constantly. They believe Room 18 is haunted by a presence, possibly of a man with acute breathing problems.

The George and Dragon Hotel
(West Wycombe, Buckinghamshire)

The present day eighteenth-century hotel is built on the site of a hostelry that dates back to the fourteenth century. According to Mr Philip Todd, the landlord and proprietor of the hotel, the eight-roomed coaching inn is built over a tunnel leading to the caves where the notorious Hell Fire Club held their meetings.

Its most famous ghost is that of a White Lady known as Sukie. According to legend she was a servant girl who once worked at the George and Dragon. She had fair hair, a beautiful face and many admirers among the local men. However, she rejected the advances of local people in an attempt to marry a wealthy man and advance herself socially. When just such a man appeared at the inn she set her sights on him. He in turn seems to have responded to her advances, though there is some story that she ignored his being a wealthy nobleman and believed the romantic notion that he was a notorious highwayman. The local boys who had also set their caps at Sukie became jealous and decided to humiliate her. They sent her a message pretending to be from her suitor and asking her to elope with him. She was to meet him at the West Wycombe caves during the night, wearing a wedding dress. Sukie believed the story and went to the caves dressed as requested, expecting to meet her dashing lover. She was confronted by three unhappy men set on her humiliation.

Quite what happened then is of course uncertain, but it is believed that a fight ensued during which Sukie was injured or killed. It is said that the men then smuggled her body back to her room where she was found dead the following morning, still dressed in her bridal gown.

Since that time it is said that Sukie's ghost has stalked the corridors of the George and Dragon and has been seen many times in the room in which she died. Sukie's room, an ornate room with a four-poster bed, mahogany wardrobe and copper topped table, has been the location of several sightings. One American guest, Mr Robbins, saw an apparition in white and 'a glowing pinpoint of light about 3 ft off the ground near the door'. The light then gradually expanded and became the image of the White Lady. As the light moved towards him he lost his nerve and turned on the light, after which it disappeared. He sensed a chill and felt his arms and legs grow heavy, and suffering considerable depression vowed never to return again. In 1972 a guest also saw a girl 'in a glorious white dress' who was drifting down a passageway and dematerialized by a bedroom door. A former landlady, Mrs Dorothy Boon, also saw a ghost sitting by a fire in the old servants' quarters and mistook it for a member of the staff, so there was no question of flimsiness or translucency in this instance. Yet it vanished before her eyes.

Another haunting frequently reported in the George and Dragon is the sound of heavy footsteps, which are believed to belong to another ghost, not Sukie. Some members of staff believe that this ghost is the shade of a man murdered on the site at some time in history.

There have also been some poltergeist activities, as is often reported in pubs and hotels; in particular articles disappearing and turning up in unexpected or almost impossible places apparently spontaneously.

In 1997 we spoke to Mrs Todd, the proprietor, who told us of her husband's strange experience. He was coming up the stairs in the hotel when he saw his wife – Mrs Todd herself – but was then shocked to see that she walked *through* a closed door into her office. She knew of course that it was not her; it seems to be a case of a 'phantasm of the living', or bilocation.

Mrs Todd has not seen 'Sukie' but she thinks it is possible that her son, when aged seven, did. They discovered him talking to an 'imaginary' friend and when asked who he was speaking to he replied 'to a ghost'. Asked what the ghost looked like, he described a girl with a pink bandage on her head. Could this be the injured and bandaged Sukie, they wondered?

Georgian House Hotel
(35 St George's Drive, London)

There have been several reported sightings of ghosts at the Georgian House Hotel over the years. The house was built in 1851 by master builder William Chinnery Mitchell and is managed now by his great-great-great-granddaughter, Serena von der Heyde.

The most frequently sighted ghosts have been children on the top floor of the hotel. A previous manager spoke to them once, saying that while they were welcome to play in the upper parts of the hotel, she would prefer them not to come lower as she had young children who could be frightened. Apparently they have been very obliging and have only been seen at the top of the hotel since then.

There have also been sightings of adult ghosts: a man sitting on a chair in one of the top rooms watching while a guest was sleeping; again a man standing in the kitchen; another man in one of the basement staff rooms. It seems that all these sightings did not cause fear, and that the ghosts at the hotel are in no way menacing.

The Grenadier Public House
(Knightsbridge, London)

The Grenadier Public House is a superbly atmospheric pub in a cobbled backstreet near Hyde Park Corner. Brightly coloured outside, the inside is decorated with dark wood, open fires, and many military antiques. On the back of their menu is the story of an officer who, one September, was flogged after being caught cheating at cards. The officer died from this rough justice in the cellar, and his ghost is said to have haunted the pub since then; the phenomena is especially noticeable during September.

Whatever the truth of this story, it seems certain that the pub is haunted. Successive landlords have reported happenings such as apparitions, presences distinctly felt but not visible, knocks and rapping sounds, and the movement of small objects, taps and electrical switches.

In 1991 we spoke to the relief manager, Peter Martin, who, although not inclined to believe in ghosts, told us of some strange happenings. First, of how one evening around midnight he was in the bar area with a witness, Mr Edward Webber, when they both saw a bottle 'lift' from approximately one foot above floor height (where the mixers are stored) to around head height in the middle of the bar space where it then exploded. Martin also told us that the pub keys would mysteriously disappear from under his mattress where he kept them and that they would be found some time later, somewhere else in the pub.

Alexandra and Paul Gibb took over as publicans of the Grenadier in September 1994. We spoke to them in 1995. The couple knew the haunted reputation of the pub but had not actively read up on it. When we showed Alexandra the report of the keys vanishing she laughed and exclaimed, 'That happens to me!' The keys are now kept behind the bar but are frequently found to be missing and will turn up later in different places. Although nothing specific frightens her, Alexandra will not go to the cellar by herself.

Alexandra went on to relate some other strange happenings such as:

- The electricity breaking down, leaving the pub without lights, and so on. It was at least two days before it could be fixed.
- While all the staff were out for a Christmas lunch, noises of someone moving about upstairs were distinctly heard. (If these noises occurred at other times it is possible that because this is a busy and lively place the sounds would not be heard.)
- A visitor staying at the pub reported the bathroom door locking by itself; this man was apparently quite shocked by his experience and was certain there was something strange about the way it happened.
- A customer, again near Christmas, reported seeing a man near the fire. 'He's over there,' the customer said, and spoke about the figure he could see. No one else in the room was able to see the figure, but they did notice that the customer was drunk.

We were also able to interview the bar staff. Joanna Tyrrell had been in the bathroom upstairs having a shower and had felt a presence in the locked room with her. She kept looking behind her, but saw nothing. There was no contact. She was not frightened, but felt it was something strange. She knew of several claims that the bathroom door would be found locked when no one should be in there. I questioned her carefully on what stories she knew of the pub, and it appears she was unaware of the suicide in that bathroom (see below).

Sally Freeman had been clearing up in the bar and saw a movement out of the corner of her eye. She looked towards it and saw a sword on the wall swinging to and fro. Another member of staff, who was also there, saw the sword moving as it came to rest. No other sightings or incidents were associated with this report. Sally knew of a girl who had now left who had woken up and seen a figure standing menacingly over her bed. She had been so terrified she had run out of the pub in the night in her nightdress and never would return.

Fergus had had no sightings but always felt apprehensive and cold in the basement area (which is not a particularly cold area – around 22 degrees throughout our investigation there). He was well aware of the history of the pub, and knew of the incidents that were alleged to have taken place in the basement.

Eddie Burks, in his book *Ghosthunter*, reports helping the ghost of the Grenadier officer move on and states that the pub has a second ghost, that of a man who committed suicide by electrocuting himself in the bathroom. It is interesting to note that the electrical failure, the upstairs noises, and the problem with the bathroom door, were told to us before Alexandra knew the story of the suicide.

The Grosvenor Hotel
(The Commons, Shaftesbury, Dorset)

'It is over 1000 years since travellers and pilgrims sought rest and shelter in some primitive inn that has grown through the centuries to be the Grosvenor as we know it,' states the literature of the hotel. 'Under its old name the 'Red Lion' the Grosvenor is often mentioned throughout the seventeenth and eighteenth centuries as the leading hostelry in the town and in the early nineteenth century the Grosvenors, Marquesses and later Dukes of Westminster, rebuilt it as we see it and gave it their name.'

At one time the building was used as accommodation for local monks. There are alleged to be many tunnels from the building to different points around the town; over time these have been closed, but those under the hotel remain as cellars. A monk-like figure has been seen in these cellars (some say he is responsible for any beer found missing!).

A further spectre seen around the hotel is a Grey Lady. She is thought to be the ghost of an abbess who was murdered when her belongings were stolen.

Mr Roper, the manager of the Grosvenor, told us of an event that happened two years ago on Hallowe'en night. Jane, a local historian, was in the hotel's Chevy Chase Lounge telling visitors of the area and the ghosts reported, when two glasses moved across a table apparently of their own accord. This was witnessed by the whole group of over twenty people.

Hallery House (Sturdington Road, Cheltenham Spa, Gloucestershire)

The hotel has two ghosts that have been seen and felt by guests; each of them reported as being friendly. Angie Petkovic told us: 'The property was built pre-1834 but we are not sure when, it is a fine villa style property that had been badly neglected when we bought it.

'When we looked at it, it felt totally unloved with no warmth at all in the place. As we restored it, and brought fun and laughter in, we felt the building change. We had lived here for approximately one year when I saw 'someone' out of the corner of my eye. I moved to where it had been and walked straight into a warm spot; this has happened many times and I and my guests who have seen/felt it think it's a young woman.

'The other presence has never been seen but is a ghost who smokes. We have a non-smoking dining-room and we periodically smell fresh smoke from one particular chair, again something that has been picked up a lot by our guests. We also have two dogs and a cat and on the days that we smell the smoke, all are reluctant to go past the dining-room.'

The Hobgoblin Public House (Maidenhead, Berkshire)

In December 1994 Paul and Dee Dean took over the Hobgoblin pub in Maidenhead, inheriting the resident ghost known as Bob. Bob appears to be a typical pub poltergeist and is credited with moving coats, making money disappear and turn up again just as mysteriously, turning the beer taps on and off. There are several reports of hearing footsteps from no obvious source. Though mischievous, Bob is generally regarded as a friendly polteregeist.

The bathroom door appears to become immovable at times, though there is no key or even lock. Different members of the family have found themselves trapped in the room. Dee stated: 'I couldn't get it open. I had to call Paul to come and open the door from the outside.'

Small items, pen lids and paperclips have been thrown at Paul when he is alone in the bar. On one occasion he was looking directly in the mirror and could see that no one was behind him.

Even shortly after moving in, the couple and their three children all began experiencing the phenomena. Just before Christmas they heard the sounds of glasses chinking when the bar was empty. While playing the board game Trivial Pursuit one of the plastic counters shifted spontaneously, moving two spaces – the number that had just been thrown on the dice. The same night a necklace went missing from a bedroom and turned up in a locked beer cellar. The barman prefers not to go into the cellar alone. 'It feels like there's someone else in there with you,' he said, 'Someone you can't see.'

Ivy Dene
(Country House, West Witton, Leyburn, North Yorkshire)

Ivy Dene is a listed building with a 300-year history set in the National Park; it is run by Bob and June Dickinson. After they had taken possession the previous owner told them some odd tales. For example, in one particular bedroom a figure could be seen from time to time sitting in the window seat, smoking an old pipe. Mr Dickinson does not believe in ghosts, but he told us: 'I have to admit that not only have guests complained of the room smelling and appearing smoky on occasion, but I myself have seen smoke in the room, with no reasonable explanation readily to hand'. The hotel is decidedly non-smoking now!

An American lady claims to have seen a figure in period dress crossing the top of the stairs. Mr Dickinson feels the American lady may have had an active imagination and is still waiting to be convinced himself of any supernatural attachments.

So if you see any ghosts while you are there – please let him know.

The King's Head Hotel
(Cirencester, Gloucestershire)

The King's Head originated in the sixteenth century as a coaching inn and saw the first bloodshed of the English Civil War. In 1688 Lord Lovelace, in the market place, was attacked by Stuart supporters, and his companion Bulstrode Whitelock was shot and died in the King's Head during the affray.

There are many ghosts reported. A night porter, Charles Anderson, saw a dim figure on a stairway in the early hours of the morning and, assuming that it was a guest, asked if he was all right. There was no reply, and this made Anderson pay a little more attention, whereupon he realized that the person was wearing a monk's robe with a cowl drawn around his face. The apparition then disappeared through a wall.

On another occasion Anderson was with a barmaid doing his rounds of the hotel. He opened the door to the Monk's Retreat, sometimes used as a skittle alley, and the barmaid screamed. Apparently she had seen a dark and faceless figure sitting by the entrance. Although the figure disappeared, the stool it had been sitting on was apparently still rocking. This room houses the entrance to a blocked-up secret passage which once led under the market place to the cellars of the abbey penitentiary.

Anderson believes that at least some of the ghosts of the hotel are friendly, and does not mind them even when they grip his shoulder, as he has reported they do. Poltergeistery in the form of moving a heavy electric fire, shaking the curtains and a pen spontaneously flung across the Whitelock Suite is attributed to the ghost; Anderson also received a report from a guest that he had felt himself pinned into his bed; this had left his arms and legs aching.

One curious apparition is of a man dressed as a Cavalier, who apparently fired a pistol at the members of staff who saw him. It is thought that this 'Cavalier ghost' is a reflection of Whitelock's death.

The Langham Hilton
(Portland Place, London)

The hotel is thought to be haunted by a German military prince, who threw himself from a balcony just before the First World War. During the Second World War the building was used by the BBC; it contained offices and dormitories for the staff. One presenter who saw the ghost,

James Alexander Gordon, spoke of the encounter in a in-flight document-ary shown by British Airways in 1993. He apparently slept in a third-floor room now known as Room 333 and awoke to see a fluorescent ball which changed shape, gradually becoming human-like. Eventually it became clear enough for him to perceive the ghost of a man in Victorian-style evening dress, including cloak and cravat, even though Gordon was still able to see through him. As the figure began to move towards him Gordon left in a hurry. He realized he needed to return for his clothes and, on doing so, saw that the ghost was still there. Gordon told the story to his colleague Ray Moore, who confirmed that he had also seen the ghost. Moore's description was slightly different: a thickset man with cropped hair wearing a jacket buttoned up to the neck.

Later, after the story was broadcast, many other reports were received. It seems that this hotel ghost most frequently appears around the month of October.

The Lodge Hotel
(Old Hunstanton, Norfolk)

This is a 400 year-old building steeped in the local history. Situated on the north Norfolk coast, the hotel occupies an area frequented in the mid-eighteenth century by smugglers. One story from the locality states that smugglers shot dead two officers of the law and could not be convicted because all the jury was benefiting from their ill-gotten gains! The officers' graves in the local church tell the tale. There is believed to be a smugglers' tunnel to the beach under the hotel, leading from one of the cellars.

Guests and past staff have reported mysterious sights and sounds in various parts of the hotel. A frequent report received by the management is of an elderly lady dressed in grey who is seen in the hotel's passages and who disappears through closed doors.

The proprietor, Carole Best, told us of a strange problem with the hotel windows. 'One unexplained occurrence many years ago was that of a window cracking in a bricked-up Georgian-style window on the first floor. The builder replaced the last pane three times in the same day and finally left it out. Last year we had all the panes removed and replaced with opaque glass to hide the bricks. The contractor reported having difficulty with the last pane of glass and had to fix a pane of toughened glass instead. Rumour has it that the old grey lady likes to climb out to haunt the little old bridge down the road, where many people have reported seeing the ghost of an old lady!'

Carole further told us of her own experience. 'I have myself once been scared to death while in a small attic room one evening. I felt something near me and felt something swish past me with a rustle and the door, which I had wedged open, slammed shut. I quickly escaped downstairs never to venture into that room after dark.'

The Longstone House Hotel
(North Sunderland, Seahouses, Northumberland)

When the present owners took over in late 1996 they knew nothing of the reputation of the building. During the initial visits to get the hotel ready – before contracts had been settled – Judy Oxley, the present owner, her teenage children and the children of the previous manageress heard a child run across the floor in the room above; no one was in the room, in fact no one was upstairs at all.

As time went on Ms Oxley heard tales of Room 6. Soon, she had her own experiences to relate. 'One afternoon, I was sitting in the bar directly below Room 6, doing some bookwork, and saw what I took to be a child. I couldn't even tell if it was a boy or a girl, I was just aware. It was like a mist, just swirling. It was strange, I felt no fear, no cold nothing – just there, then gone. Somebody else has told me that they have also seen a child there; I hadn't told them anything. People have just come to me and told me. One visitor in the bar even asked me if I had seen the ghost yet – I was able to tell him I had. We take school parties and of course children are full of ghost stories but twice this year they have mentioned Room 6. There have also been stories from Room 1, directly above Room 6. So it's always in that area – the bar, Room 6 and Room 1, all above one another.'

Even on the night previous to our interview Ms Oxley was told by some children – a sensible, not mischievous group, she assured us – that they were being disturbed by someone knocking on their door. They were in Room 6. They waited for the knocking to occur again and – when they heard it – they immediately pulled open the door. There was nobody there.

The Lord Crewe Arms Hotel
(Blanchland, near Consett, Durham)

The Lord Crewe Arms Hotel was originally built as the abbot's lodge, guest house and kitchens of Blanchland Abbey. The main entrance leads into what was the abbey kitchen. The Hilyard Room and Crypt Bar were store rooms where crops from abbey lands would have been kept. The giant fireplace in the Hilyard Room was used for the smoking and curing of meat. High inside the chimney you can see the priest's hiding hole! We spoke to Mr Peter Gingell, who told us of three ghosts. We quote from the hotel's own literature on its ghostly history. The first concerns a family that once owned the house: 'Tom Forster was a military commander of the Jacobite forces during the 1715 uprising. He had no qualifications whatever for such a post and, at Preston, surrendered to the government troops without even trying to put up a fight. He was taken to London and imprisoned in Newgate gaol, from where he managed to escape three days before he was due to be tried for high treason. This escape was planned by his sister Dorothy Forster II, who it is said, disguised herself as his servant, rode to London behind the village blacksmith and made good her brother's escape.

'It is believed that Tom and Dorothy returned to the Lord Crewe Arms, which had previously been their family home, and that Tom was hidden in the Priest's Hole until he was able to escape to France where he died. Dorothy has remained at the Lord Crewe ever since . . . in spirit, of course! Her presence has been felt by many in the part of the hotel where she had her apartment. Dorothy haunts the Bamburgh room asking anyone who will listen to take a message to her brother, still in France, that all is well and he can safely return to England.'

The second report is from just a few years ago: 'A couple were sleeping in the Radcliffe bedroom. They did not know that the room that they were in was part of the Abbot's lodging of a monastery and they knew nothing of the White Cannons. The wife woke during the night to see a monk in a white habit kneeling at the bottom of her four poster bed, she put her hand out and he was quite solid and then, she reported, he slowly dematerialized. Her husband was asleep beside her and we know that they had drunk very little at dinner time the previous evening.' We were told that the monk appears mostly during the winter months.

The third account: 'Some years ago a woman, who knew the hotel well, was the only person sleeping in the ancient part of the building. Early in the morning she heard an outside door open and close, then footsteps, then she saw a light under her door. The footsteps receded into the hotel and the light was extinguished. Next morning she mentioned to the manager that she had heard old Tom coming into the hotel to light the fires. But the manager knew that Tom had died some months earlier. The outside door was bolted and it was quite certain that no one beside herself had been in her part of the building all night.'

Peter Gingell is an amateur historian at the hotel and we suggest that any visitor speaks to him for more information on the hotel, Blanchland Abbey and Blanchland village.

The Lord Haldon Hotel
(Dunchideock, Near Exeter, Devon)

The Lord Haldon Hotel and Restaurant claims it has a ghost: the spectre of a maid who once worked for Lord Haldon himself. The building was once owned by Robert Palk, Lord Haldon, who is said to have had an association with this servant, who became pregnant. Lord Haldon not wishing a scandal to ensue, enticed her to one of the lakes in the grounds and drowned her, making it look like accidental death. It is said that she reappears today looking for him. She appears in only one of the hotel's guest bedrooms, which in Lord Haldon's time was part of the servants' quarters.

Simon Preece told us that some years ago a séance was held in the lounge bar using a Ouija board. The date 1813 and the name Isabella were spelt out when questions were asked about the maid. We cannot be certain that this is the same ghost but the date certainly suggests it.

The Mermaid Inn
(Rye, Sussex)

The Mermaid Inn is a hotel with over 500 years of history to draw from. An American woman staying at the inn is reported to have been shocked almost into paralysis by the sight of two swashbuckling smugglers duelling in her room. It was several minutes, the witness thinks, before she realized that the figures were making no sound. The fight ended when one of the ghosts killed the other, whereafter the witness watched as the victor rifled through the victim's pockets. The apparitions ended when the victor hid the corpse behind a panel in the room.

New Hall
(Walmley Road, Sutton Coldfield, West Midlands)

New Hall was bought by Thistle Hotels in 1985, and Ian and Caroline Parkes were asked to oversee the conversion. Since May 1988 they have run New Hall as a luxury country house hotel. New Hall is a leading hotel in the Birmingham and West Midlands area, receiving many awards and accolades since its opening, and has become famous for looking after many of the stars that perform in Birmingham and the National Exhibition Centre. Although a hotel for only twelve years, New Hall has a long history. It is reputedly the oldest listed inhabited moated house in England, dating back to the twelfth century.

In 1995 Ian and Caroline provided us with the Hall's own literature on its ghosts from which the following is extracted: 'New Hall has witnessed many historic events during its 800 years history, and numerous families have lived and worked within its walls, so it is not surprising that there are a number of ghost stories associated with the house. However, ghosts tend to have rather disobliging habits; they elude the most dedicated ghost hunters, but materialize without warning before people who claim not to believe in them, and though darkness is their element, they are frequently seen in broad daylight. Such are the ghosts of New Hall.

'Inside the house a lady in white is said to haunt the Red Landing. No one is certain who she is, but perhaps she is the wife of Henry Sacheverell who died at the beginning of the seventeenth century, and the many coats of arms which decorate the timbers of the ceiling on the landing remind her of the lost heritage of her own children, for her husband bestowed New Hall on Valens, the elder of his two illegitimate sons by 'Mistress Keics'.

'Sometimes it is the audible rather than the visual effects of a ghost which are experienced and this is the probable explanation of the loud crashing noise which may be heard in the area adjacent to the dining-room. A former resident of New Hall relates how one evening when sitting in what is now the dining-room she heard a loud crashing noise nearby, which she likened to the sound of a large dresser falling. When she rushed to see what had happened, she found everything in perfect order. The noise remains unexplained, but the area where it occurs is where the secret study of George Sacheverell was found. At the beginning of the eighteenth century he was known as 'The Alchemist of New Hall'. Maybe it is George up to some of his old tricks!

'Another ghostly happening which is heard and not seen may be experienced after dark in the circlet of trees at the end of the Yew Tree Walk. Here voices and the noise of a carriage being driven with galloping horses may be heard. Who is riding with such haste and calling with such urgency? The answer may be found to relate to the period of the Civil War. In 1645 Valens Sacheverell was charged with 'compounding for delinquency in deserting his house for enemy quarters' and he was fined a sum of £542. Valens supported the Cavaliers, and it is said that Charles II stayed one night at New Hall during his flight from England.

'Outside there has been seen on the driveway of New Hall, a lady in dark clothing, with a dog, who is likely to have been a local woman who worked at the manor. It is often said that small children have natural psychic abilities and can evoke responsiveness from ghosts. This was the case when the lady was seen near the old kennels by the children of a gardener at New Hall, she held out her hand to them, as a mother would offer her hand to her child.'

Old Colehurst Manor
(Colehurst, Market Drayton, Shropshire)

Old Colehurst Manor is owned and run by Bjorn and Maria Teksnes. They took seven years to restore the building to create an atmosphere of times past. Guests are invited to live 'in the seventeenth century' during their stay there. The manor positively revels in history: open fires, candlelit dining and all staff in period costumes. Guests are also invited, but not obliged, to dress in period clothing, which is provided.

Maria claims to have 'encountered' what the hotel charmingly calls 'absent friends'. They have nicknamed the most prominent ghost 'Fred', a common enough nickname for a ghost we have found, but a name which the Teksnes point out means 'peace' in Norwegian. His presence – and they believe guidance – was felt during the reconstruction work. As the couple explained: 'Many times when uncertain or about to do something which would have been dangerous, Bjorn has felt a guidance which he followed, only to find out later the dire consequences that would have resulted without this guidance. Maria describes 'Fred' as a short pleasant faced man in period costume, with long curly hair, always smiling as if pleased with the work that is returning Old Colehurst Manor to its former glory.'

Other ghostly reports include sightings of a man and woman comforting a child, sitting under the window in the 'Prison Cell'.

Overwater Hall
(Ireby, near Keswick, Cumbria)

A hotel set in eighteen acres of gardens and woods in the Lake District is the setting for a gruesome ghost report. There have been sightings of a figure tapping on the hotel windows, a woman with no hands, just severed stumps. The same figure has also been seen passing through the closed door of Room 3. Inexplicable voices have also been heard occasionally in the corridors.

The origin of the ghost is lost in legend; the favoured story is that the original owner of the building, Joseph Gillbanks, tried to drown his pregnant mistress in Owerwater Tarn by rowing her out in a boat and throwing her into the waters. When she tried to climb back into the boat he chopped off her hands with an axe.

Pengethley Manor
(near Ross-on-Wye, Herefordshire)

Pengethley Manor sports a friendly ghost known as 'Harriet'. She is thought to have been a maid at the Manor House when it was owned by the Symmonds family. There was a fire in the Manor in the late 1800s; perhaps she died in that incident. Harriet is particularly fond of two bedrooms and there are reports of people who sense her presence at the foot of their beds. Sometimes reported is the noise of a party coming from an empty bedroom.

Last year a party of Americans staying at the hotel took some Polaroid pictures in the hotel and these showed some strange lines which they thought were 'paranormal'. Paul Forster, the general manager to whom we spoke, could not find any easy explanation for the images.

In Christmas 1996 a colleague of Paul's was closing the bar when a brass doorstopper moved away and the door closed by itself. He was shocked. Paul has himself felt a presence in the reception area, and along an upstairs corridor.

The Prestbury House Hotel and Restaurant (The Burgage, Prestbury, Cheltenham, Gloucestershire)

The hotel is a 300-year-old Georgian country manor house owned and operated by Jacqueline and Stephen Whitbourn. Stephen provided us with the hotel's own literature on its haunted heritage, from which the following is extracted:

'The most famous ghost dates back to the atrocities of the English Civil War. Cromwell had his officers billeted at Prestbury House, whilst his own headquarters was just up the road, when a King's messenger from Sudeley Castle galloped the length of the Burgage trying to get through. This brave but foolish man did not see the wire strung between the beech trees that once stood outside and his head was neatly severed, as if by a surgeon, from his Royalist body. This ghost is not seen but the sound of his galloping horse is heard by some on certain nights.

'The second ghostly happenings are of a tea party in the Spinney not 200 yards from the West Wing. It is thought that this is from the time when King George III held a tea party there.

'But the hotel's favourite ghost is a beautiful servant girl with a water pitcher seen in the garden. She is certainly lost in time and destiny, as her clothing suggests she is of an age long before a house ever stood on these grounds.'

The Prince Rupert Hotel (Butcher Row, Shrewsbury, Shropshire)

The Prince Rupert Hotel is situated in the heart of Shrewsbury, particularly conveniently located for an exploration of Wenlock Edge. It has a contemporary record of hauntings of its own.

In Room 6, in the historic part of the hotel, a young lady is said to haunt this room looking for a single young man willing to marry her. She apparently committed suicide in that same room after having been jilted at the altar. Before the hotel was refurbished, Room 6 was a staff room area: over a period of time there were several minor but none the less unexplained happenings of objects moving, book markers being several chapters further on from where they were left, etc.

Rooms 4 & 5, the honeymoon suite, have a recent report. In 1991, not long after the refurbishment of the Prince Rupert, a couple on their wedding night completed a guest questionnaire as follows: 'You may think that I am mad, that's up to you, but the recent renovation work has disturbed atmospheres that were very settled. You have disturbed several buried 'spirits', i.e. old memories of the Jones Mansion part of the hotel (despite most major refurbishment being in the connecting corridor). These 'spirits' kept me (a clairvoyant) awake most nights and the sudden changes in atmosphere when going from one part of the hotel to another are quite unnecessary. May I recommend that when the refurbishment is absolutely complete, you get the hotel blessed by a local vicar (NOT exorcized; you want to keep these friendly (but disturbed at present) spirits here). This will settle the atmosphere down a bit. Was someone ever buried in the cellar, or 'walled up' at this end of the Jones Mansion? Have you ever found a small brass box/chest in a fireplace with an important document inside ... behind/above the beams over fireplace in chimney! Why were gunshots fired in the Prince Rupert Lounge long ago? Ask Margaret Patience (old housekeeper 1690–1720). I may be absolutely loony, but as a professional at this sort of thing, it wouldn't be the first time I was right!'

In 1997 the hotel confirmed another sighting in the 'Rupert Lounge', which is just outside rooms 4 and 5. Guests considering holding a wedding reception there were being shown around, and one of the ladies asked the manager: 'Can you see him?' The manager was a little perplexed; the woman's daughter explained that her mother often saw ghosts and spirits and that in this case there was a 'a gentleman sitting on a chair in the entrance to the lounge wearing period dress'. The woman told the manager that he was psychic even though he might not be aware of it, due to his being a Pisces (which, it turns out, he is).

From Room 105, in the modern section of the hotel, another recent story was reported. Just after Christmas 1994 a married couple were in bed asleep on their first night in the room, when the woman awoke to the feel of cool breath on her cheek. She said the room suddenly turned ice cold and then the end of bed depressed as if someone was sitting down. On the second night, exactly the same thing happened and this time her husband awoke and also witnessed it.

The Queen's Hotel
(City Square, Leeds, West Yorkshire)

The present day Queen's Hotel, was built in 1937 on the site of the first Queen's Hotel which was established in 1863. It is the original Queen's Hotel that was host to many ghosts, one of which still haunts the new building; the ghost of Mrs Karen Fleet.

Karen Fleet was housekeeper at the Queen's in 1916. She was widowed with one son, and was heartbroken when she heard of his untimely death during the monstrous battle of the Somme. Naturally, her motherly instincts were to have her son's remains returned to her for Christian burial in his native city of Leeds, and after much pleading and many weeks of correspondence to the War Office by her and the hotel's general manager, Mr John Garden, they at last received notification that his body would be despatched from France on a frigate bound for Dover.

In the meantime Karen Fleet had resigned her employment, purchased a suitable grave and had it prepared to receive her son's body. Every day at 11 a.m. precisely Mrs Fleet arrived at the hotel to discuss progress with Mr Garden.

Shortly after sailing from France the frigate bearing her son, Edward Adrian Fleet, was attacked from all sides by enemy superior forces and was sunk with all hands, twenty-five miles off the French coast beyond all possible recovery. In those days it was often considered wiser to suppress bad news to the British public and the news of the frigate's loss was submerged in a complex of bureaucracy that not even the Member of Parliament, Mr Thornton, was able to penetrate, so Mrs Fleet continued to visit the Queen's at 11 a.m. precisely every day for news of her son's arrival. These visitations continued for three weeks until finally Mrs Fleet, overcome by grief and malnutrition through self-neglect, collapsed and died in Mr Garden's waiting-room.

It is a ghostly legend passed on from hotel to hotel via the working generations of the two Queen's that Mrs Fleet continues to visit the hotel at 11 a.m. precisely every day in her tormented search for her lost son. The administration suite of offices for the previous building is now the sub-basement of the present Queen's Hotel, specifically the boiler house area; mysterious sightings have taken place there as recently as 1989, when the general manager, Mr Steven Maslen, and an assistant manager,

Mrs Heather Riley, saw a white figure pass through the double doors leading to the old coal-fire boiler-house and, despite the obvious warmth to be expected in the boiler-house area, experienced a swift and chilling reduction in the temperature which lasted as long as the apparition was in sight.

The hotel engineer, Mr Peter Dickinson, in whose area of responsibility the boiler-house is, cannot explain the reasons behind padlocked doors falling unlocked, valves and dials and temperatures altered and interfered with and – most strange of all – the gentle sounds of a woman sobbing often heard in the far corners of the area beneath the hotel.

It should be considered a consolation for all guests to the hotel to know that Mrs Karen Fleet was a very thoughtful, caring, gentle and hospitable person and by all accounts is now a very friendly ghost.

Red Lion Hotel
(Colchester, Essex)

In 1997 the hotel told us of two ghosts, both from long ago in the building's history. The first ghost is named Alice, thought to be a girl of around fifteen or sixteen years of age. Two stories purport to explain this white figure that has been seen particularly around the kitchen area. One suggests that she was murdered by her lover, who returned after serving in the Army and believed – rightly or wrongly – that she had taken other lovers. The second story is that she was murdered by her father, though there is no explanation offered as to why.

The second ghost is that of a monk-like figure known as Father Peter. In part of the original building in which the hotel is presently situated there was a fire, during which several children in Father Peter's care were in danger. Father Peter is said to have perished saving his charges.

Redworth Hall Hotel and Country Club
(Redworth, near Newton Aycliffe, Durham)

Legend has it that a Lady Catherine died in the building 200 years ago, committing suicide by jumping off the tower. On Hallowe'en night 1990, a team of psychics, mediums and investigators held a séance at the hotel in an attempt to identify its hauntings and to win an unusual prize:

a bounty of £5,000 if they were able to prove to the hotel managers the existence of paranormal phenomena. The team included psychic Matthew Hutton and medium Tony McQueen.

As reported in the *Northern Echo* of 15 October, prior to the vigil, the pair had already visited the premises and obtained impressions of someone who had hanged themselves. Tony became convinced that a death had occurred in the tower, which was when the management revealed that that was where Lady Catherine was said to have committed suicide. The newspaper reported a summary of the Hall's phenomena by psychic Steve Pearce, consisting of rapid temperature drops, a feeling of a presence, the apparition of a female form, mysterious footsteps and children's voices.

In the *Northern Echo* of 1 November 1990, the morning following the vigil, the summary was: 'The general consensus was that there was something there – but it has left the uninitiated wondering'. During the séance they apparently received a great many impressions: 'a boy tripping up and down the stairs, psychic mist, the babble of voices'. As the paper points out, the building was once a reformatory. Of the sound of footsteps it was believed that nobody could have been in the location without the team knowing it, which seemed to suggest some paranormal activity. Of Lady Catherine, Tony detected the names Rupert, Charles, Geoff and Granville but without being able to attribute them to any part of Lady Catherine's story.

The management did not feel that sufficient proof had been offered to merit the £5,000 reward.

The Royal Castle Hotel (Dartmouth, Devon)

There are several hauntings associated with the Royal Castle Hotel. One in particular is the apparition of a female form and the sound of what appears to be a horse-drawn carriage being driven through the middle of the hotel in the dead of night. The carriage is held by some to be a portent of an untimely death to follow. It is said that William of Orange sent a carriage to collect his wife, Princess Mary, who was staying at the Castle Hotel in November 1688 when William came to claim the throne of England from Mary's father, King James II. This, however, does not meet historical accuracy. Princess Mary was in Holland at the time when William left for England. It was not until 12 February 1689 that the crown of England was offered jointly to William and Mary and it was not until the following day that Mary arrived in England. On 14 February they were proclaimed King and Queen at Westminster and there is no record of Mary ever having visited Dartmouth up until her death five years later.

However, the fact that the local legend and beliefs can be proven to be inaccurate means only that the attribution of the sound is wrong. It does not mean that the sound has not been heard but only that its origin has yet to be discovered.

If these paranormal events are the result of death or suffering then we can at least locate one death at the Castle Hotel, sufficiently strange to allow for the possibility that the deceased might be somehow trying to explain or accuse. In 1895 William Hingston Tabb, an ostler at the Castle Hotel, was found dead in a horse trough in the stable-yard at the rear of the hotel, according to an edition of the local *Chronicle* of the time. The water in the trough was eighteen inches deep. The medical evidence was that he had died by drowning and he had a small abrasion on his forehead. This would be consistent with a murder, with the victim forced into the trough and perhaps cutting his head in a struggle. However, because he had been depressed following the recent death of his wife and because the stable-yard was locked when his body was found, the verdict given was: 'Found drowned – probably accidental'. So it is unclear whether Tabb died accidentally, committed suicide or was murdered. Tabb had worked all his life with horses and carriages and if the paranormal represents at least in part a reaching out from beyond the grave then perhaps that is why this particular 'attention-seeking' takes the form it does.

In 1997 we spoke to Nigel Way at the hotel, who told us that: 'In the last three years we have had four night porters hand in their notice due to ghostly apparitions in the central courtyard – originally open to the sky, and now covered in glass. Their stories were always similar: two men fighting and tumbling over each other. One porter even indicated that it rained at the same time once, and that some but not all of the furniture showed signs of wet patches.

'In Room 22 more than one guest has awoken to find their clothes removed from the chest of drawers and deposited on the floor.'

Ruthin Castle
(Ruthin, Denbighshire)

Since 1963 this splendid castle has been a luxury hotel featuring medieval banquets where 'twentieth-century guests pursue the pageantry of the sixteenth century with obvious relish'.

On a walk through the grounds visitors are invited to inspect the drowning pit, where prisoners were interred either to drown themselves or to perish when their strength ran out. Further on you can visit the dungeons and the whipping pit. You should also look out for the grave of the castle's ghost: The Grey Lady.

There are many different stories surrounding the Grey Lady, described as such because she is dressed from head to foot in grey. The most popular of these stories is that she was the wife of the second-in-command at the castle when it was a fortress and inhabited by the armies of Edward I. The Grey Lady discovered that her powerful husband was having an affair with a local lady, so she took the necessary action and murdered her husband's lover with an axe. When her dreadful deed was discovered, the Grey Lady was sentenced to death. As she could not be buried in a churchyard (as this was consecrated ground) it was decided that she should be buried just outside the castle walls and her grave can be seen to this day.

The Grey Lady is reportedly seen in the banqueting hall, which was once the castle chapel. She has also been seen roaming the castle battlements, and, from time to time, wandering around the grounds outside the present castle.

Shipman's Public House
(Northampton, Northamptonshire)

The Shipman's pub is over 200 years old and, like many pubs and old buildings, has a reputation for being haunted. When Diane West took over as landlady of the pub she soon heard of its reputation but dismissed the stories as just that – stories. One day, however, she photographed the pub, took the film for developing at the local chemist's, and was shocked to discover on looking at the prints she got back that there seemed to be a ghostly figure standing next to the fruit machine in the bar area.

Two weeks later more manifestations broke out. 'Drinks glasses started to move. Full pint glasses just slid to the end of the table, stopped, jumped up and dropped off,' described Diane. After several years, she became used to the poltergeistery. She has heard footsteps on the stairs and mysterious noises from the bathroom.

Perhaps the ghost, if it is a restless spirit, is identified by a newspaper cutting Diane located. It described Harry Franklin, a manager of the pub around 100 years ago, who committed suicide by slitting his own throat and taking a week to die.

The Smithfield Public House (Derby, Derbyshire)

Poltergeist-type activity of a type frequently found in pubs arose in 1996 in the Smithfield, in Meadow Road. Pipes to the beers somehow got switched around, resulting in, for example, lager coming out of the cider taps. On other occasions the pipes would deliver beer even when the gas taps were switched off – which, as landlady Yvonne Greaves pointed out, is impossible. 'If the gas isn't working then the beer won't travel through the pipes.'

One night the landlord, Dick Greaves, came down into the public area to check the doors were locked and found an old man sitting in a chair. The corner where he was seen sitting is always inexplicably cold. It is believed that he is the ghost of a man who was killed in the stables that used to exist behind the present building, and is well known to locals, who warned the new tenants about the ghost when they moved into the pub.

The Stag at Redhill (Alcester Road, Redhill, near Stratford-upon-Avon, Warwickshire)

The Stag at Redhill is a post house built in the sixteenth century and retains many original features. The walls within the centre of the building are made of local Binton stone and the hotel rooms around the courtyard are converted from the original stables. The restaurant was the archway through which coaches entered. The Medieval Banqueting Suite was used by the travelling circuit judges; cells existed at the rear of the room and also above the new staircase, where two of the original cell windows have been retained. (Visitors should look out for the original cell door, now in the hallway.) Prisoners found guilty were hanged nearby, at the crossroads by the Billesley Manor.

A phantom old lady has been seen on a number of occasions in the rear car park, and is thought to be visiting her son, who was a prisoner here before being taken to the gallows. She is most often seen on Midsummer's Night – presumed to be the anniversary of her son's death – but in 1997 she was seen in January. A businesswoman saw and spoke to the old lady in the car courtyard, and it was not until she asked the proprietor of the hotel, Mr John Hunt, that she was told it was a ghost.

Inside the hotel is a haunted bedroom. This was visited by a psychic, who explained that the ghost there is one of Cromwell's officers who visited the building after leaving nearby Edge Hill. Although this ghost is not always seen, many people have felt and commented on a coldness in that room. To discover which is the haunted room, visitors should speak to Mr Hunt, the proprietor.

Talbot Hotel
(Leominster, Herefordshire)

The hotel dates from the fifteenth century, although the premises have been altered over the years. The following experience took place in a bedroom which was once a small adjacent cottage used by coachmen of the day. One off-duty evening Mr Creswell, the managing director of the hotel, retired early after having only very little alcoholic drink and wanting a good rest. He told us: 'During the early hours of the morning I was woken by pressure on my legs; jumping on my bed was a male person wearing a grey monk's habit with hood which was covering the rear of his head. I pulled myself up in bed and the monk jumped from the bed to the floor to the left, he continued to jig up and down, tittering as he did so. The window from the bedroom opens to an interior well of the hotel. I first thought that the monk image was a reflection from outside against a full length mirror in the room. When looking through the window there was no light to be seen. Although startled but not frightened, my reaction was to then switch on the bedroom light, the switch being adjacent to the headboard. When turning on the light the monk disappeared.'

Leominster is a town to which a number of monks moved to escape the religious persecution of religious orders in earlier centuries. A monk was also seen in 1996 by a visitor who told Mr Creswell the story and asked if the hotel was haunted. This sighting took place in the corridor outside the bedroom where the grey monk was seen.

The hotel stands at a point which was known as 'The Iron Cross'. According to local historians, a monk by the name of Cadwallader was hung, drawn and quartered at this spot. Tales say that on this occasion the ritual was very messy, being carried out by a local butcher.

The Thorn Hotel
(Mistley, Manningtree, Essex)

As the Thorn Hotel's own literature states: 'The Hotel exudes memories of its historic past and the décor reflects this with its oak beams and wood panelled walls'. The hotel 'raises the memory of the port's most notorious resident, Matthew Hopkins'. Matthew Hopkins was of course better known as the Witchfinder General and started his work in Mistley. It is believed a good many of his interrogations took place in an upstairs room at the Thorn. Anne Leech of Mistley and four women from Manningtree were amongst the first twenty-eight women hanged as witches as a result of Hopkins's 'work'.

The Thorn Hotel is said to have several ghosts, including a Grey Lady and a hooded figure seen by many residents and a few of the previous landlords. The Thorn Hotel, in a letter to us, commented: 'The locals have numerous stories of various 'appearances' over the years but the most recent was from a couple staying in our 'witches' room. They claimed to have seen a figure two nights running during the early hours of the morning'.

John Parker, the hotel proprietor, had been there just six months when we spoke to him in 1997. He has noticed that lights in one bedroom turn on by themselves. He finds them on when he knows they should be off. A guest staying in that same bedroom complained of being woken three times by a presence. The woman also went down into the cellars, and found that an unpleasant experience. It is worth noting that the cellars, in the days of the witchhunts, were used to temporarily imprison women waiting for 'trial'.

Ghosthunters should speak to Mr Parker to book themselves into the haunted bedroom – and he would be grateful for your comments on your night's stay!

The Tudor Rose Hotel
(Kings Lynn, Norfolk)

The buildings which now house the Tudor Rose Hotel date back to the twelfth century. The nearby area has a long-standing reputation as being haunted. At one time the Tudor Rose was virtually derelict and became known locally as the 'Haunted House' or 'Haunted Castle'. It was one of those buildings that young boys took a 'dare' to run close to. It was also generally thought that young people ran past it at night rather than walked.

Legend has it that a horrific murder was committed in the building during a wedding. The new bride, bridegroom and guests got themselves into a huge quarrel and the bridegroom stabbed his wife to death. The bride is said to haunt an upstairs room; the scene of her brief marriage. There is an alternative version of the legend; that a jilted ex-suitor of the bride broke into the wedding ceremony, killing both the bride and groom. A sad and pitiful presence is said to invade the hotel from time to time, an echo of whatever reality might lie behind these tragic stories perhaps.

Mrs Sally Hunter lived at the Tudor Rose Hotel from 1977 till 1984. Although she received many complaints of hauntings from guests, her concern was professional and she did not personally concern herself with the story. Until, however, Mrs Hunter had her own experience. On a busy Saturday night she asked a waitress to get a glass of port from downstairs for a restaurant customer. After a while she realized that the waitress was taking too long and walked to the stairs to call down to her. There she saw coming up the stairs towards her a small woman in a long dress. Her face was infinitely sad, and Mrs Hunter perceived that although looking solid she also 'seemed ethereal'. As she watched, the figure dissipated into a mist. At that point the waitress came up the stairs flapping her hands and said, 'It isn't half smoky on the stairs,' and walked straight through the mist. Mrs Hunter reported that the atmosphere was depressing for two days after the sighting.

During a Christmas period the staff were on holiday and Mrs Hunter had her mother and father staying. This resulted in a curious claim of bilocation or projection. Sally's father saw the night porter, Tom, go into his cubbyhole, yet Tom was away from his job enjoying a holiday. On another occasion during heavy snow in January a receptionist reported that a man was in the yard clearing the snow away. This seemed unlikely, but Mrs Hunter felt it was only right to go to the door to thank him. As they looked out they could see that there was no one there and the snow was untouched, not even a footprint on it.

There were several poltergeist accounts from the bar, again particularly at Christmas. Glasses taken from shelves, a heavy tray smashed on to the floor, one woman reported footsteps behind her but never found anyone there. Mrs Hunter found some of the poltergeistery annoying, in particular giving the impression that customers were waiting in reception by footsteps of 'presence' but finding that no one was there.

Mr John Bull and his wife are now the proprietors, and we asked if they had experienced anything since moving in. We were told that they themselves had not but that their son, aged ten, had seen a ghostly nun in his attic bedroom in 1996. Mr and Mrs Bull accept that it could be a nun but have also speculated if it could be the shade of a bride in her wedding gown and veil.

More recently, in 1997, a cleaner walked into the restaurant and saw a person sitting at a table. The cleaner walked out, unsure about cleaning while a guest was present, but on turning back found that the room was completely empty. We were assured that there was no way anyone could have left without being seen. Soon after that the cleaner also left the hotel, and she has not been seen since either!

The White Hart Hotel
(Bridge Street, Andover, Hampshire)

Simon Hughes, the proprietor, told us: 'It is true that many reported sightings of a lady dressed in green roaming the corridors have been made, both by guests and staff of the hotel, the latest being in 1995. An account was of the lady in a bedroom: a person recently asked at reception, 'Do you have a ghost?' He had been staying in Room 14 and had noticed someone standing over his bed during the night.

'Other reports of repeated knocking on bedroom doors in the middle of the night, when answered, no one being there, are not uncommon.

'One particular duty manager has also heard her name whispered late at night, when there was no one else around to whisper it.'

The Wig and Pen Public House
(St Giles Street, Northampton, Northamptonshire)

The 'low-level' poltergeistery typical of pubs is a factor in the hauntings at this public house. Dozens of people have been disturbed or become aware of the activity, which has included lights mysteriously switching on or off, objects moving without obvious cause, and dogs refusing to enter the cellar which is thought to be the centre of the activity.

Wold House
(Wold Road, Nafferton, Near Driffield,
East Riding of Yorkshire)

Jonathan Owen, the proprietor, of Wold House, told us: 'Our hotel dates from 1854 and although not endowed with any known history of tragedy we have had a few instances of unexplained events. A number of guests who have stayed in one particular room have commented on their watches stopping unexpectedly in the night – these are only the instances remarked upon at breakfast – at least half a dozen times over the last couple of years – there may be others not commented on by guests.

'In the same room, on two occasions recently, people have commented on the noise made by other occupants in the night, i.e. doors opening followed by footsteps along the corridor, followed a few minutes later by return footsteps and a door closing again – always in the early hours. But there were no other guests in the hotel on the nights in question – on both occasions our guests assumed it was members of our family who had been around – but we live in separate accommodation always locked from the main hotel at night.

'One of our reception rooms was used as a Catholic Chapel for a number of years and staff have often commented on chill in the room – even though totally unaware of its history.'

Ye Olde Dog and Partridge Inn
(High Street, Tutbury,
Burton-upon-Trent, Staffordshire)

Ye Olde Dog and Partridge was originally built as a manor house and then became a coaching inn and a staging-post for the London-to-

Liverpool coach. It now boasts a well-loved and friendly ghost named Gracie, who appears as a child of about ten or eleven years old; she has been seen and more often heard many times by both guests and staff at the hotel. Some say that Gracie was hanged in Room 33, now one of the guest rooms in the fifteenth-century part of the hotel.

Gracie seems to love Christmas decorations, and is very evident at Christmas time. One of the guests reported that during the night he heard someone singing and skipping and bouncing a ball, although he failed to see her. Another guest staying in Room 33 said that he saw her standing at the bottom of his bed. Surprised, he put his head under the covers until his early morning call.

There have been reports of doors being opened and closed by unseen hands, items being moved from one place to another, and a ball being bounced against a wall in the dead of the night. There has also been other poltergeistery in the hotel. In the early hours of one morning the photocopier mysteriously leapt to life – no one had touched it, and a few minutes later it did it again. A pint of beer leapt off the counter and was spilled across the floor one evening.

Sue Yelland told us: 'Our Gracie seems to be a typical child doing what children do. We do not fear our Gracie, we love her, our quaint picturesque hotel in Tutbury would not be the same without the charm of "Our Gracie".'

REFERENCES AND RECOMMENDED READING

Not all of the following books have been used as references for *The Ghost Handbook* but they all have information relating to ghosts included herein, or to other sites of hauntings around Britain, many of which are accessible to the public.

Bord, Janet and Colin, *Mysterious Britain*, Garnstone Press, 1972.

Bord, Janet and Colin, *Modern Mysteries of the World*, Grafton, 1989.

Brooks, J. A., *Ghosts of London*, Jarrold, 1991.

Brooks, J. A., *Ghosts and Legends of the Lake District*, Jarrold, 1988.

Brooks, John, *The Good Ghost Guide*, Jarrold, 1994.

Burks, Eddie and Cribbs, Gillian, *Ghosthunter*, Headline, 1995.

Cady, Michael (ed.), *The Book of London*, AA Publications, 1980.

Chapman, Robert, *UFO – Flying Saucers over Britain?*, Arthur Baker, 1969.

Devereux, Paul, *Earth Lights Revelation*, Blandford, 1989.

Devereux, Paul and McCartney, Paul, *Earthlights*, Thorsons, 1982.

Downes, Wesley H. (ed), *Essex Ghosts and Hauntings (magazines) and Ghosts and Hauntings (magazines)*, Wesley's Publications.

Folklore Myths and Legends of Great Britain, Reader's Digest Association, 1973.

Forman, Joan, *The Haunted South*, Jarrold, 1978.

Forman, Joan, *Haunted East Anglia*, Robert Hale, 1974.

Forman, Joan, *Haunted Royal Homes*, Harrap, 1987.

Fry, Plantagenet Somerset, *Castles of Britain and Ireland*, David and Charles, 1996.

Fuller, John G., *The Airmen Who Would Not Die*, Souvenir Press, 1989.

Green, Andrew, *Haunted Houses*, Shire Publications, 1994.

Green, Andrew, *Haunted Inns and Taverns*, Shire Publications, 1995.

Green, Andrew, *Ghosts in the South East*, David and Charles, 1976.

Green, Andrew, *Our Haunted Kingdom*, Wolfe Publishing, 1973.

Greeves, Lydia and Trinick, Michael, *The National Trust Guide*, National Trust, 1995.

Hallam, Jack, *The Haunted Inns of England*, Wolfe Publishing, 1972.

Harper, Charles G., *Haunted Houses*, Senate, 1994 (orig: 1907).

Harris, Paul, *Ghosts of Shepway*, privately published.

Hauntings Time-Life, 1989.

Hippisley Coxe, Anthony D., *Haunted Britain*, Pan, 1973.

Hole, Christina, *Haunted England*, Fitzhouse, 1990 (orig: 1940).

Innes, Brian, *The Catalogue of Ghost Sightings*, Blandford, 1996.

Jackson, Michael, *Exploring England*, Collins, 1979.

Jones-Baker, Doris, *Tales of Old Hertfordshire*, Countryside Books, 1987.

McEwan, Graham J., *Haunted Churches of England*, Robert Hale, 1989.

Metcalfe, Leon, *Discovering Ghosts*, Shire Publications, 1972.

Montgomery-Massingberd, Hugh (ed.), *Burke's Guide to the British Monarchy*, Burke's Peerage, 1977.

Moss, Peter, *Ghosts over Britain*, Elm Tree Books, 1977.

Norman, Diana, *The Stately Ghosts of England*, Dorset, 1963.

Paget, Peter, *UFO – UK*, New English Library, 1980.

Phantom Encounters, Time-Life, 1989.

Phenix, Penny (ed.), *Illustrated Guide to Britain*, Automobile Association, 1996.

Rogers, Ken, *The Warminster Triangle*, Coates and Parker, 1994.

Spencer, Brian (ed.), *Byways of Britain*, Moorland Publishing, 1990.

Spencer, John, *The UFO Encyclopedia*, Headline, 1991.

Spencer, John and Anne, *The Encyclopedia of Ghosts and Spirits*, Headline, 1992.

Spencer, John and Anne, *The Encyclopedia of the World's Greatest Unsolved Mysteries*, Headline, 1995.

Spencer, John and Anne, *The Poltergeist Phenomenon*, Headline, 1997.

Spencer, John, Wells, Tony, *Ghostwatching*, Virgin, 1994.

Steel, David and Judy, *David Steel's Border Country*, Weidenfeld & Nicolson, 1985.

Sykes, Homer, *Mysterious Britain*, Weidenfeld & Nicolson, 1993.

Underwood, Peter, *Ghosts of North-West England*, Fontana, 1978.

Underwood, Peter, *Ghosts of Dorset*, Bossiney, 1988.

Underwood, Peter, *The Ghosthunter's Guide*, Blandford, 1986.

Underwood, Peter, *The A–Z of British Ghosts*, Chancellor, 1992.

Underwood, Peter, *Ghosts and How to See Them*, Brockhampton Press, 1993.

The Unexplained (magazines), Orbis, 1982.

The Visitor's Guide to English Heritage, English Heritage, 1995.

Warren, Melanie and Wells, Tony, *Ghosts of the North*, Broadcast Books, 1995.

Wells, Tony, and Warren, Melanie, *Ghost Stories of the South-West*, Broadcast Books, 1994.

Westwood, Jennifer, *Albion – a Guide to Legendary Britain*, Granada, 1985.

Wilson, Ian, *In Search of Ghosts*, Headline, 1995.

WE WOULD BE PLEASED TO HEAR OF READERS' EXPERIENCES. THE AUTHORS CAN BE CONTACTED:

BY LETTER TO:
   The Leys
   2C Leyton Road
   Harpenden
   Herts
   AL5 2TL
   England

or by fax: 01582 461979

or by e-mail: paranormal@dial.pipex.com

If you who would like to take a more active role in ghostwatching, write to ASSAP (The Association for The Scientific Study of Anomalous Phenomena) at:
   Saint Aldhelm,
   20 Paul Street,
   Frome,
   Somerset BA11 1DX
   Contact: Hugh Pincott
   e-mail: assap@dial.pipex.com

PLACES INDEX

INDEX